HEART OF BEIRUT

Samir Khalaf

HEART OF BEIRUT

Reclaiming the Bourj

SAQI

British Library Cataloguing-in-Publication Data
A catalogue record for this book is available from the British Library

ISBN 0-86356-542-5
EAN 9-780863-565427

First published 2006 by Saqi Books

copyright © Samir Khalaf, 2006

SAQI
26 Westbourne Grove
London W2 5RH

www.saqibooks.com

To

Ghassan Tueni

A man for all seasons but, above all,
a quintessential cosmopolitan

Contents

Foreword and Acknowledgements

Writing this book was largely serendipitous. The project was propelled by considerations unrelated to those that initially sparked it, and thus acquired a life of its own.

In June 2004 Solidere – the private land development company established by the late Rafik Hariri to spearhead the reconstruction of downtown Beirut – launched an international competition to rehabilitate Martyrs' Square, the once historic and cosmopolitan center. The competition drew over 400 participants from forty-six different countries, and a seven-member international jury was appointed to select the winning designs.

As the only social scientist on the jury familiar with the social and urban history of Beirut, I was asked to prepare a position paper elucidating the historic transformations of the Bourj. The provisional report I submitted in April 2004 ended with a prophetic and promising conjecture. Throughout its checkered history, I maintained, the Bourj has displayed a relentless proclivity to re-invent itself in order to accommodate the changes generated by regional and global events. Indeed, it had undergone a dozen striking mutations in its official identity and the popular labels it assumed.

Three such labels stand out: First, as *Place des Canons*, connoting its colonial legacy; second, as *Martyrs' Square*, to commemorate martyrdom and to celebrate the country's liberation from Ottoman control; finally, as the *Bourj*, perhaps its most enduring label, in reference to its medieval ramparts.

Despite this perpetual change in its collective identity, it managed to retain its basic character as an open, mixed and cosmopolitan central space. It was this malleability which rendered it more receptive in fostering high and popular culture, mass politics and the mobilization of advocacy groups, popular entertainment and, as of late, global consumerism. The latter has brought the disheartening manifestations of excessive commodification, kitsch and the debasement of the already threatened legacy of the arts and the spirited intellectual debate the Bourj once nurtured during its 'golden' or 'gilded' heydays. This receptivity, eclecticism and cross-cultural context helped the Bourj become a porous, tolerant and pluralistic setting.

The treacherous residue of three decades of strife and political instability, compounded by other regional and global uncertainties, suggests why Lebanese people now seem inclined to seek refuge either in religious and communal affinities or in the faddish and seductive appeals of consumerism. Herein lies the challenge for urban planning and design. Participants in the competition were urged to consider strategies through which the redemptive and healing features of the Bourj as a public sphere might be embraced while safeguarding it from slipping into a sleazy touristic resort or a ritualized sanctuary for sectarian communities to assert their threatened public identities. The prospects of neutralizing both forms of 'false consciousness' and, by doing so, reclaiming its vibrant legacy, seemed close at hand for the first time in over three decades. I concluded my report by declaring that the Bourj was now poised to become the harbinger of yet another watershed. What, I wondered, were the forces that might usher in these fateful transformations?

It was not long before these prospects surfaced again, amidst cataclysmic forces which brought about a national tragedy transcending the benign and parochial history of the Bourj. By embracing these forces of change, the Bourj, Beirut and Lebanon – let alone neighboring regimes – are bound never to be the same again.

On 14 February 2005 a massive bomb blasted Rafik Hariri's motorcade, killing him and Basil Fuleihan (an Member of Parliament, former minister and one of his closest associates), along with twenty-one others. It also devastated much of the fashionable Saint-Georges bay area, the site of the explosion. Hariri's martyrdom was epochal for the events it unleashed. His poignant funeral procession, the succession of public protests and demonstrations and his makeshift shrine next to the Martyrs' monument, propelled the Bourj once again to play host to momentous transformations. From then on, I felt irresistibly impelled to recapture the unfolding events of the story within the context of the dialectical interplay between the social production of space and political and socio-cultural transformation – how and why, in other words, a particular setting may invite certain forms of socio-cultural mobilization, and how in turn they are bound to redefine the character of that spatial setting.

In narrating this story, another serendipitous circumstance dictated the nature of my own 'participant observation', as it were. Our residence in Saifi Village is barely 50 yards away from Martyrs' Square. Hence I had a front-row seat in a theatrical spectacle played out before my own eyes. I vividly recall stretches of research and writing done against the background commotion of collective enthusiasm sparked by the populist uprising of the 'Cedar Revolution'.

By reworking the report into narrative form, I had to redirect its basic thrust and tone. The intention shifted to illuminating the Bourj's ebullient and enigmatic past and, hopefully, to enlighten the quality of the impending public debate and the future prospects it is bound to invite. The timing is most propitious. At the moment, the Bourj is still largely an empty strip of about 50,000 square meters, sandwiched between the massive profusion of religious edifices and the seductive venues and artifacts of mass consumerism and popular entertainment. Ironically, it was both the ruinous devastation of protracted strife, together with the bulldozers of reconstruction schemes, that made this unique prospect possible.

The international competition, it must be pointed out, was intended as a competition for ideas and not for the production of a definitive design or master plan. The foresight and intuitive judgment of Solidere's Urban Planning Division must be complimented in this regard. There is, then, considerable latitude for public intervention in shaping the defining features of the envisioned schemes. It is my earnest hope that this book will play a role in enhancing the quality of public awareness and informed debate so urgently needed in such critical moments of our urban history and threatened civility. To this effect, I have toned down the heavy academic jargon in the hope of rendering the 'Bourj story' more accessible to a wider audience.

Written during such a short interval, suffused with a scurry of unpredictable events, I had to rely often impetuously on the informed judgments and documentation extracted from a variety of sources. The extensive number of references I dipped into reveal how much I borrowed from others. I also benefited from conversations with architects, town planners, colleagues and friends. The late Pierre El-Khoury, Sheikh Michael El-Khoury, Myrna Boustani, John Keane, Walter Wallace, Touma and Leila Arida, Hashim Sarkis, Angus Gavin, George Arbid, Nabil Azar, Bernard Khoury, and Amira Solh, among others, were particularly helpful. Nouhad Makdisi and her technical staff at Solidere must be praised for their assistance in selecting images. Nor did I spare my students: as a captive audience, they were often compelled to listen, in paraphrase or verbatim, to many earlier drafts of the book.

Throughout my career I have been blessed with a loving family and a long-lasting circle of caring colleagues and friends. They never ceased to inspire and offer the critical and sobering counsel one needs. Hence I never felt short in returning the favors to those passionate few who merit the gratitude a book dedication carries. Such modest tokens are almost always self-selected.

This is Ghassan Tueni's book from beginning to end. Perhaps more than any other living Lebanese individual, he has been tireless in inciting the discourse on how to safeguard our maligned archeological troves, built and natural environment and cultural heritage from being debased further by the mindless aggrandizement of greedy capitalists and corrupt and self-seeking politicians. As in other threatened realms of our public life, he has been our lightning rod. His sharp, acerbic Monday morning editorials – rare for their staying power, range and erudition – are matchless even among the world's most accomplished journalists. But it is his tenacious, often combative and adversarial actions and campaigns on behalf of the cherished virtues of civility, liberalism and free-spirited cosmopolitanism that I acknowledge here. Much like Kant and his Stoic mentors, whom I know Ghassan admires, he has gone beyond mere contemplation and study. By grounding his thoughts in action he has enriched the common good and quality of our public life. Like the Stoics, he too harbors the view that in being a *world citizen* one does not need to break away from his local affiliations. It is in this sense that he is the godfather of the kind of cosmopolitanism I celebrate in this book. In a culture so anemic for role models, he towers luminously, and has continued to inspire and dazzle for the best part of six decades.

Like earlier works of mine, this one was achieved by withdrawing 'quality time' from Roseanne, George and Ramzi. Over the years they have been understanding and appreciative of such lapses. They have also become my sounding boards, unwavering in their eagerness to question and debunk. Roseanne, as usual, has done more than her due share in polishing the rough edges of my prose. For these and much more, I am grateful.

I have also been privileged during the past eight years to enjoy the sustained support of the Andrew Mellon Foundation. Without the summer research awards which allowed me to devote uninterrupted stretches of time to research and writing this, like the rest of my recent output, would not have been possible.

Finally, I wish to acknowledge the devoted professional attention of Saqi Books. Mai Ghoussoub and André Gaspard were generous in accommodating some of my seeming idiosyncrasies. Thanks are also due to Ken Hollings for his editorial labor and Ourida Mneimné for her aesthetic skill in designing the layout of the book. The research assistance of Ghassan Moussawi, particularly in scouting for sources, scanning images and preparing the final manuscript for publication, were invaluable. His technical proficiency and spirited enthusiasm are disarming. Mrs Leila Jbara, my devoted administrative assistant, displayed her noted keyboard skills in preparing the multiple versions of the manuscript.

Rafik Hariri's Martyrdom and the Mobilisation of Public Dissent

'The spatial dimensions in which we live our everyday lives are not as natural or innocent; they are shaped by social forces and are, in turn, a shaping force in social life'

Edward Soja, *Postmodern Geographies*

'Only by engaging with the changing fabric of the city and by acknowledging change as both loss and enrichment can we adequately approach the experience of living in urban space, without being caught between utopia and decay'

Elizabeth Wilson, *The Contradictions of Culture*

Ring the bells that still can ring;
Forget your perfect offering.
There is a crack in everything
That's how the light gets in.

Leonard Cohen

As a Lebanese, I feel at long last a bit redeemed by the startling and exultant events that took place during February and March of 2005. For almost four decades of my active life as a social scientist and humanist, I have been documenting and accounting for Lebanon's enigmatic and contested existence, but this is the first time I genuinely feel more than just a flush of elusive enthusiasm.

Throughout its chequered history, the country has been bedevilled by an almost Janus-like character. During interludes of relative stability and prosperity, its admirers described it euphorically as the 'Switzerland' or 'Paris' of the Middle East. The more chauvinist went even further to depict the country, often in highly romanticised tones, as a 'wondrous creation', a 'valiant little democracy', a 'miraculous' culture and economic experiment. In the late-1960s and early-1970s, when the country started to display early symptoms of political instability (largely the by-product of internal disparities compounded by unresolved regional rivalries), it became fashionable to depict Lebanon as a 'precarious', 'improbable', 'fragmented', 'torn' society: so divided and fractured, in fact, that it was deemed impossible to piece together again.

No sooner had the country lapsed into the abyss of violent strife in 1975 than it became the easy target for outright disparagement. To many of Lebanon's detractors, and to the obituary writers who came out in droves, the country was dismissed as an artificial creation. Others rushed to vilify it as a congenitally flawed entity doomed to self-destruction. Indeed, by the mid-1980s, Lebanon was reduced in the global media to an ugly metaphor: a mere figure of speech that conjured up images of the grotesque and unspoken or, worse, only to highlight the anguish of others.

More grievously, the country's history and some of its vivid accomplishments were either overlooked or maligned. Lebanon, as it were, was only acknowledged when it was being held accountable for the havoc and collective violence with which the country was beleaguered, although repeated scholarly and diplomatic evidence revealed that it was no more than a proxy battlefield for other peoples' wars.

There is a painful irony in this. This once vibrant republic, after nearly three decades of political subservience to one of the most autocratic and ruthless regimes in the region, should continue to be declared unfit to govern itself or to enjoy the most basic civil virtues, namely autonomy, balloting and constitutionalism (the 'ABC' of any viable democracy). The only country in the Arab world that could boast of carrying out periodic and free national elections, imperfect as they were at times, has had to suffer the indignity of putting up with uninspiring and inept leaders not of its own choosing.

Those who harboured a deep-seated resistance to the futility of violence and other belligerent strategies of change (and I am one of them) sought instead to expose the more redemptive features of Lebanon's pluralism and its consociational democracy. We also felt that silence, muted discontent and impotent rage are fundamentally antithetical to democracy. If the disruptive consequences of global incursions and unresolved regional rivalries were beyond our control, we shifted instead to more accessible and redeemable problems of post-war rehabilitation and reconstruction: enhancing municipal autonomy, civil liberties, advocacy groups and voluntary associations, urban planning and landscape design and efforts to pronounce and safeguard our habitat and architectural heritage. Most of all, we sought to resuscitate the public spheres and other venues for collective mobilisation in an effort to forge transcending and hybrid cultural and national identities.

We took heart from other troubled spots in the world. We marvelled how, often in the least likely of places (Budapest, Gdansk, Silesia, Estonia, Beijing...), the springtime of nations, so to speak, ushered in blissful signs of change. These and other collective icons of defiance, the voices of resistance, wrath and determination, shook and reawakened the conscience of the world to lingering injustices and crushing brutalities. The cynics among us thought that Lebanon had become much too mired and duplicitous to entertain, or be the beneficiary of, such redemptive outbursts. This is why the momentous events of February and March 2005 are destined to become a historic milestone.

Naturally, one must temper this first rush of contagious enthusiasm with some of the disheartening realities of local and geopolitical considerations. The raw and unalloyed sensibilities they have already aroused are, however, unlikely to be quelled. They were unleashed by the solemn funeral procession of Rafik Hariri. The hushed outpouring of grief, as throngs meandered through the streets and neighbourhoods of Beirut to Hariri's final resting place in the city's central square, was transformed into a resounding collective protest that transcended all the fractional loyalties and divisions within society. Enigmatic in his spectacular rise to public prominence, his cold-blooded murder inspired and galvanised a national uprising of immense proportions. Rather than laying him to rest in Saida, his birthplace, his family had the presence of mind instead to settle on Martyrs' Square next to the imposing al-Amin Mosque he had bequeathed to the nation's capital.

This seemingly serendipitous choice has made all the difference. Judged by the momentous changes it has generated thus far, particularly at the level of popular culture, it is destined to become a watershed in Lebanon's political and urban history. More compellingly, it might well turn out to be another pacesetter for other peoples' grassroots uprisings elsewhere in the region.

If the seething and repressed rage needed a tipping point, the moment and the setting could not have been more auspicious. The Bourj, in particular, has historically served as a vibrant public sphere and testing ground for collective mobilisation. Indeed, nowhere else in the Arab world could such a spectacle of unalloyed national sentiment and the voices of dissent have been released with such stupendous expression. The initial uprising, together with the countermobilisations it has provoked, displays all the uplifting elements of pure and spontaneous consciousness-raising happenings. Unlike other forms of protest, they are emotionally charged rallies, not riots. They have, thus far, remained expressive but peaceful and measured. Above all, the makeshift grave of Hariri was turned into a national shrine for the evocation of collective grief and deliverance from the oppressive designs of our 'sisterly' Syrian regime and its hapless cronies in Lebanon.

By acquiring a life of its own, the uprising was 'Lebanonised' into a mélange of seemingly dissonant elements: a Woodstock or a Hyde Park gathering, a triumphal post-World Cup rally or a bit of a carnival, a rock concert, a 'be-in' or other rejectionist manifestation of early-1970s 'counterculture'. Youngsters, who could never finish a basketball match without the intervention of the army, were now in restrained frenzy. They observed candlelit vigils, formed human chains, scribbled artistic manifestos, graffiti and posters beseeching Syria to 'get out'. Little children in white overalls offered flowers to stunned soldiers. Others, propped on their parents' shoulders, cheered joyously. Most touching to see were the Christians and Muslims praying in unison or bearing cross-religious placards as they observed moments of silence over Hariri's gravesite.

To commemorate the thirtieth day of Hariri's murder, the coalition of opposition forces called for a public gathering in Martyrs' Square on 21 March 2005 to reinforce their demands and sustain the peaceful mobilisation of public dissent the youth had been staging there. The gathering, both in sheer numbers and form, was truly stunning: clearly the largest and most compelling display of collective dissent the country has ever witnessed. It dwarfed the pro-Syrian public demonstration staged by Hizbullah and its allies a week earlier. Estimates of the numbers attending range between 800,000 and a million: more than twice the size of that of its political adversaries. This is almost one quarter of the entire population of the country. In the United States this would have meant close to eighty million protesters; just imagine what would have happened had the equivalent of twenty million agitated Egyptians hijacked the streets of Cairo!

Riad el-Solh Square, its adjoining courtyards, parking lots and construction sites were dense with overzealous crowds. All major arteries and thoroughfares converging on the city's centre were clogged with heavy traffic. Those from the northern coast crossed over by boats. Countless numbers were unable to reach their ultimate destination. More striking was the composition, mood and character of the rally. While the Hizbullah demonstration was sombre, stern, homogeneous and almost monolithic in its composition and message, the 14 March event was altogether a much more joyous, ebullient and spirited spectacle. It was also a hybrid of all the sectarian and regional communities, most visible in their outward demeanour, slogans and placards and the rich diversity of dress codes: from traditional horsemen in Arab headscarves and clerics in their distinctive robes and turbans to young girls with bared midriffs and pierced navels. But the most resounding image was the red, white and green hues of the Lebanese flag. From a distance, the flickering flags along with the white and red scarves of the protesters seemed like a flaming sea of dazzling gladiolas. Those who were not carrying flags had them painted on their faces or tattooed and inscribed on visible parts of their bodies. This was one event in the history of the country when such a unifying and patriotic national symbol transcended all other segmental and sub-national loyalties.

Lebanese youth, often berated as a quietist, disaffected, self-seeking generation in wild pursuit of the ephemeral pleasures and consumerism of the new world order, have been reawakened with a vengeance. To the surprise of their own parents and mentors, they have emerged as the most recalcitrant disparaging voices against the sources undermining the sovereignty, resources and well-being of their country. On their own, and without the support of political parties, blocs and mainstream voluntary associations, they are forming a variety of advocacy and emancipatory grassroots movements to shore up national sentiments and sustain modes of resistance. Most refreshing is the new political language of resistance they are offering, which is in stark contrast to the belligerent overtones of car bombs, suicidal insurgency and counterinsurgency that continue to beleaguer the political landscape in the region.

Also, generations too young to have participated in or to recollect earlier episodes of national emancipation are now receiving their own overdue tutelage in national character-building. They are giving notice, at a time when the gaze and conscience of the world are attentive, that the future architects of sovereign, free and independent Lebanon have just made their exultant entry into public life.

Once again, Lebanon's destiny seems delicately and precariously poised between such aroused aspirations and the impervious dictates and vengeful ploys of the 'benevolent' regime expected to shelter us from such calamities. The unsettling episodes of those few days – when massive explosives devastated the four suburban neighbourhoods of New Jdeideh, Kaslik, Sad al-Boushrieh and Broumana, part of the country's Christian heartland – are stark reminders of such grim prospects.

For once, however, thanks to the tragic martyrdom of Rafik Hariri and the treacherous legacy of Syria's thirty years of ruthless hegemony over Lebanon, the voices of dissent seem more tenacious and united than ever before. Both inside and outside sources have a rare moment to capture and act upon such propitious times. Otherwise, the renewed victimisation of Lebanon is bound this time to have ominous implications for stability in the entire region.

This fateful coincidence between the startling transformations incited by Hariri's tragic death and the role that the Bourj is currently playing in hosting the momentous events and then serving as a compelling setting for political mobilisation is not that unusual. Throughout its chequered history the Bourj was receptive in embracing a diversity of subcultures and ideological perspectives, playing host to some of the more resourceful artists, performers, advocacy groups and political activities. Most compelling was its proclivity to attract marginal groups, unconventional activities and deviant lifestyles. Groups who continue to harbour reservations or misgivings about mixing freely with others somehow find their reservations disappear around the Bourj.

As a vibrant, open space, almost akin to a 'commons' ground or a public 'maidan', the Bourj always managed to encourage people to let down their inhibitions: to melt, as it were, in the intensity and transcending encounters nurtured there. It is then that groups become freer to experiment with, or cultivate, new visions and collective identities. What has transpired in the wake of Hariri's assassination, and as of the time of this writing (15 April 2005), the momentous changes sparked by the uprising continue to be formidable sources of collective mobilisation. Indeed, in their magnitude, diversity of expression and likely consequences, the unfolding events are unprecedented in Lebanon's history.

What accounts for the emergence of such public spheres? What socio-cultural and historical circumstances are associated with their emergence, growth and demise? When posed in this manner, inevitably the query turns into an exploration of the interplay between social structure and spatial forms. More explicitly, how are particular spatial settings socially produced and reproduced? By virtue of its commanding historic pedigree, as the birthplace of the world's most ancient civilisations, Beirut's Bourj has always displayed some curious attributes and defining elements which account for its survival as a cosmopolitan urban setting in the throes of persistent change.

I will first situate the thrust of this book within a few salient conceptual concerns that inform most current debates on the social production of space. I will then provide a historical overview and an exploration of Solidere's massive reconstruction and rehabilitation of downtown Beirut. I will then move on to consider how the Bourj managed to incorporate and reconcile pluralistic and multicultural features and be so inventive in reconstituting its collective identity and public image. The last two chapters will focus on the Bourj as a cosmopolitan public sphere and how it evolved into an effective venue for self-expression, public entertainment, the commercialisation of sexual outlets, nurturing the press in its formative years and as a forum for public discourse and political mobilisation.

In effect, what we are witnessing at this critical interlude in Beirut's spatial and socio-cultural history is yet another metamorphosis in what Kevin Lynch calls the 'imageability' of a city.[1] To Lynch, and other associated reformulations by Frederic Jameson[2] and Jim Collins,[3] imageability is an expression of the predisposition of certain cities to generate strong visual impressions in the minds of their inhabitants. In the context of our interest in the social production of space, this will certainly allow us to substantiate more explicitly the relationship between 'self-identity' and 'self-location'.[4] Jameson's notion of 'cognitive mapping' is also of relevance. What these perspectives suggest is that new cultural forms may be *learned* as they are *made meaningful* through the appropriation of individuals of exigent modes of behaviour as they face new circumstances demanding instant accommodation. This is, after all, how mass culture is converted into folk-cultural phenomena exhibiting all the spontaneous and organic qualities associated with popular cultural movements. By playing host to such momentous transformations, the Bourj is reclaiming and extending its historic legacy in this regard.

The pictorial character of the book is, in my view, inevitable and desirable. Given Beirut's appealing natural endowments and distinct architectural heritage, an image-bound representation will certainly enrich the textual analysis. An intuitive synthesis of both will highlight more concretely how these attributes, and other derivative elements, might inform the envisioned prospects for reclaiming and reconstituting the Bourj once again as a vibrant public sphere.

On Collective Memory, Central Space and National Identity

Observing Beirut in the throes of reconstruction is a bewitching, often beguiling, experience, both existentially and conceptually. From a close and intimate range, one is not only struck by the massive physical and material transformations under way but one also gains insight into how new socio-cultural spaces and territorial entities are being invested with new meanings. One becomes aware of how disembedded groups and communities are recreating and reinventing their familiar daily rhythms and the city's social fabric. More compellingly, we become conscious of the artefacts, objects and spaces in the built environment which are being effaced and discarded and those which are being restored, embellished and rendered more pronounced.

Beirut today is akin to a living laboratory where one is in a sustained state of being captivated by the perpetual thrills of new discoveries unfolding, as it were, before one's very eyes. It is a marvel to live in such an urban milieu where one, literally, never encounters the same familiar and unchanging street or neighbourhood. One is liberated, in an existential sense, from the deadening effects of habit and the sterility of familiar places. A daily stroll always carries with it the visceral sensation of surprise and the prospects of levitating, as it were, into another world. It always heightens one's visual and aesthetic sensibilities. To borrow one of the metaphors of Ghassan Hage, one is in a sustained state of being pushed, pulled, propelled upward and whirled downward at one and the same time.

More compellingly still, Beirut is at another critical threshold in its chequered history. A restless and buoyant city is in the throes, once again, of redefining itself. I say 'once again' because it has been in this predicament many times before. It has reinvented itself on numerous occasions. This is, however, the first time that the process has incited such a contested and public debate regarding the rehabilitation scheme itself and its impact on the envisioned or projected public image of Beirut. Indeed, in the popular imagination a plurality of images is invoked: a future Honk Kong or Monaco, a Mediterranean town or Levantine seaport, a leisure resort, a playground or tourist site. Incidentally, we are not only talking about tourism in its ordinary or conventional form. At least two new types have become salient recently: health or medical tourism and war tourism engendered by the curiosity of travellers to behold sites of the ravages of war and how they are being reconstructed. Beirut is also envisioned as a tempting hub for services, communication networks, popular mass entertainment and faddish consumerism. It is rather ironic that the appeals of Beirut, at this moment in its contested collective identity, are embodied and informed by the dissonant forces of ruination, havoc, loss but also rehabilitation, restoration and well-being.

The spectacular events sparked by the 'Independence Uprising' in the wake of Rafik Hariri's assassination on 14 February 2005 have been so riveting in their manifestations and consequences that they have drawn the attention of the world and driven global powers to take remedial action. Spontaneous and self-propelled, the uprising – largely because it could exploit the commanding setting of Beirut's historic centre – displayed so much daring and inventiveness that it evolved into a formidable public sphere. Sustained demonstrations and expressions of collective grievances allowed the protesters to articulate a coherent set of demands and to mobilise normally passive and quiescent groups to participate in popular grassroots movements in support of the uprising. Thus far, the by-products have been vast in their immediate consequences and promise to be more consequential in their anticipated future reverberations. The massive sustained uprising forced the resignation of the government and precipitated a sharply contested political crisis. It expedited the formulation of two decisive UN resolutions: 1559, calling for the immediate withdrawal of Syrian troops and security agencies from Lebanon, and 1595, to set up an international commission of inquiry into the assassination of Hariri. Perhaps more compellingly, in view of its future fallouts, the uprising initiated the country's youth into a hands-on and direct tutelage in civic virtues and emancipatory political struggle.

By virtue of its centrality and commanding historic setting – almost akin to an open museum of the world's most ancient civilisations – Beirut's central square has always displayed curious historical features that account for its survival as a fairly open, pluralistic and cosmopolitan urban district. Archaeological findings repeatedly show that this very site, often dubbed the 'nursery of Homo sapiens', has served as an abode for humanity almost since its first appearance on the face of the earth. Indeed, some of the implements (mainly stone artifacts) that continue to be unearthed on site may be traced back to the Lower Palaeolithic period, roughly two or three million years ago. The relentless succession of dynasties and civilisations that have left their indelible legacies on this site is truly overwhelming. The massive reconstruction efforts under way, particularly around Beirut's historic centre, continue to come across almost daily finds that reconfirm the most distinguished heritage of its ancient past.

Stunning as its archaeological relics are, one need not be misled by the prehistoric eminence of Beirut. Nor should one go too far back into the past to disclose the circumstances associated with the distinctive role its central square came to play. Despite its momentous history, its emergence as a modern, cosmopolitan urban centre is of recent vintage. In fact, the most definitive symptoms of urbanisation – rural exodus and the spill of the population beyond its medieval walls – did not really appear in any substantial form until the 1860s. Of course, there were earlier signs of rural exodus. Dislocation in native crafts, the decline in silk production and the shift in the pattern of trade, particularly during the Egyptian occupation (1831–41) had generated a shift in population movement towards coastal towns. These and earlier movements, however, were limited in scale. For example, when Volney visited Beirut in 1773, he described it as a small town with no more than 6,000 people. There was not, it must be noted, any perceptible increase in the population during the next six decades. By 1830 the population was still in the neighbourhood of 8,000.

The decade of Egyptian presence, with its concomitant commercialisation and opening up of Mount Lebanon to western incursions, added only another 2,000 to Beirut's population. This relatively slow rate of increase (about five hundred annually) was maintained during the 1840s and 1850s. In short, it was not until the outbreak of civil disturbances in the late-1850s and early-1860s that the impact of a massive shift in population began to be felt. Beirut's population leaped from 22,000 in 1857 to 70,000 in 1863, an annual increase of almost 10,000. During the height of civil disturbances and in the short span of only two months (from August to September 1860), an Anglo-Saxon committee of local missionaries gave aid to more than 20,000 refugees in Beirut.[5]

Every description of Beirut prior to the 1860s attests to this. Until then, it was no more than a small, fortified medieval town with seven main gates and about half a square kilometre surrounded by gardens. The central core of the city was built around its historic port and mole with defences on the landward side and two towers at the entrance of the port. As in most European towns before industrialisation, people in Beirut lived and worked within the same area and carried on nearly all their daily routines within the same urban quarter. Ethnic and religious affiliation created relatively homogeneous and compact residential neighbourhoods. Daily routines were carried out within clearly defined quarters, and the neighbourhood survived as an almost self-sufficient community with which the individual identified. There was a strong sense of neighbourliness, and patterns of behaviour were largely regulated through kinship and religious ties. Physical and social space, in other words, were almost identical. More importantly, these neighbourhoods offered the urban dweller a human scale and types of social networks that he could comprehend and in which he could find a uniquely individual space.

Gross density was high – around 300 per hectare – and the town gave an overwhelming impression of congestion. Lamartine, who visited Beirut in 1832, said, for example, that the roofs of some houses served as terraces to others. Except for *souks*, *khans*, baths, places of worship and other public buildings which dominated the town, the prevailing house types were flat-roofed farmhouses and the traditional two or three-storied, red-tiled villas with elaborate facades and decorative railed stairways and balconies. Sandstone blocks, quarried in the area, were the predominant construction form. Lush, subtropical vegetation graced the well-tended gardens of its houses and lined its winding alleyways.

The cactus-lined alleys were soon converted to macadamised streets. Urban construction leaped beyond the medieval walls of the city to accommodate the persistent inflow of rural migrants into Beirut. The construction of the wharf in Beirut's port in 1860 to accommodate the increasing maritime traffic, like all the other infrastructural developments and public amenities undertaken throughout the second half of the nineteenth century (e.g. harbour facilities, Damascus railways, gaslights, potable water, electric tramways, telegraph and postal services, quarantine, dispensaries and hospitals along with schools, colleges and printing houses) assisted naturally in the expansion and urbanisation of Beirut. As a residence for consul generals, headquarters for French, American and British missions and a growing centre of trade and services, it gradually began to attract a cosmopolitan and heterogeneous population. It is then that some of the early symptoms of cosmopolitanism, marked by elements of sophistication and savoir-faire in public life, started to surface. This was particularly visible in the opening up and receptivity of seemingly local and provincial groups and neighbourhoods to novel and mixed lifestyles and mannerisms.

But Beirut's swift urbanisation (the consequences of both internal migration and natural growth rates in the population) carried with it other more disheartening consequences. Since nearly two-thirds of the rural exodus was directed toward Beirut, the capital trebled its residential population between 1932 and 1964 and grew by nearly tenfold between 1932 and 1980. This rapid growth of Beirut was not only due to internal demographic factors, but to a large extent it was also a reflection of external pressures that generated increased demand for urban space. First, the Armenian Massacres of 1914 brought over 50,000 Armenian refugees from Turkey. The waves of Palestinian refugees after 1948 and the political instability in neighbouring Arab countries intensified this demand, as did the subsequent inflow of capital from the Gulf States and foreign remittances, which poured into the already lucrative real-estate and construction sectors of the economy. The building boom of the 1950s and 1960s, with its manifestations of mixed and intensive land-use patterns and vertical expansion, was largely a by-product of such forces. The resulting uncontrolled and haphazard patterns of growth were maintained during the early-1970s. Shortly before the outbreak of civil disturbances in 1975, greater Beirut was probably absorbing 75 per cent of Lebanon's urban population and close to 45 per cent of all the inhabitants of the country. In addition, its already overcrowded 101–square kilometre area had to accommodate an estimated 120,000 daily commuters from adjoining suburbs.[1]

By the early-1970s Beirut's annual rate of growth was estimated at 4 per cent, which implied that the city was bound to double in less than twenty years. The magnitude of this change may be expressed in more concrete terms: if the current rates of growth were maintained, Beirut would have had to accommodate and provide housing, schooling, medical services, transportation and other services for at least 40,000 new residents every year. It is in this sense that Beirut was associated at the time with the phenomenon of primacy and over urbanisation. Insofar as the degree of urbanisation was much more than would be expected from the level of industrialisation, then Lebanon was among the few countries – along with Egypt, Greece and Korea – that may be considered over urbanised.[2] We will subsequently explore some of the spatial and socio-cultural implications of such over urbanisation. Suffice it to note that this is one of the most critical problems Lebanon continues to face: a problem with serious social, psychological, economic and political implications. Urban congestion, blight, depletion of open spaces, disparities in income distribution, rising levels of unemployment and underemployment, housing shortages, exorbitant rents, problems generated by slums and shantytowns and, to a considerable extent, the urban violence of the war years, were all by-products of over urbanisation. In short, the scale and scope of urbanisation had outstripped the city's resources to cope effectively with continuously mounting demand for urban space and public amenities.

Hence, Beirut has always been gripped by a nagging dissonance between conceived and lived space. The city, as we shall see, has never been short on blueprints or the often idealistic conceptions of how planners and builders perceive the defining elements and shape of the spatial environment. For a variety of reasons, such perceptions were not consistent with the concrete spatial realities. In other words, lived space almost always assumed a life of its own, unrelated to its original or intended expectations.

From its eventful past, much like its most recent history, a few distinct but related features stand out. Together, these defining elements continue to be vital in informing the way Beirut, and its central square in particular, could continue to serve as a vibrant and transcending public sphere amenable for collective mobilisation and for forging a hybrid popular culture for tolerance and peaceful coexistence.

City and Mountain

First, and without doubt one of its most striking attributes, is the dual role Beirut managed to embody throughout its eventful history as a port city and a national capital linked to its hinterland. Hence, any understanding of this distinctive feature requires an elucidation of the timeless interplay between the accidents of its geographic and ecological endowments, namely the sea and its mountainous hinterland. Indeed, to many of its historians, philosophers and writers who often evoke these natural gifts with emotive hyperbole, much of their country's accomplishments are seen as an outgrowth of such seemingly dissonant attributes. Some, like Charles Malik, Michel Chiha, Said Akl and Kamal el-Hajj, speak with more than just a hint of geographic determinism of the 'horizontal' effects of the sea and the 'perpendicular' effects of the mountain to account for the two most distinctive characteristics that informed its distinguished history: the open, adventurous, itinerant and worldly predispositions generated by its seafaring heritage, along with the role its mountains served as a secure asylum for displaced minorities and dissident groups.

To Albert Hourani, Lebanon's political culture, particularly its republican and liberal features, managed to reconcile two distinct visions or ideologies which had been tenuously held together since the creation of Greater Lebanon in 1920:

> On the one hand, there was the idea of Mount Lebanon: a society rural, homogeneous, embodied in an institution, the Maronite church, with a self-image ... and with a vision of an independent and predominantly Christian political community. On the other, there were the urban communities of Beirut and other coastal cities, mainly Sunni Muslim but with Orthodox and other Christian elements, and with a different idea: that of a trading community open to the world, and serving as a point of transit and exchange, and therefore a community where populations mingled and coexisted peacefully; of a society which needed government and law, but preferred a weak government to which the leaders of its constituent groups had access and which they could control.[3]

Hourani traces the theoretical basis of this vision and its embodiment in the *mithaq* or 'covenant' of 1943 to the writings of Michel Chiha, in which we can see the marriage of the two ideologies: the mountain and the city. To Chiha, this largely accounts for what he termed Lebanon's 'spiritual dominance':

> Lebanon the mountain of refuge and Lebanon the meeting place, rooted in its own traditions but open to the world, with bilingualism or trilingualism as a necessity of its life; possessing stable institutions which correspond with its deep realities, an assembly in which the spokesmen of the various communities can meet and talk together, tolerant laws, no political domination of one group by another, but kind of spiritual domination of those who think of Lebanon as part of the Mediterranean world.[4]

Chiha's optimistic vision notwithstanding, the marriage was strenuous from its very inception. It was, after all, an arranged liaison: a contract, not a romantic bond. With all the bona fides of its architects and the noblesse oblige of the consenting parties, the *Mithaq* could not have possibly survived the multi-layered pressures (local, regional and international) with which it was burdened. It was a partial covenant. It did not fully express the changing demographic and communal realities of the time. With the creation of Greater Lebanon, Christians as a whole were no longer in a majority, although the Maronites were still arguably the largest single community. The annexation of the coast and the Beqaa also ushered in an unsettling variety of political cultures and disparate ideologies.

Incidentally, it is these 'New Phoenician' voices who captured the attention of the American Legation offices in Beirut at the time: particularly those of Chiha, Gabriel Menassa and Alfred Kettaneh, and their extended network of families and close associates of the commercial and political elite. As staunch advocates of free trade, they were opposed to any form of central planning and protectionism, shunned industrialisation, jealously guarded the sources of their new wealth and lived by the edict 'import or die'. Writing to the secretary of state on 19 August 1947, Lowell Pinkerton of the US Legation had this to say:

> The ancient commercial craft of the Phoenicians is still very evident ... perhaps it will prevail upon more modern counsels, or be more effectively supplemented by expert foreign advice. In any case, here are vigorous exponents of the capitalist system who now look only to the United States for ideas and encouragement.[5]

Chiha himself, incidentally, was fully aware that his vision was far from an exemplar of stability and harmony. His liberal image of Beirut as a cosmopolitan city-state coexisting with the more archaic tribal and primordial loyalties of the mountain and hinterland was, to say the least, a cumbersome and problematic vision. This was compounded, particularly after 1920, by the impassioned claims of the rival ideological currents taking root in the coastal cities. The 'Lebanism' of the Christians was pitted against the 'Arabism' of the Sunni Muslims with reverberations among the Shi'ites and Druze of the hinterland. No wonder that during the 1930s the neighbourhoods of Beirut were periodically 'the scene of violent clashes between Christian and Muslim gangs, one side brandishing the banner of Lebanism, the other of Arabism'.[6]

The shortcomings of the *Mithaq*, it should be noted, are not inherent in its basic philosophy or *modus vivendi* to arrive at a compromise between communities seeking to contain potentially explosive issues of sovereignty, collective or national representation and peaceful coexistence. The *Mithaq* was also addressing perhaps the more delicate problems associated with the 'fears' of the Christians and the 'demands' and 'grievances' of the Muslims. Like most pacts, it involved mutual renunciation. The Christians undertook to renounce their traditional alliances with the West, and France in particular, while the Muslims promised to abandon their pan-Arabist aspirations. In effect both communities were to turn away from the larger world to help galvanise their loyalties to Lebanon. George Naccache's pungent aphorism notwithstanding – '*deux negations ne font pas une nation*' – this double renunciation seemed both feasible and appropriate at the time.

The Ta'if Accord of 1989 has not fared any better in allaying some of the disheartening manifestations of such persistent fragmentation and conflict-filled images regarding Beirut's collective memory and national identity as the nation's capital. The Accord is often heralded as an innovative and remarkable pact marking the threshold of a new republic. It is credited with putting an end to nearly two decades of protracted violence and for laying the foundation for reconciling differences over the three implacable sources of long-standing discord and hostility: namely, political reforms, national identity and state sovereignty.

The tensions between the two seemingly dissonant 'ideologies' – those of the city and those of the mountain – have been compounded by yet another unsettling feature: the 'ruralisation' of Beirut as seen in the tenacity and survival of large residues of non-urban ties and loyalties. Repeated studies have shown that the swift and extensive urbanisation Lebanon was experiencing at the time was not associated, as is the case in most other societies, with a comparable decline in kinship and communal loyalties.[7] In other words, the intensity and increasing scale of urbanisation as a physical phenomenon was not accompanied by a proportional degree of urbanism as a way of life.

What this suggests, among other things, is that a sizable portion of Beirut was, in an existential sense, *in* but not *of* the city. To both recent migrants and relatively more permanent urban settlers, city life was predominantly conceived as a transient encounter, to be sustained by periodic visits to rural areas, or by developing rural networks within urban areas. In practice, urbanisation in Lebanon has not meant the erosion of kinship ties, communal loyalties and confessional affinities and the emergence of impersonality, anonymity and transitory social relations.

As in other dimensions of social life, the network of urban social relations, visiting patterns and the character of voluntary associations still sustain a large residue of traditional attachments, despite increasing secularisation and urbanisation. In many respects, Beirut remains today more a 'mosaic' of distinct urban communities than a 'melting pot' of amorphous urban masses. Often neighbourhoods emerge that consist of families drawn from the same village and the same religious group, resulting in patterns of segregation in which religious and village ties are reinforced. The survival of such features has been a source of communal solidarity, providing much of the needed social and psychic supports, but they also account for much of the deficiency in civility and the erosion of public and national consciousness. More importantly, as will be shown later, they may obstruct rational urban planning and zoning.

The protracted civil disturbances between 1975 and 1992 not only reinforced the communal character of neighbourhoods but also generated other problems of a far more critical magnitude. Vast areas, in addition to the central business district, were totally or partially destroyed. Massive population shifts generated further disparities and imbalances between the various communities and intensified religious hostilities and feelings of paranoia and/or indifference towards the 'other'.

We are, of course, concerned here with the implications such unresolved socio-cultural and political realities have for the spatial and architectural heritage of Beirut and its central square. More particularly, what role can urban planning and landscape design play in providing spatial settings conducive to allaying some of the segmental and divisive loyalties which continue to undermine prospects for forging transcending and cosmopolitan urban environments?

Post-War Setting

Another compelling reality, with substantial implications for the envisioned role the Bourj can play in providing venues and outlets for forging the desired collective and spatial identities, has much to do with the process of post-war reconstruction. Such ventures, even under normal circumstances, are usually cumbersome. In Lebanon, they are bound to be more problematic because of the distinctive character of some of the residues of collective terror and strife with which the country was besieged for almost two decades and which set it apart from other instances of post-war reconstruction. The horrors spawned by the war are particularly galling because they were not anchored in any recognisable or coherent set of causes. Nor did the violence, ugly as it was, resolve the issues that might have sparked the initial hostilities. It is in this poignant sense that the war that devastated Beirut was wasteful, futile and unfinished.

As such, the task of representing or incorporating such inglorious events into Beirut's and the country's collective identity becomes, understandably, much more problematic. But it needs to be done. Otherwise, the memory of the war, like the harrowing events themselves, might well be trivialised and forgotten and hence, more likely to be repeated. The disheartening consequences of unfinished wars are legion. Two are particularly poignant and of relevance to the concerns of this study. The first of these is the salient symptoms of 'retribalisation' apparent in reawakened communal identities and the urge to seek shelter in cloistered spatial communities. The second is a pervasive mood of lethargy, indifference and weariness bordering at times on 'collective amnesia'. Both are understandable reactions that enable traumatised groups to survive the cruelties of protracted strife. Both, however, could be disabling, as the Lebanese are now considering less belligerent strategies for peaceful coexistence.

Both manifestations – the longing to obliterate, mystify and distance oneself from the fearsome recollections of an ugly and unfinished war, or efforts to preserve or commemorate them – coexist today in Lebanon. In fact, retribalisation and the reassertion of communal and territorial identities, perhaps a few of the most prevalent elements in post-war Lebanon, incorporate both these features. In other words, the convergence of spatial and communal identities serves both the need to search for roots and the desire to rediscover or invent a state of bliss that has been lost; it also serves as a means of escape from the trials, tribulations and fearful recollections of the war.

Expressed more concretely, this reflex or impulse for seeking refuge in cloistered spatial communities is sustained by two seemingly opposed forms of self-preservation:

to *remember* and to *forget*. The former is increasingly sought in efforts to anchor oneself in one's community or in the reviving and reinventing of its communal solidarities and threatened heritage. The latter is more likely to assume escapist and nostalgic predispositions to return to a past imbued with questionable authenticity. The two, however, as will be seen, are related. It is only when certain artifacts and objects are remembered that, by exclusion, they begin to cause others to be forgotten.

If there are, then, visible symptoms of a 'culture of disappearance' evident in the growing encroachment of global capital and state authority into the private realm and heedless reconstruction schemes which are destroying or defacing the country's distinctive architectural and urban heritage, there is a burgeoning 'culture of resistance' which is contesting and repelling such encroachment and dreaded annihilation, as well as the fear of being engulfed by the overwhelming forces of globalisation.

One unintended but compelling consequence of all this is that through this restorative venture, and perhaps for the first time in recent history, a growing number of Lebanese are becoming publicly aware of their spatial surroundings. It has enhanced, in appreciable ways, their spatial sensibilities and public concern for safeguarding the well-being of their living habitat. By doing so, consciously or otherwise, they are transforming their tenuous, distant and instrumental attachments to 'space' into the more personal and committed identities engendered by deep, more meaningful and supportive loyalties to one's 'place'. It is these loyalties, after all, which are receptive to the needs of urbanity and civility. Hence, rather than berating and maligning one's 'roots' and primordial attachments (religious, sectarian, kinship, communal and otherwise) as sources of retrograde or infantile nostalgia, they could, if judiciously mobilised, become routes for forging new cosmopolitan identities and transcending loyalties and commitments.[8]

Global, Regional and Local Encounters

Lebanon is not only grappling with all the short-term imperatives of reconstruction and long-term needs for sustainable development and security, but it has to do so in a turbulent region with a multitude of unresolved conflicts and contested strategies for steering post-war rehabilitation and the broader issues of national development. Impotent as the country might seem at the moment to neutralise or ward off such external pressures, there are measures and programmes already proven to be effective elsewhere, which can be experimented with to fortify Lebanon's immunity against the disruptive consequences of such destabilising forces. Such efforts can do much in reducing the country's chronic vulnerability to these pressures. A central premise of this book is the belief that urban planning and design, architecture and landscaping, among other overlooked forms of public intervention, can offer effective strategies for healing symptoms of fear and paranoia and, also, offer a way to transcend parochialism.

This is not, after all, the first time that the country – Beirut, in particular – faces such predicaments. As will be seen, during earlier confrontations with both Ottoman and French attempts at the production of social space, local builders, architects and other indigenous groups displayed considerable awareness, knowledge and skills relevant to the processes of construction and reconstruction under way at the time.

Since Beirut, as capital and imposing port city, was subjected to successive planning schemes – the construction of monumental edifices, thoroughfares and public squares – it is instructive to re-examine how such attempts were perceived and implemented. Were local groups, in other words, merely passive recipients in such instances of struggle for power and control over lived space? Or were they active participants who often succeeded in resisting and changing the imperial and colonial impositions? The experience of Beirut, particularly its central square and contiguous urban spaces, becomes instructive in conceptual and comparative terms. In this respect, Beirut offers another grounded and living instance of the production of social space that departs from other common experiences and patterns observed in other settings.[9] Beirut's experience, as will be argued, was not – and is not – merely a process of transfer, transplantation or imposition of external visions and schemes on a willing, compliant and non-participative public. More vitally, perhaps, by disclosing the interplay between this inevitable plurality of forces – local, regional and trans national – that are involved in the construction of the collective identity of a particular settlement, one is also probing into the elements which make up the 'imagined community' of the Bourj, Beirut and Lebanon as a nation-state.

Regardless of what perspective or paradigm one adopts for contextualising the nature of spatial identities – i.e., the perspective of world systems, globalisation, postcolonialism or postmodernism – in the final analysis this requires an understanding of both the broader structural transformations along with the nature, scale and the particular manner in which local considerations continue to make their presence felt in redefining and reconstituting social space. Indeed, in some instances, so-called 'postmodern' attributes – i.e., fragmentation, fluid and multiple identities, the mixing of different histories, pastiche, irony, the destruction of the vernacular and the provincial – were present in Beirut long before they had appeared elsewhere, including Europe and America.

No matter how we define globalisation it involves, as Roland Robertson reminds us, 'an increasing consciousness of the world as a whole'.[10] He goes on to suggest that:

> the contemporary concern with civilisational, societal (as well as ethnic) uniqueness – as expressed via such motifs as identity, tradition and indigenisation – largely rests on globally diffused ideas. In an increasingly globalised world ... there is an exacerbation of civilisational, societal and ethnic self-consciousness. Identity, tradition and indigenisation only make sense contextually.[11]

While Anthony King is in agreement that identities are established and validated contextually, he is not of the view that they are usually the outcome of the broad and distant forces of 'globalisation'. Instead, he argues that they are usually 'constructed in relation to much more specific, smaller, historical, social and spatial contexts'. He goes on to say that people 'express their resistance to the global political and economic situations that engulf them, and at the same time may also immerse themselves within these situations'.[12]

Such state of consciousness and the proclivity to engage with cosmopolitan encounters were also present in Beirut before the advent of globalism and postmodernity. The identity of some urban Beirutis – if one were to infer this from the architectural styles of their residences, their mannerisms, fashions and other cultural manifestations of everyday life – was also a hybrid of seemingly dissonant and inconsistent features. Expressed more concretely, the Lebanese are certainly becoming more interconnected at all three levels: globally, regionally and locally. They cross over with greater ease. At least they seem less guarded when they do so. They visit areas they never dared to visit before. These and other such symptoms of interconnectedness should not, however, be taken to mean that the Lebanese are becoming more alike or that they are becoming more homogenised by the irresistible forces of globalisation and postmodernity.

On the contrary, and in many instances, geography and attachments to place are becoming more important, not less. Geography, location, territorial and spatial identities have become sharper and more meaningful at the psychic and socio-cultural levels. Such manifestations should not be dismissed as nostalgic or transient interludes destined to 'pass' into 'secular', tenuous and more impersonal or virtual encounters. Indeed, one of the central premises of this chapter is that we can better understand the emergent socio-cultural identities – even the political and economic transformations – by seeing their manifestations in this ongoing dialectic between place and space. How, in other words, are spaces being transformed into 'places' and how, in turn, do places degenerate into mere spaces to be occupied and exploited for commercial and mercenary pursuits? Of course, notions like space and place are ordinary, everyday terms. Yet they are suffused with meaning and symbolism and, hence, vital to individual and group identity. It behoves us to explore how they are being played out in Beirut's post-war setting.

Manifestations of such fluidity and hybridity have become more pronounced today. A cursory stroll through the rehabilitated districts of central Beirut, as well as those under reconstruction, quickly reveals symptoms of such dissonance. First, and doubtlessly the most striking, is the pronounced dominance of religious edifices: mosques, cathedrals, churches and shrines. In the process of rehabilitation some have appropriated additional property and, through the stylistic use of modes of architectural illumination, electronic digital amplification, they have been rendered physically and audibly more overwhelming. While mosques are restrained from extending the utility of their premises to non-sacred activities, churches and Capuchins have been making efforts to host musical recitals, poetry readings and other secular performances and events. Incidentally, Greek Orthodox churches are also restrained from using their premises for other than Gregorian Chants and religious choral recitals.

The gargantuan al-Amin Mosque, about to be completed, occupies a massive space of about 4,000 square metres. It literally dwarfs everything in proximity. It is a joint by-product of three benevolent foundations: Walid ibn Talal, Rafik Hariri and the al-Amin Mosque Association. Because of its colossal proportions, it has been a source of contested negotiations to scale down its height and the number of its protruding minarets so that it will not overshadow the adjoining Maronite St Georges Cathedral.[13]

If the sacred features have become more conspicuous and redoubtable but then so have the profane, to invoke Durkheim's classic dichotomy. Any land-use mapping of the district is bound to reveal the dominance of mass consumerism, retail shops, boutiques, restaurants, coffee shops, sidewalk cafes, nightclubs and bars. But here as well the global and postmodern (i.e., shopping arcades, internet cafes, fast-food franchises and elegant fashionable boutiques) coexist symbiotically with some of the provincial outlets. Quite often global franchises (i.e., McDonalds, KFC, Pizza Hut, Dunkin' Donuts etc ...) 'go native' – so to speak – by appropriating local elements such as valet parking and other semiotic images of the vernacular to enhance the appeal of their products and services. Likewise, traditional outlets often assume the scintillating features of their global counterparts to validate their own public images and marketing ploys.

Within such a context, it is no longer meaningful to talk about conceptual oppositions such as local/global, provincialism/cosmopolitanism, vernacular/universal, space/place, being/becoming, village-in-the-city/global-village etc as though they are distinct, irreconcilable dichotomies. Such polarisation and ideal typologies, much like the earlier misplaced dichotomies between sacred and secular, traditional and modern, mechanical and organic are not a reflection of what is, in fact, grounded in the real world.[14]

Such realities must be borne in mind as we explore or anticipate the future national image or collective identity that Beirut's central square is likely to assume at this juncture in its chequered history. We are, after all, dealing with the convergence or interplay of three problematic and tenuous realities or considerations: post-war Beirut, regional uncertainties and global incursions. Hence the emergent identities in Beirut are blurred and are in perpetual states of being reconstituted and redefined. The views of a growing circle of recent scholars – Ulf Hannerz (1996), H. Bhabha (1994), A. Appadurai (1996), J. R. Short (2001), among others – are in support of such expressions of cultural diversity and hybridity.

Collective Memory vs Collective Amnesia

Beirut is not only grappling with all the trials and tribulations of a post-war setting, local fragmentation and the unsettling manifestations of unresolved regional and global rivalries. These are not new to Beirut. What is fairly recent, however, are some of the compelling consequences of post modernity and globalism: a magnified importance of mass media, popular arts and entertainment in the framing of everyday life, an intensification of consumerism, the demise of political participation and collective consciousness for public issues and their replacement by local and parochial concerns for nostalgia and heritage.

Within this context, issues of collective memory, contested space and efforts to forge new cultural identities begin to assume critical dimensions. How much – and what – of the past needs to be retained or restored? By whom and for whom? Common as these questions might seem, they have invited little agreement among scholars. Indeed, recent views seem to vary markedly. For instance, to Ernest Gellner,[15] collective forgetfulness, anonymity and shared amnesia are dreaded conditions resisted in all social orders. Perhaps conditions of anonymity, he argues, are inevitable in times of turmoil and upheaval. But once the unrest subsides, internal cleavages and segmental loyalties resurface. MacCannell goes further to assert that the ultimate triumph of modernity over other socio-cultural arrangements is epitomised not by the disappearance of pre-modern elements but by their reconstruction and artificial preservation in modern society.[16] Similarly, Jedlowski also maintains that a sense of personal identity can only be achieved on the basis of personal memory.[17]

Paul Connerton likewise argues that it is collective memory – i.e., commonly shared images of the past – which legitimise a present social order.[18] To the extent that peoples' memories of a society's past diverge, then its members will be bereft of common experiences, perspectives and visions. These memory-claims figure significantly in our self-perceptions. Our past history, imagined or otherwise, is an important source in our conception of selfhood. In the final analysis, our self-knowledge – our conception of our own character and potentialities – is, to a large extent, shaped by the way in which we view our own past actions.[19] Likewise, Halbwachs argued persuasively that it is primarily through membership in mediating groups such as religion, national ideological or class membership that people are able to acquire and then recall their memories.[20] These become the venues for creating and sustaining shared memories. We often forget that for man, as for no other creature, to lose his past – to lose his memory – is to lose himself, to lose his identity. History, in this case, is more than just a record of how man becomes what he is. It is the largest element of his self-conception.

Persuasive as such pleas on behalf of collective memory are, particularly with regard to their impact on reconstituting the frayed symptoms of social solidarity and national allegiance, a slew of other scholars make equally persuasive claims on behalf of collective amnesia and social forgetfulness. Benjamin Barber, for example, argues that successful civic nations always entail a certain amount of 'studied historical absentmindedness ... Injuries too well remembered,' he tells us, 'cannot heal.'[21] What Barber is, of course, implying here is that if the memories of the war and its atrocities are kept alive, they will continue to reawaken fear and paranoia, particularly among those embittered by them. Without an opportunity to forget there can never be a chance for harmony and genuine coexistence.

David Lowenthal, in his preface to an edited volume entitled *The Art of Forgetting*, goes further to underscore the close etymological connection of 'amnesia' with 'amnesty'. He invokes one of the basic premises of Hobbes who, he reminds us, treated forgetting as the basis of a just state and amnesia as the 'cornerstone of the social conduct'. What he termed 'remedial oblivion' was a common strategy of seventeenth-century statecraft.[22] Lowenthal advances another compelling inference in this regard: that much forgetting turns out to be more beneficent and enabling than bereavement; a 'mercy' rather than a 'malady': 'To forget is as essential as to keep things in mind, for no individual or collectivity can afford to remember everything. Total recall would leave us unable to discriminate or generalise.'[23]

To reinforce his plea in favour of forgetting as a merciful as well as a mandatory art, Lowenthal makes a distinction between individual and collective forgetting. While the former is largely involuntary, on the other hand, collective oblivion is mainly:

> deliberate, purposeful and regulated. Therein lies the art of forgetting – art as opposed to ailment, choice rather than compulsion or obligation. The art is a high and delicate enterprise, demanding astute judgment about what to keep and what to let go, to salvage or to shred or shelve, to memorialise or to anathematise.[24]

Adrian Forty, in supporting the view that forgetting is an intentional, deliberate and desirable human response, invokes the classic tradition, particularly the perspectives of Durkheim, Freud, Ernest Renan, Walter Benjamin, Martin Heidegger and a sampling of a few contemporary cultural theorists and philosophers like Michel de Certeau and Paul Connerton.[25] By fulfilling this universal need to forget, which to Forty is essential for sustaining normal and healthy life, groups normally resort to, or take shelter in, two rather familiar and well-tried strategies. They either construct an artifact by building monuments, war memorials and the like – such as a material proxy – as substitute for the delicate and fragile nature of human memory. The trauma, senseless destruction and sacrifices are in this case redeemed. Or, and more likely, society resorts to iconoclastic predispositions by effacing and destroying much of the relics and material heritage of the past.

Both these traditions, as we shall see, have been quite salient in Beirut. Indeed, they have provoked an ongoing, often heated, polemic over the architectural heritage of the city and how to memorialise the country's pathological history with protracted civil strife. Critics of Solidere's massive rehabilitation scheme for downtown Beirut continue to decry and berate how much of the city's distinctive archaeological heritage was needlessly destroyed in the process of reconstruction. If the belligerent and recurrent cycles of random violence had devastated much of the city's centre and adjoining urban neighbourhoods, the reconstruction schemes, the critics often charge, compounded the ruthless destruction by acting more like a merciless bulldozer. When the more divisive issues associated with the war's collective memory – how, where and in what form can they be recalled – are invoked, manifestations of discord and ambivalence become equally contentious. They always generate and reawaken sharp and heated debate and, thereby, give vent to layers of hidden hostility and unresolved fear.

These, clearly, are not merely rhetorical and benign concerns. Nor are Beirut's experiences in this regard unique or unusual. They are embroiled with the testy issues of collective memory, space and national identity. More explicitly, they inform the entangled discourse regarding the connection between objects, memory and forgetting. Adrian Forty, in fact, takes us back to the Aristotelian tradition to show us how it was inverted by Freud, Ernest Renan and, more recently, by Michel de Certeau.

To Forty, the Western tradition of memory since the Renaissance has been founded on the Aristotelian premise that material objects, whether natural or artificial, can act as the analogues or correlates of human memory. What this also came to mean is that such objects may be interpreted as the means by which members of a society may get rid of what they no longer wish to remember. This was predicated on the assumption that memory loss is inevitable through the passive attrition of time.

Freud's theory of mental process is the antithesis of such an Aristotelian conception of memory. He questioned this presumed relationship between objects and memory. Since to Freud memory is no more than a mental process, he advanced the thesis that in 'mental life nothing that has once been formed can perish – that everything is somehow preserved and in suitable circumstances ... can once more be brought to light'.[26] In other words, rather than memory-loss taking place through the passive attrition of time, as Aristotle had assumed, Freud considered that memory and, thus, forgetting is an active, intentional and desired force, not passive, natural and involuntary. The French philosopher Michel de Certeau views this connection between memory and objects from an interesting and telling perspective. He writes, intuitively, that 'memory is a sort of anti-museum: it is not localisable'. For him, the defining element of memory is that 'it comes from somewhere else, it is outside of itself, it moves things about.'[27] This is taken to imply that, if and when it ceases to display such alteration, when it becomes fixed to particular objects or local artifacts, then it is destined to decay and may well suffer oblivion. Seen in such a light, objects become the enemy of memory. Confining memory will most certainly dispel its forgetfulness.

Within this context, it is understandable, considering the natural reactions of the Lebanese to all the unbearable atrocities and traumas with which they were beset, that they should try to forget or at least distance themselves from and sanitise, as they appear to be doing, the scars and scares of almost two decades of cruel and senseless violence. As the country was preparing itself to commemorate the thirtieth anniversary of its misbegotten civil war on 14 April, a score of voluntary associations were declaring their birth and pronouncing their envisaged programs and strategies for healing, reconciliation and enhancing national consciousness through voluntary and cross-communal work camps and social welfare projects which cut across and transcend sectarian and local attachments. Interestingly, leaders and spokespersons of these associations are, on the whole, youthful groups who are too young to have witnessed firsthand any of the treacherous events of the war. They are also perceptive in launching their programmes on the dreaded 'green line' adjoining the National Museum, a site that conjures up images of demarcation, distance and the bounded territoriality of warring factions.

The Heritage Crusade

It is the ambivalence and uncertainty with which we behold the past, along with the fear of disappearance, which account for the concern for what Lowenthal aptly calls the 'heritage crusade'. In post-war Lebanon this crusade has become so pervasive that it is beginning to assume all the trappings and hype of a national pastime and a thriving industry. Escape into a re-enchanted past has obviously a nostalgic tinge to it. This tinge, however, need not be seen as a pathological retreat into an illusionary past. It could well serve, as Bryan Turner has argued, as a redemptive form of heightened sensitivity, sympathetic awareness of human problems and hence, could be 'ethically uplifting'.[28] In this sense it is less of a 'flight' and more of a catharsis for human suffering.

This nostalgic longing among a growing segment of disenchanted intellectuals is a form of resistance or refusal to partake in the process of debasement of aesthetic standards or the erosion of *bona fides* and veritable items of cultural heritage. Impotent as such efforts may seem, they express a profound disgust with the trivialisation of culture so visible in the emptiness of consumerism and the nihilism of the popular culture industry. They are also an outcry against the loss of personal autonomy and authenticity. Even the little common place, mundane things and routines of daily life – street smells and sounds and other familiar icons and landmarks·of place – let alone historic sites and architectural edifices, are allowed to atrophy or be effaced.

Here, again, this nostalgic impulse is beginning to assume redemptive and engaging expressions. A variety of grassroots movements, citizen and advocacy groups and voluntary associations have been established recently to address problems related to the preservation and protection of the built environment. Earlier special-interest groups have had to redefine their objectives and mandates to legitimise and formalise their new interests. A succession of workshops, seminars and international conferences has been hosted ʾto draw on the experience of other comparable instances of post-war reconstruction. Periodicals and special issues of noted journals, most prominently perhaps the feature page on 'heritage' by the Beirut daily *an-Nahar*, are devoting increasing coverage to matters related to space, environment and architectural legacy.

At the popular cultural level, this resistance to the threat of disappearance is seen in the revival of folk arts, music and lore, flea markets, artisan shops and other such exhibits and galleries. Personal memories, autobiographies, nostalgic recollections of one's early childhood and life in gregarious and convivial quarters and neighbourhoods of old Beirut are now popular narrative genres. So are pictorial glossy anthologies of Beirut's urban history, old postcards, maps and other such collectibles. They are all part of a thriving business. Even the media and advertising industries are exploiting such imagery and nostalgic longing to market their products.

Another mode of retreat or escape from the ugly memories of the war and the drabness or anxieties of the post-war era is the proliferation of kitsch. While kitsch is not normally perceived as a mode of escape, its rampant allures in Lebanon, as will be shown, are symptomatic of the need to forget. Hence, it feeds on collective amnesia and the pervasive desire for popular distractions.

Mediating Agencies of Social Forgetting

What are the mediating agencies or artifacts in the Bourj able to evolve into effective vectors for the process of social forgetting, or what Hobbes had termed 'remedial oblivion'? There is no shortage of candidates. The envisioned 'Archaeological Trail', the 'Garden of Forgiveness', under construction: some of the distinct architectural icons or edifices can easily play such a role since they all embody elements of cultural pluralism, tolerance, hybridity and peaceful coexistence. Likewise, some of the proposals also addressed issues of how to incorporate the Martyrs' Monument, which commemorates the national heroes executed by the Ottomans in 1915 and 1916, or how to envision a war memorial or a monument to celebrate or memorialise all the victims and sacrifices of the civil war. Such efforts become pertinent not by way of helping us dwell on the pathologies of civil and uncivil violence; they can also serve as the socio-cultural venues for cultivating the sorely needed outlets for forgetting. Generations of Lebanese, either directly or vicariously, are still old enough to remember those years. In no way have they – or can they – forget such dark and misbegotten episodes in their past. Indeed, they often remember them so well that they deeply resent being reminded of them. Indeed, as will be elaborated below, much of the carefree abandon and exuberance – together with the proclivity of the Lebanese to embrace novelties, crazes and popular pastimes – are largely symptomatic of their eagerness to distance themselves from the dreaded memories of the war.

Here again, the longing of the Lebanese for a respite from the beleaguering elements of their collective memory finds parallels in other comparative instances of internecine hostility. For example, the outbreak of violence in former Yugoslavia may well be seen as the outcome of the refusal to forget past events. Likewise, the Northern Irish protracted conflict is symptomatic of the fact that the protagonists – both political parties and religious groups – were reluctant to forget the elements of their belligerent past that other groups might no longer feel the urge to remember. Neil Jarman's account of the Irish in Belfast graphically epitomises the consequences of a people so trapped in their past, so embroiled in reliving their contentious and bloody history that they are unable to free themselves from the constraints of such conflict-prone history.[29] Such selective retention certainly implies that some of the more redemptive and beneficent elements of that past are not celebrated or commemorated with the same passionate intensity. In short, what we remember and what we forget is socially constructed.

From these and other such instances, it is clear how essential to stable political life – indeed, to the well-being of individual life as well – is a certain measure of amnesia or social forgetfulness. By re-examining the chequered history of the Bourj, it is our hope to reconstruct from its rich and diverse past a history, to paraphrase Forty, 'not of memorials but of amnesiacs!!'[30]

It is in this sense that the experience of the Lebanese – particularly their ambivalence regarding how to cope with, let alone incorporate, the barbaric legacy of the war – is not at all unique. The setting in post-war Europe is very instructive in this regard. Indeed, as some historians argue, the relative stability of Western Europe since 1945 has in part been due to that colossal act of collective, consensual forgetting. For example, the divisions between wartime partisans and collaborators, whatever may be said in private, have been largely forgotten in public.[31] As indicated earlier, the very word 'amnesty' denotes a certain measure of public forgetfulness. As Ernest Renan reminds us, most of the social contract theories of the state, upon which modern democracies are based, assume that their members are prepared to forget the more divisive differences that on occasion pull them apart. Renan was unequivocal when he asserted that the 'essence of a nation is that all individuals share a great many things in common also that they have forgotten some things'.[32]

Recently Jens Hanssen and Daniel Genberg have coined the term 'hypermnesia'[33] to refer to instances in post-war Lebanon of the abundance of overlapping, conflicting and rivalling memories of the war. In their view, such celebratory conceptions of history – indeed, the frequent public debates about collective forgetting – have served to amplify and reinforce this notion of 'collective hypermnesia'. To them, the loss of memory is no more but an 'antonym to amnesia ... the inaccessible, passive *other* memory that is triggered inadvertently, to denote a situation where memory is constantly present, multiple and celebrated'.[34] In this sense, the whole experience of Solidere in the reconstruction of downtown Beirut became a hotly contested public debate precisely because it was emblematic of, and embodied, the discourse over versions and visions for the past and future of city and country.

The threatening effacement of dilapidated vestiges of the past falling prey to early 'clean slate' ideologies ironically produced a public sphere pregnant with divergent versions and visions for past and future of city and country. At this particular juncture the debate represented an effort and commitment to effect a moratorium on the seemingly inevitable and ever-accelerated, globalisation-induced forgetting.[35]

The relentless polemics over the remembrance of the Holocaust, America's experience in Vietnam, the repeated *naqbas* (disasters) and *naqsas* (setbacks) that Arabs have had to suffer in their misbegotten confrontations with Israel – from the colossal defeat in the Seven-Days War to other equally treacherous failures, including the collapse of the

Saddam regime in Iraq – and other such atrocities of modern times always re-invite the same poignant and anguishing public debates. Of course, forgetting always runs the risk of repetition. In this sense, had the Lebanese recalled and learned from all their earlier encounters with civil strife, perhaps the atrocities would not have been as recurrent. The basic dilemma the Lebanese face today is to know how to remember all the ugly atrocities of the war without lessening their horrors. To put it differently, the problem is how to recall the hideous episodes of the war without sanitising them by making them more tolerable to remember. To attribute the war to external forces by which the country, and Beirut in particular, became no more than a proxy battlefield for other peoples' wars is one such effective strategy or alibi to which the Lebanese continue to resort. It obviates their guilt and, hence, their direct responsibility for partaking in the horrors. They become no more than surrogate victims of other warring and belligerent groups.

These matters, incidentally, are not merely of conceptual and abstract interest. As I write, Solidere has just completed the first phase of the International Urban Design Ideas Competition for Martyrs' Square and the Grand Axis of Beirut. The competition was launched on 18 June 2004 under the auspices of the Union of International Architects (UIA). By the time the website for the event was made accessible, it was inundated during its first week (the last week of June 2004) by some 6,000 to 8,000 hits per day! By the time registration ended on 31 July, some 420 applicants (from sixty-five countries) had submitted proposals for the competition. The international jury, after three days of deliberation, arrived at a shortlist of seven finalists. During the second phase of the competition the finalists are expected to submit their detailed final projects. The winning projects, including a special category for students, was announced on 6 May 2005: National Martyrs' Day.

Virtually all the finalists, in one way or another, addressed the issue of what, how and where in the reconstructed central square of the city's capital can we memorialise or celebrate some of the disparaging elements in the country's chequered history with civil strife. This too is a testy and probing issue. It is bound to invite heated polemics, given the disparate and contested views the Lebanese continue to hold about the war. Will the commemoration be a sober, subdued memorial to recall and dwell upon tragic, lamentable and mournful events? Or will it be a celebratory monument to revel and bask in the glories of past heroic events?

We often associate dramatic iconoclastic reactions – the deliberate acts of destruction of national symbols – with efforts to mark or celebrate moments of transition from one political era or regime to another. Such riddance of monuments (e.g. the destruction of the Berlin wall, Lenin's statue, the Buddha statues in Afghanistan and, more recently, Saddam Hussein's statue in Baghdad), often accompanied by the frenzy of aroused masses, is more than just a vengeful act of sheer retribution. It must be seen as a collective attempt to permanently erase or withdraw representations of the maligned or discredited old system that might serve again as vehicles for popular recollection.[36]

The importance we conventionally assign to memorials or monuments, or any visual imagery, is clearly not an invention of the modern world. In his fascinating work,[37] Frances Yates persuasively traced this back to the age of scholasticism and medieval memory where *memoria,* the conscious evocation of past experience through visual imagery, served to facilitate the spread of devotional learning to laymen. From medieval times onwards, the destruction of such visual imagery appeared to be tantamount to acts of forgetting.[38]

Although we are often inclined to use terms like 'memorials' and 'monuments' interchangeably, James Young insists on clarifying the distinct meanings of each. To him, memorials 'recall only past death or tragic events and provide places to mourn'. On the other hand, there is an element of triumphalism in monuments: 'They remain essentially celebratory markers of triumphs and heroic individuals'.[39]

Bearing this subtle distinction in mind, Arthur Danton, in his assessment of the contested Vietnam Veteran Memorial, situates his observations within the polemics of collective memory or the social art of forgetting. Danton is very explicit in this regard. He tells us that:

> we erect monuments so that we shall always remember and build memorials so that we shall never forget. Thus, we have the Washington Monument but the Lincoln Memorial. Monuments commemorate the memorable and embody the myths of beginnings. Memorials ritualise remembrance and mark the reality of ends ... Monuments make heroes and triumphs, victories and conquests, perpetually present and part of life. The memorial is a special precinct, extruded from life, a segregated enclave where we honour the dead. With monuments, we honour ourselves.[40]

It is hoped that these introductory considerations, conceptual and otherwise, will serve as a meaningful context to situate and inform the 'story' I wish to narrate about the Bourj's historical transformation and the role it is envisaged to play at this critical juncture in Lebanon's history. From its eventful past, much like its most recent history, a few distinct but related elements stand out: first, the predisposition of the Bourj to incorporate and reconcile pluralistic and multicultural features; second, its inventiveness in reconstituting and refashioning its collective identity and public image; third, its role in hosting and disseminating popular culture, consumerism, mass entertainment and often nefarious tourist attractions.

Most of all, as amplified by the riveting, popular and emancipatory expressions unleashed by the murder of Hariri, the Bourj can also nurture and play host to some formidable socio-cultural and political transformations. Further, and perhaps unavoidably, the uprising has given free vent to some of the festive, light-hearted and frivolous forms of popular entertainment and fun-loving activities. These, however, should not detract from the weightier consequential concerns and public issues it has already aroused.

Beirut's Encounters with the Social Production of Space: A Historical Overview

The often-made claim that the site of the Bourj – Beirut's quintessential central square – is the nursery of Homo sapiens is not a vain or hollow one. Since its inception, the site has always served as a compelling node of human settlements, a magnet for the world's most vibrant civilisations.

It is customary in tracing its prehistoric origins to single out its Phoenician pedigree. It was the Phoenicians, after all, who launched its maritime and trading vocations. One tradition claims that the city was built by the god Illion, who had married a goddess named Beirut. The first recorded reference is in the Tell El-Amarna tablets, in which Ammunira, a Phoenician vassal of Akhenaton (1379–1362 BC), mentions Beirut's strong defences and prosperity.

Many conquering armies have descended upon the city, from the time of Ramses II of Egypt (thirteenth century BC) to 1941, when British forces took the city. Destroyed by Tryphon, a usurper of the Syrian throne, in 140 BC, it later flourished under Roman rule (64 BC onwards), doubtlessly one of its most glorious periods. Marcus Agrippa, Augustus's admiral, had visited in 15 BC, after which it was granted the status of a Roman colony. The Herodian kings of Palestine embellished Beirut with hippodromes, an amphitheatre, baths and porticoes.

As an imposing Roman colony, it evinced clear symptoms of rational planning. Following the Roman invasion, as social historians remind us, Beirut was built over the urban grid of the Hellenistic city. The Emperor Augustus honoured Beirut by making it a colony and named it after his daughter, Julia Augusta Felix Berytus. He bestowed upon the city Roman rights and privileges. More visibly, he endowed it with all the icons

Bronze Age wall   *Middle Bronze Age*

of a Roman colony. The end product was so elegant that it was referred to as the 'most handsome Berytus, the Jewel of Phoenecia'.[1] Like other Roman colonies, the city was laid out in an orthogonal plan with two main axes, the *Decumanus Maximus* and the *Cardo Maximus*, intersecting at the main crossroad of the city and dividing it into the four quarters which prefigured much of the subsequent layout of modern Beirut. Compelling as these physical edifices were, Beirut's prominence at the time was also attributed to its intellectual standing, a reflection of the Roman School of Law that flourished between the third and sixth centuries. A few of its imposing columns and other archaeological artifacts continue to adorn the city centre today.

Like many other prehistoric cities, Beirut had its full share of calamitous disasters, both natural and man-made. In 551, a tidal wave, accompanying one of a series of earthquakes, destroyed the city, reducing the population to a few thousand. In view of the catastrophic devastations of the recent Indian Ocean tsunami, W. M. Thomson's graphic description of a similar visitation that beleaguered Beirut deserves quoting in full:

> On the ninth of July AD 551, one of those awful earthquakes, which repeatedly shook the Roman world in the time of Justinian, seems to have entirely destroyed Beirût, overthrown her colleges, churches, temples, theatres, and palaces, and buried multitudes of inhabitants beneath the ruins; and, although the city was re-built, it never regained its former magnificence. You can scarcely walk through the gardens or dig a foundation for a house without coming upon the memorials of that dreadful calamity. It is amazing to see how deeply some of those ruins are entombed, suggesting the idea that the very terraces on which such costly structures stood were upheaved and precipitated on those below. And this corresponds with the history of that fearful time. We are told that 'enormous chasms were opened, huge and heavy bodies were charged into the air, the sea alternately advanced and retreated beyond its ordinary bounds,' and a mountain was torn from that bold promontory – then called Theoprosopon, the face of God, and now Râs esh Shukkah – and cast into the sea, where it formed a mole for the harbour of Batrûn. Perhaps its Arabic name, implying the cape of the split or cleft open, may be a witness of that catastrophe.[2]

The Arabs occupied the city close to five centuries, from 635 to 1110. Shortly afterwards, it was captured by Baldwin I, the Flemish leader of the First Crusade. Beirut was again devastated by a raft of other misfortunes. In 1151, it was pillaged by an Egyptian fleet and, from then until 1187, when it was captured by Salah El-Din, it was the scene of constant battle. During the 200 years of its largely uneventful history during the Crusades, Beirut was captured several times by Saracens and Christians. Judging from the scanty and unsubstantiated accounts of the pilgrims of the Middle Ages, the number of its inhabitants, from about five to ten thousand, engaged in commerce and in the manufacture of olive oil, soap, and silk, which for several centuries continued to be the staple productions of this region.[3]

Historical accounts indicate that the city declined considerably under the Mamluks (1291–1516). It started, however, to revive after the Ottoman conquest. Much of the most enduring architectural heritage of the city is the outgrowth of four centuries of Ottoman sovereignty over Lebanon. Initially, Druze emirs, who had won Ottoman favour, became masters of central and southern Lebanon. The most illustrious of them, Fakhr al-Din II, who ruled from 1593 to 1635, made Beirut his winter residence. Trade relations with Western powers were revived. The city was once again fortified, and its picturesque pine groves were restored. It was Fakhr al-Din II, incidentally, who had carried with him notions of building design and landscape gardening back from his five-year exile at the Court of Florence between 1613 and 1618. The picturesque palace he built in 1623, with its refined architecture, embellished by effusive water fountains

Amir Mansour Mosque (built in 1572)

St Georges Cathedral (built in 1767)

Italian attack in 1912

and fragrant orange groves, dazzled successive generations of visitors. An even earlier landmark, the Emir Mansour Assaf Mosque (built in 1572), which has recently been restored, deserves recognition. The next architectural landmark worthy of note is, doubtlessly, the Greek Orthodox St Georges Cathedral, built in 1767, on the site of a medieval Episcopal monastery.

In 1772, Beirut was beset with another interlude of conflict and decline. As an offshoot of the Crimean War, a Russian fleet attacked the city. An even fiercer and more devastating assault in 1841 by the joint forces of England, Austria and Turkey put an end to the ten-year occupation of Muhammad Ali of Egypt. The combined assault left the city, once again, a virtual ruin.

After the civil strife of 1860, the by-product of protracted hostility between Maronite Christians and Druzes in Mount Lebanon, a massive influx of Christians encroached upon the city. It was then that the growing density of the town started to spill out beyond its already demolished medieval walls. The post-war period was marked by major infrastructural developments, particularly the construction of harbour facilities and the completion of the Damascus railway. More strikingly, as a headquarters for French, British and American religious and evangelical missions and as a growing centre of trade and services, the cosmopolitan character of Beirut became more visible. By then, the population had leaped to 120,000.

This brief auspicious interlude was marred, once again, by the disruptive consequences of WWI. In 1912 the Italians, at war with Turkey, attacked Beirut by sea. In 1918 the allies entered the city. During the early years of WWII, Beirut remained under the control of the French and British until it was declared the capital of an independent Lebanon in 1941.

This historic overview will be necessarily brief and sketchy. The intention is twofold: first, to highlight some of its striking spatial and architectural heritage; and second, to account for the failure of successive attempts at urban planning to curb Beirut's haphazard and unguided growth. Or, more specifically, why agencies empowered to safeguard the city's habitat and living space always failed to exercise their responsibilities. An effort will also be made to show how the distinctive features of the urban landscape and architectural heritage came to be socially constructed and reproduced. This will naturally involve identifying how local architects, town planners and other indigenous groups were instrumental in adapting and rearranging transplanted and borrowed schemes to local socio-cultural exigencies and expectations.

Urban Landscape and Architectural Heritage

All historical accounts of Beirut, particularly narratives of travellers, reinforce the view that by the end of the eighteenth century Beirut was still no more than a small harbour with relatively safe anchorage. In fact, most travellers who happened to disembark in Beirut were en route to other more appealing spots in the Orient. It should be recalled that for three centuries (and only after the battle of Lepants in 1571 had ended Turkish and the Barbary Corsairs' domination of the Mediterranean), there was virtually no interest in the Orient as a beguiling melting pot and epicentre of the world's religious movements.

However, between 1780 and 1840 (an interlude associated with the emergence of the Renaissance, the Romantic movement and humanism) the Orient became a source of literary, cultural and artistic imagination. A relentless list of legendary poets, writers and painters (Byron, Flaubert, Chateaubriand, Delacroix, Lamartine, Nerval, among others) trickled in. They sometimes preceded and at other times followed in the wake of evangelists, diplomats and military expeditions. This nascent curiosity in the Orient, which in the Western imagination stretched from Persia to the Maghreb, was incited and sustained by a myriad of personal and historical circumstances. Doubtlessly, the image of the Orient as an immutable, unchanging but enchanting topo, in contrast to the political and economic restlessness of Europe, must have played a part in reinforcing this heightened sense of interest for pilgrims and tourists in the region. This was, after all, the Holy Land, and throngs of pilgrims came to reconnect with the divine footsteps of Christ or the shrines, sacred spaces and architectural icons of Islamic art and architecture. To many others, it was the bucolic, pristine and exotic natural endowments, suffused by the sheer delight of that enchanting Mediterranean light which bathed virtually everything within its reach, which aroused this sense of adventure.

But even then, I would argue, Lebanon was rarely sought out directly. Beirut was no more than a station or port of call on the way to the more legendary cities of Damascus, Baghdad, Cairo or Mecca and Medina. Indeed, as Fouad Debbas notes in his exquisite collection of postcards of historic Beirut between 1880 and 1930,[4] the engravings of Lebanon bought by the early travellers tended to deal almost exclusively with Baalbeck, Sidon or Tripoli. This neglect was also apparent in the first systematic studies and ethnographies of the period. If, and when, an incidental reference was made to Beirut, it was always beheld as a charming, labyrinthine medieval enclosure surrounded by an unspoiled natural habitat with a fresh, healthy and seasonable climate. Indeed, it was these beneficial natural endowments that had initially drawn the attention of itinerant missionaries and other travellers coming from the harsh and unforgiving desert-like interior. Beirut, and its plush and more temperate surroundings, always seemed more inviting.[5]

In identifying the early symptoms of Beirut's urbanisation, social and urban historians are often prone to single out events associated with the sectarian hostilities of 1860. The influx of Christians fleeing their plundered homes and villages could not all be accommodated within the already congested quarters of the walled town. Hence, the demographic spill beyond the medieval ramparts was always assumed to have begun at that time. The evidence extracted from missionary reports and diaries and those of other travellers, sketchy as they seem, suggest that these symptoms were already visible at least three to four decades earlier.

By the time, for example, Issac Bird and William Goodell stopped in Beirut in 1824 on their way to Palestine, it already seemed a 'safer and more agreeable seaport than Smyran'. Although it was no more than a small settlement of little more than half a square kilometre with a resident population of 5,000, it was already being dubbed as a 'great emporium' and 'eastern Naples' with 'Frank' residents seeking it as a summer resort.

The overriding image one can extract of the city beyond its cloistered walls was generally desolate, squalid and unsafe. Residents ventured outside the walls during the day, only to return to their homes at night. Yet to a seasoned traveller like Stephen Olin, it was these same groves and gardens that seemed so 'luxuriant' and 'verdant'. This is what he recorded as he approached the city in 1835:

We approached the city through a region of luxuriance and beauty such as seldom greets the eye in the environs of an Oriental town. It is covered with gardens and mulberry trees now literally burdened with their rank and deeply verdant foliage. The best houses of Beyrout, including those of most of the foreigners and merchants are, in the midst of these gardens.[6]

The impression Beirut left on the missionaries, at least initially, was equally auspicious. Perhaps because they had suffered all the travails of restless wandering, along with the discomforts and ill-treatment at the hands of suspicious and resentful officials, Beirut seemed like a pleasant surprise! Yes, of course, they had much to complain about. Goodell's account of their disembarkation, on 16 November 1823, captured much of the bizarre and inconsistent features of the local culture. He was stunned by both the 'verdant and lovely' beauty of the habitat, as captivating as the 'hills, dales, fruits and flowers of our own happy country', but also by the 'half naked and barbarous Arabs' who carried them ashore on their shoulders because the port was still without a wharf at that time:

> At eleven o'clock in the morning we came to anchor at four miles' distance from the city. It was a morning without clouds; and we discovered on the sides of Lebanon and in the environs of Beyrout, many trees, and more that appeared verdant and lovely, than we have before seen, since we left the hills and dales and fruit and flowers of our own happy country. May the countenance of our Redeemer ever be to us 'as Lebanon, excellent as the cedars.' In a short time, boats came, and we found ourselves surrounded by half naked and barbarous Arabs, of whom we have often heard say, 'who can stand before these sons of Anak?' Our hearts are indeed sometimes ready to faint within us; but we remember the years of the right hand of the Most High: 'What time we are afraid we will trust the ...'
>
> There is no wharf at Beyrout, and when our boat struck the sand, the fierce Arabs leaped out, and carried us on their shoulders, through the billows to the dry land amidst the multitude who ran to witness so novel scene. We were in the English costume and the ladies were without veils. The Turkish Governor sat with his pipe, looking on with great composure ... The filth of the city, together with its dampness in winter, and its heat in summer, renders it a very undesirable place for a family.[7]

Although he had considered Beirut an 'undesirable place for a family' because of its filth, damp winters and hot summers, he had some pleasant things to say about the spacious house in which they were living and the fairly lush habitat beyond the city walls. More importantly, he provided evidence to the effect that as early as 1824 there were already more than 200 cottages beyond the walled city:

> The plain to the south of Beyrout was covered with olive, palm, orange, lemon, pine and mulberry trees, enriched with vines and enlivened by numerous cottages ... From

the terrace of the house, we can count without the walls of the city, no less than 200 of these cottages, scattered here and there in the fields of mulberry trees.[8]

Fisk's initial impression, at least the one he relayed back to the board, was also favourable. He too spoke of all the attractions it possesses, particularly with regard to its favoured position as a missionary field station:

> Beyrout seems to me to possess many important advantages as a missionary station. It is situated at the foot of Mount Lebanon, and a missionary might very profitably spend the hot months of the summer among the convents and villages of the mountains, many of which are within a few hours ride of the town. Occasional visits might be made to Damascus, which is only three days off. On the other hand, it is only one or two days sail to Cyprus. On the coast south of Beyrout you reach Sidon in one day, and Tyre in two: and to the west, in two or three days, you arrive in Tripoli, where I understand there are many Greeks. It would be easy to maintain correspondence with all these places, and supply them with books, in Beyrout itself a missionary who could preach in Italian might, I think collect a small congregation immediately: and if he were disposed to open a school, there are probably few places in Syria that would be so promising. Another circumstance which, though not perhaps very important in itself, will yet weigh something in the mind of a missionary, is, that here he will find, oftener than anywhere else in Syria, opportunities to receive and forward communications. Here too he will enjoy the protection of an English consul, and the society and friendship of several other consuls and their families. I think a missionary family would be more comfortably situated at Beyrout, than at any other place which I have seen in Syria.[9]

It is of interest to note here that the appeals of Beirut were also attributed to its proximity to the mountains with their scenic beauty and temperate climate. To the roving, fatigued and often afflicted missionaries from other stations in the region, the country served as an inviting place for refuge and recovery. To those returning from exhausting trips to the desert and hinterland, or others weary and jaded by fruitless labour, a brief respite in the mountains always seemed invigorating.

Thomson was so taken by how refreshed his colleagues became after one such restful reprieve in the mountains that they seemed to him as vigorous as if they were back in beloved New England:

> Our brethren have all returned from the mountains, where they have spent a very pleasant and profitable summer. The health of all, old and young, has been much improved by the mountain air: and they return with more like the life and vigour of our native land, than I have seen since I arrived in this country.[10]

Returning from a trip to Damascus and Alepyo in June 1824, where they encamped in a 'dirty Mussulman village of a thousand inhabitants and suffered much from exposure to the heated air, filled with sand and dust', they had this to say:

> There was neither tree nor rock to shade us. The strong wind was almost as hot as if it came from a furnace, and we had nothing to eat but curdled milk, called *leben*, and bread that had been dried and hardened by the heat of eight or ten days.[11]

The prospects of re-entering Beirut and the joyous anticipation of reunion with comrades were always specially cheery and refreshing to drooping and weary spirits. Fisk, after another disheartening trip to Jaffa in the spring of 1824, recorded how rejoiced he felt in this happy and favoured land:

> These days of busy, friendly, joyous intercourse have greatly served to revive the spirits that drooped, to refresh the body that was weary, and to invigorate the mind that began to flag. I came here tired of study, and tired of journeying, but I begin to feel already desirous to reopen my books, or resume my journeys. We have united in praising God for bringing us to this land. I suppose we are as cheerful, contented and happy, as any little circle of friends in our favoured county.[12]

On his second visit to Beirut forty years later, in 1876, Thomson continued to be impressed by the comparatively felicitous advantage the city enjoyed because of its proximity to the invigorating climate of the mountains:

> It is surprising to see how speedily the cool, invigorating air of the mountains will revive not only the little sufferers, but also the emaciated victims of the malignant Syrian fevers. Lebanon is destined to become erelong a favourite summer retreat for invalids and for those who occupy the sultry valley of the Nile, the sea board, and the hot plains around the eastern end of the Mediterranean.[13]

Of special concern to the missionaries, given the preponderance of epidemics, plagues and other associated hazards, was the overall quality of sanitation and public health. Here, as well, Beirut seemed comparatively advantageous. In their periodic reports, they repeatedly recognised these blissful attributes and considered themselves fortunate for being there. Yet they remained chronically restless about the unhealthy sanitary conditions, were understandably fastidious about bracing themselves to face the ravages of illness, disease, pestilence and the blustering and tempestuous elements. Indeed, they wrote special detailed reports monitoring changes in weather and climatic conditions. They were naturally most apprehensive about the recurring onslaught of epidemics and plagues:

Beyrout is certainly healthy, and it is probably the most healthy place on the coast of Syria. I have known several cases of intermittent fever, during the rainy season: but none that proved mortal. It is said, that the plague never rages here. Last spring two Turkish men-of-war brought the plague with them from Egypt. Many on board were sick, some were dead, and others dying. But they came on shore, went into every part of the city and continued three days in Beyrout. We were a little alarmed, and kept ourselves in close quarters: but no instances of infection occurred. We unlock our doors, and ventured abroad, after the expiration of a week.[14]

As alluded to above, all spatial descriptions of Beirut around the middle of the nineteenth century continued to reinforce this traditional image of the old town as an 'Old Seraglio', which, much like a medieval citadel, was a gated enclosure. May Davie traces the origins of this edifice to the Mamluks and perhaps even to the Crusades.[15] Regardless of its prehistoric origins, all travellers' accounts, spotty as they may be, reinforce the view that by the end of the eighteenth century, Beirut was still no more than a little town of about 6,000 inhabitants, huddled rather comfortably within its cloistered ramparts. Although often dubbed as 'Square Beirut' the fortified enclosure was more rectangular in shape. Debbas, in fact, offers explicit dimension: 570 metres from north to south and

Gated medieval town (1850s)

370 metres east to west.[16] Ahmad Pasha al-Jazzar, typical of his rapacious and oppressive hegemony over Mount Lebanon while governor of Sida (1776–1804), had reconstructed the city walls beyond its former enclosure to permit greater freedom of movement of his soldiers against potential aggressors. Likewise, he also managed to clear much of the plush orchards and extensive mulberry-tree plantations beyond the walls to ward off the likelihood of such surprised attacks. Debbas makes reference to Montfort's engravings and the Royal Navy map of Beirut in 1831 as evidence of such gross mutilation of both the physical and natural heritage of a city to comply with aggrandising whims of a despot.[17]

Egyptian, Ottoman and French Legacies

During the latter part of the Egyptian decade, Ibrahim Pasha had begun the process of demolishing part of the ramparts in an effort to extend the town beyond its walls. But we know, from various sources, that inhabitants were already building more than makeshift and temporary residences outside the city walls. While Presbyterian missionaries – Bird and Goodell – counted, about 200 cottages in 1824, by 1837 Leon de Laborde indicated that as much as half the town's populations were, in fact, living in the surrounding groves. He also noted that law and order were virtually non existent at night. Thieves and vagabonds were legion. They went on a rampage under the cover of dark. Hence, inhabitants had no choice but to return to the security of the inner town protected by its gates that were locked at night.[18]

It should be remarked that Beirut's prominence as a trade centre was more than an accident of geography and natural harbour facilities. Muhammad Ali took a keen interest in encouraging and stimulating trade. Commercial treaties, intended as a compromise between the provisions of the old capitulatory privileges and modern requirements, were introduced to regularise customs duties and facilitate the circulation of goods.[19] The opening of Damascus to Europeans, the shipment of Western goods to the interior, growing public security and safety in the transport of goods and travels, growth of foreign community and freedom granted to missionaries to expand their activities: all, in one way or another, assisted in Beirut's development as a major Mediterranean seaport. During the decade of Egyptian occupation, Beirut's population rose rapidly from 10,000 to nearly 15,000, and tax returns for the same period increased by fourfold.[20]

These new forces for regeneration – introduction of order and security, revival of foreign trade, easing of restrictions from which Christians had previously suffered, opening up the hinterland by extending agriculture and stimulating economic activity – had compelling social implications. Some of the most visible consequences, symptomatic of the genesis of cosmopolitanism, were the changes in taste and lifestyles. Travellers in the late-1830s and early-1840s were already describing Beirut as the 'Paris of the East'. Beirut was 'rapidly increasing in wealth, population and dimensions ... Stupendous new mansions, the property of opulent merchants, were daily being built; beautiful country houses, summer residences of the wealthy; hotels and billiard rooms and cafes, elegantly fitted ... Everywhere utility was blended with magnificence.'[21] Travellers, particularly those coming to Beirut after visiting other towns and cities in Syria and Palestine, were all struck by how 'European' the character and amenities of the city had become. The British traveller Frederick Neale, like several others, was almost rhapsodic when describing the stylish lounging bars and Italian *locandas* 'with the latest European journals and French papers'.[22] He wrote amusingly of the evening quadrille, parties, musical reunions and balls to which 'all the elite of every religion and costume are invited'[23] and where the latest polkas and waltzes were admirably performed. 'The ordinary reunions break up before midnight; the people are a strictly mercantile set and late hours would interfere with their daily business'.[24] He spoke of European bazaars and shops kept by Greeks, Ionians, Maltese and Italians selling 'a little of everything that comes from the West'.[25] Others were more impressed by the freedom of movement and the new liberties people were beginning to enjoy in their dress and appearance in public places. Lady Stanhope's physician and author of her *Memoirs*, revisiting Beirut in 1837 after an absence of six years, was moved to observe the following changes:

> The city of Beyrout had undergone great changes since the conquest of Syria by Ibrahim Pasha; not in the tortuosity of its streets, not in its broken pavements and the filthy entrances to its houses, but in the appearance of its population. Formerly, a few straggling Europeans, or Levantines in European dresses, were seen hanging about the doors of a warehouse or two in the Frank quarter; and occasionally a European woman, the wife of a consul or a merchant, would steal from one house to another, as if afraid, in her way, of insult from a fanatic Turk. Now, the bustle of a crowded mart was visible, and Europeans and their ladies walked about with a freedom which showed that a strong arm kept the haughty Mussulman under control. In 1831, the appearance of a French lady in the streets, wearing a green silk gown, was signalised as a feat of great hardihood; such an assumption of the colour peculiar to the prophet Mahomet's descendants generally entailing vexations on the wearer: and a gentleman would never have dared to give his arm to a lady out of doors: but now, both the one and the other passed on without any loud remark, although, internally, the grave Mussulmans cherished a feeling of vengeance against those who so openly violated their religious and moral institutions.[26]

Of the extensive economic changes introduced during the Egyptian period, no factor had as significant an impact on the local economy as the change in the scale and pattern of foreign trade. This was also largely responsible for the transformation in the basic character of Beirut, which was becoming less of a hinterland city and more of a seaport and Mediterranean city. Prior to the Egyptian invasion, the little international trade that did exist was predominantly Asian. Beirut, although still confined to its medieval

Mansions and villas of the new urban elite (Sursok, Sursok quarter, Melhame, Ghandour, Pharaon)

walls, was just emerging as a major *entrepôt* for the hinterland. Until then, and because of the traditional 'caravan navigation', the main cities of Syria, such as Damascus and Aleppo, were inland cities oriented toward the desert. Ports on the Syrian and Lebanese coast were, by comparison, relatively small towns. Beirut's population before the Egyptian occupation barely reached 10,000, for example. The rise of Beirut, as Dominique Chevallier has argued, is linked with the shift of trade from the interior to the Mediterranean.[27] This shift would not have occurred without the revolution in shipping and the introduction of steam navigation lines into the eastern Mediterranean. Vessels with deeper drafts for mass cargos were established first by the British in 1835; shortly afterwards, competition from French and Austrian lines increased the number of vessels operating in the Mediterranean. Beirut's harbour was naturally more endowed to accommodate deeper vessels and began to attract the bulk of growing traffic. Other coastal cities, without such natural advantages – such as Sidon, Tripoli and Tyre – began to witness a decline.

In his famous 1840 report to both Houses of the British Parliament, Dr Bowring provides evidence of this increase in the number of ships visiting Beirut's harbour. From fifteen ships in 1824, the number rose to twenty-two in 1830 and twenty-eight in 1833. By 1840 about 150 British ships alone arrived in Beirut.[28]

The physical facilities of the harbour cannot and should not, however, be overstated. At best, judging by the accounts of travellers and engravings of the period, the port had very modest anchorage: mostly relics from the Crusaders. Two towers – Bourj al-Silsilah (Chain Tower) and Bourj al-Fanar (Beacon) – guarded the entry into the old harbour.

Steamers, particularly sizeable ones, could never dock inside the harbour. Quite often heavy seas and overcrowding at the wharfs compelled them to remain offshore. Some of the most picturesque images capture sights of such ships being surrounded by small fishing boats, coasters with makeshift awnings waiting to deliver passengers ashore. Travellers' accounts also provide evidence that the entrance to the harbour was often blocked with sand to ward off the entry of pirates and hostile ships.

That last stretch of disembarkation, again as recounted by spellbound travellers, is fraught with elements of drama and surprise. Distraught and bewildered passengers were greeted by an eager, often overzealous, coterie of agents, custom officers, porters and hotel-keepers loudly extolling the attractions of their *locandas*, rooming houses and other amenities amid scenes of appalling chaos and boisterous noise. Most dishearteningly, the beleaguered travellers never made it to their destinations before being quarantined for about ten days: more so if their ships had stopped en route in seaports of countries afflicted with epidemics. The more fortunate passengers, particularly those with local connections or an ingratiating *bakhsheesh*, made it instead to a *lazaret* nearby which served as a proxy quarantine.

Modest as they were, the harbour facilities did not survive for long. In 1840, a European fleet allied to the Ottomans that had come to oust Ibrahim Pasha, bombarded and damaged the port's historic towers and embankments. In 1849, a heavy storm swept away the remaining bridge that had provided the only access to the mainland.

The Ottomans were fully aware of the deficient harbour facilities but were rather slow in executing the necessary changes consistent with the sharp and sustained increase in steamship traffic. In 1860 they filled in Bab al-Silsilah and constructed a wharf (*sansoul*) in the hope that such measures could cope with both the volume of traffic and the size and tonnage of steamers and cargo ships. But by 1863 the port was being regularly served by

Beirut's harbour (1840s)

seven sea routes.[29] The piecemeal adjustments became patently inadequate to cope with the increased traffic. It was not, however, until 1888 that an imperial *firman* granted the port (with its wharfs and warehouses) to the Compagnie Imperiale du Port with directions to construct and eventually utilise its expanded and modernised facilities. A string of successive bad winters and another ravaging epidemic (more likely alibis for Ottoman inefficiency), delayed completion until October 1894. The construction of the 800–metre jetty, a new, imposing landmark of its seafaring legacy, rendered the port more amenable for deeper vessels with much greater draft to call at Beirut. Incidentally, in 1925 the company was taken over by the French, who subjected the port to further developments. By 1934, a new dock was added and a jetty was extended by another 450 metres.

It was then that the port, much like other Mediterranean seafaring cities, started to consolidate itself as the most imposing and defining feature of the emerging city. It was the mixed and hybrid attributes of the edifices it attracted that stand out. In addition to the ordinary quays, wharfs, warehouses, postal, telegraph services and banks, there were also *khans*, elegant caravan *serais* to accommodate not only travellers but also the headquarters of foreign consulates. Interestingly, these were to prefigure some of the most recent developments and rehabilitative ventures of the port and its seafront areas. Many of these additions, then like now, were made possible by reclaiming the sea or the refilled land from the ruins and debris of the old town. For example, the old landing platforms became Marseillaise Street. Likewise, the landing stage of Khan Antoun Bey, doubtlessly one of the most elegant architectural icons that had graced the city since it was built in 1860, became Quai Street.

Beirut's wharf (1860s)

French post office   *Ottoman post office (1880s)*

    Providing even a relatively exact date for Beirut's urbanisation may be difficult. It is
also unnecessary. All that could be asserted is that, although a small town of barely 6,000
inhabitants, it was already a city early in the nineteenth century. Typical of other nascent
cosmopolitan settings, it had started to display signs of growth as a commercial, seafaring
and cultural centre of considerable appeal to those who sought it at the time. Indeed,
by then, it had already overtaken Acre's regional hegemony in this regard.[30] During the
decade of Egyptian occupation in the 1830s it witnessed, as we have seen, further such
developments. Furthermore, what is uncertain was that, as soon as these symptoms
appeared, processes and forms of swift urbanisation and urban growth were swift and
unabated.

    Naturally, not all relics of its past were swept aside. For example, its imposing
ramparts and watchtowers lingered on. So did the tempo and routine of daily life within
its medieval enclosures. Travellers continued to be captivated by the dense, congested
traffic – both human and donkey-borne – in its labyrinthine *souks* and gate entrances. By
dusk, all became calm and quiet. Except for one gate (whose keys were entrusted to the
Wali), all the entrances to the inner town were barred at night. Engravings of the period
also reveal an outer belt of watchtowers that circled the town for further security. In the
likelihood of an imminent threat, beacons and torches were lit on the elevated parts of
the towers. Sentries on duty were roused to repel assailants.

    The exact number of gates varies slightly, depending on the source. For example,
while the map cited by May Davie,[31] identifies six gates, Fouad Debbas provides vivid
descriptions of seven. All the appellations of the gates reflected designations or identities
associated with either the site they occupied or a function they served. For example, Bab
Dabbagha ('the Tanners'), on the north eastern stretch of the wall, was adjacent to a
tannery. By avoiding the compact and narrow street system of the inner courtyards, this
gate provided easy access to the port. Next to it, in the middle of the eastern flank, was

Coffee house: El-Kezaz (1920s)

Bab Es Saraya, located close to the picturesque seraglio of Emir Fakhreddine and, hence, its title. Abou En Nasr was the southeast gate. The derivation of its name is uncertain. Its popularity was largely due to its proximity to El-Kezaz café ('the Glass Coffee house'), one of the most frequented of popular ḥaunts: a rendezvous for commoners. Bab Ed Derkeh, another unknown appellation, lies squarely at the centre of the southern end of the walls. It is always identified as the most beautiful and imposing. It is the gate, apparently, which Ibrahim Pasha used when he victoriously entered the city in 1831. Because of its prominence, this is also the only gate that was kept open at night, particularly for latecomers and foreigners who were in no need for chaperoning. Bab Yacoub was at the corner of the south western flank of the wall that was built by Ahmad Pasha al-Jazzar at the beginning of the nineteenth century. A certain Yacoub Kesrouani lived above the gate, it seems. Hence, it was named after him. Just opposite Bab Es Saraya on the eastern front stood Bab Edriss, named after the Edriss family who must have built their residence in that neighbourhood. Over the years, Bab Edriss provided access to the sprawling quarters and suburbs of the western flanks of the city, such as Minet El Hosn, Zokak al Blat, Ain Mraisse, Sanayeh, Hamra and Ras Beirut. It also evolved into a fashionable shopping and recreational area. Finally, at the northern tip stood Bab Es Santiyeh, which opened onto the adjacent Muslim Santiyeh graveyard.

There was more to the old town than the prime location of its harbour or its imposing gated ramparts. Between its watchtowers and medieval walls, three other striking fortresses and fortifications stood out. First, there was Bourj al-Hashesh, a Crusaders' fortress at the north eastern tip of the rampart. Because of its commanding view of the harbour, it offered a strategic location to protect the entrance to the port. Today, it is earmarked as the 'Archaeological Tell' and awaits incorporation in the envisioned international competition for the rehabilitation of the Bourj Square. Another fortress, to the west, was Bourj al-Jadid (literally, 'the New Fortress') on the hilltop where the Grand Serail was eventually built in 1853. Finally, and perhaps most significantly, given its historic transformations in prefiguring what was to become the Central Bourj Square, was Bourj al-Khashef on the south eastern tip of the rampart. For a while the Bourj Square bore its name until it was demolished in 1874 to make way for the reconstruction of the square.

Towards the end of the nineteenth century, the old town started to show a few of the early symptoms of urbanisation. By the 1880s Beirut's population had already reached the 100,000 mark and its compact labyrinthine alleyways and dirt roads were much too dense with human and animal traffic. More importantly, it was also at this time, due to the growing problem of security and law and order, that a growing number of Beirutis started to build their permanent residences outside its walls. On his return visit to Beirut in 1873, after a lapse of forty years, William Thomson had this to say:

Forty years ago, when I came to Beirut, there was scarcely a house outside of the walls

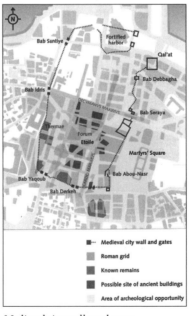

Medieval city walls and gates

fit to live in; now hundreds of convenient dwellings, and not a few large and noble mansions, adorn its beautiful suburbs, and two-thirds of the population reside in the gardens. The massacres of 1860 led many of the inhabitants of Damascus, the Lebanon, and elsewhere, to settle in Beirut, which added largely to its inhabitants, and many of the public buildings that attract the notice of visitors now have been erected since that deplorable event.

The population is now estimated at eighty thousand, more than one-half of which is made up of the various Christian sects and denominations. No city in Syria, perhaps none in the Turkish Empire, has had so rapid an expansion. And it must continue to grow and prosper, with but one proviso to cast a shade of doubt upon its bright future. Should a railroad ever connect the head of this sea with the Euphrates and the Persian Gulf, that will inevitably dictate where the emporium of Syria is to be. If Beirut can attract that line of trade and travel to its door, it will rank amongst the important cities of the world; if it cannot, then must it wane before some other rival queen of the East.[33]

It is of interest to note Thomson's prophetic projection of Beirut's future role as 'emporium' of Syria and other regions of the Turkish Empire. The spatial and land-use character of the old town became less residential and started to attract more commercial and business activities. The old dirt roads and alleyways gave way to rectilinear streets and paved, avenue-like thoroughfares. The first to be converted, in the summer of 1894, into a broad street was souk al-Jamil (literally, 'the Elegant' or 'the Beautiful'). Because it was at the time the only street in the city which could boast of paved sidewalks, it attracted a large number of craft shops and makeshift hawkers. Somehow, it managed to retain its character as a fashionable venue for the latest European products.

The old Roman road, Decumanus Maximus, a vestige of the old Roman grid, was rendered more visible as it dissected the town from east to west: that is, from Bab Edriss to Bab Es Saraya. For a while it acquired the nickname of 'El-Fashkah' (literally 'a stride' or 'step') to epitomise the diminutive character of the central avenue of the old town. Fouad Debbas recollects a story handed down by a distant uncle of his, claiming that he had arranged a kind of pulley system across the street which saved him the trouble of going back and forth through the mud and dirt to attend to the needs of his clients in both stores![34] Incidentally, during the Mandate, El-Fashkah was renamed Weygand Street in 1924.

Part of this narrow street, which originally bordered the eastern side of Bab Edriss, survived as Souk el-Frange. With its colourful and vibrant tiny shops, mostly selling perishable local produce, it became a favourite haunt for foreigners and residents of the western neighbourhoods. Another street which witnessed this structural transformation was Serail Street, which was formerly entirely residential. This once picturesque street, which began south of Bab Es Saraya and skirted the former Emir Fakhreddine Palace and was bordered by colourful Japanese lilacs, evolved first into Souk Sursock, since prosperous Greek Orthodox families such as Sursock and Tueni were the prominent

Old roads, alleyways

property-holders in the neighbourhood. Ironically, after WWI this same street was 'degentrified' into Souk el-Nourieh, the site of the city's bustling open and popular retail market for fresh agricultural produce, knick-knacks, household items and second-hand products.

The fairly swift urbanisation of Beirut demanded more than just feeble and piecemeal efforts of planning and control. The first such efforts to subject the bourgeoning city to some concerted organisation along civic lines, particularly with regard to hygiene, quarantine regulation and policing of law and order, dates back to the Egyptian occupation from 1831 to 1840. But these and subsequent efforts were imposed by a distant authority not too receptive to local interests. It was not until the first municipal or town council was officially set up in 1867 that local citizens, particularly the emancipated and civic-minded intellectual and business elites, who were instrumental in prodding Ottoman administrators to enact more extensive schemes for the modernisation of their city. It was then, for example, that measures were taken to prevent sheep, goats and other domestic animals from passing through the centre of the town en route to the harbour. The maze of congested and narrow dirt roads and alleyways gave way to the novel appearance of rectilinear, broad thoroughfares and parallel arterial road networks. Most obvious were streets like Foch, Allenby and Fakhreddine whose southern stretch was later called al-Maarad in commemoration of the first international fair hosted in Beirut's centre in 1921.

Of course, this surge of new developments meant the disappearance of some of the distinctive icons and vestiges of the old town. The devastations of WWI and the ravages of epidemics and other treacherous visitations had left their debilitating imprint on the city. Ottoman authorities were equally unsparing in their determination to subject the city to further destruction. Indeed, a few historians have been inclined to suggest that such demolition projects, often executed with much fanfare, were frequently undertaken to distract the attention of the famished and beleaguered population.[35] The old dense courtyards with their private dwellings and paved *souks* gave way to broad fifteen-metre wide avenues. Jamal Pasha, the Turkish governor at the time, inaugurated these projects as part of a 'renovation' policy. The expropriation of large tracts of private property was done with hardly any regard for due and fair process of compensation. In addition to those debilitated by famine and disease, a countless number were rendered homeless by a reckless project of urban renewal. Fouad Debbas extracts the following journalistic entry about the official opening of the demolition programme:

On Thursday, 8 April 1915, the official programme of demolition of the old souks began under the auspices of the Wali Azmi Bey. All the town dignitaries were present and Azmi Bey himself struck the first blow with a silver pick-axe supplied by the town council, to the accompaniment of the band of the Islamic School. Allenby Street, Maarad Street, Fakherddine Street, Marechal Foch Street were shortly to come into existence.

Souk El-Nourieh

Ottoman bank (1870)   *St Louise hospital (1912)*

During these works, the demolition workers uncovered the remains of a Byzantine basilica which may now be said to serve as a supporting structure for the Avenue des Francais. The façade of the Great Mosque, the former Church of Saint John, was also bared for a while.[36]

In quick succession, from the mid-nineteenth century onwards, a string of other monumental buildings and imposing infrastructural facilities (particularly port, rail, postal services, *khans*, *aswaqs*, *sahas*, electric tramways, gaslights and the like), did much to embellish the edifying quality of the urban setting. It was, however, a handful of prodigious and towering structures which started to overwhelm Beirut's skyline and define its character: The Grand Serail (1853), the Ottoman Bank (1856), Capucine St Louise (1863), the Petit Serail (1884), Beirut's Train Station (1895), the Ottoman Clock Tower (1898), Orozdi-Back, the Ottoman department store (1900) and Sanayeh, Arts et Metiers Vocational school (1907). Highlighting the distinctive features of a few of these is in order.

Doubtlessly, the Grand Serail, constructed during the Crimean War as the imperial barracks, stands out as the most conspicuous reminder of Ottoman state power, both in terms of its lofty location and austere façade. To this day it remains the most massive and towering structure. Its location on the Qantari hilltop overwhelming the amphitheatre-like landscape, its stern and severe façade, the diverse stately functions it came to host, all attest to its venerability as an architectural icon. Although only two storeys in height, its two identical wings, rendered more pronounced by three rows of sixteen similar windows, the building stretches well over eighty metres. The meticulous restoration to which it has been recently subjected, along with the landscaping of the adjoining grounds, has made it seem much more imposing. The commanding character of the Serail was also enhanced by the momentous functions it has hosted over the years. Although initially built as a military barrack, Fuad Pasha, the Sultan's special envoy to Mount Lebanon after the civil disturbances of 1860, converted it into his official residence. Shortly afterwards, it served as Beirut's main prison, and eventually it housed the Ottoman medical units. After the creation of the Province of Beirut in 1920 it was used for ceremonial occasions on commemorative events and high-profile parades.[37] Today, the rehabilitated Serail is headquarters of the Office of Prime Minister. Because of its picturesque and appealing premises, it is also used for ceremonial events.

The Petit Serail, on the northern fringe of the Bourj, stood in stark contrast to the magisterial Grand Serail. Built originally in 1830, it served first as headquarters for the Ottoman Postal Service. It was remodelled completely in 1882 by Fakhry Bey, then president of municipality who, it seems, had a keen interest in architecture, and served as a seat of local government. From 1926 until its unfortunate demolition in 1960 (to become the Cinema Rivoli), this picturesque building was used as official headquarters of successive Lebanese presidents. What the diminutive Serail lacked in size it made up in its exquisite and eclectic architecture: a representation of the neoclassical and neo-Baroque styles current at the time among European trained architects.

The mixture of playful ornamentation and solid, geometric structure was very much a reversal of Orientalising trends in European architecture at the time. It consisted

Petit Serail (1920s)

of two storeys above a semi-basement, erected on a rectangular ground plan with a central courtyard. The two storeys were lined with windows set off by neo-Baroque marble frames producing a marked contrast to the darkish Beiruti sandstone façade. The monumental white marble portal opening onto Sahat al-Bourj stretched over the basement and the first floor, recalling the entrance to an Italian Renaissance palace. Over the entrance a flowing gable with ornate vaults decorated the roof. The corners of the protruding rectangular corner towers and the central part of each façade were topped and accentuated by octagonal miniature towers which, in harmony with the miniature battlements lining the roof, evoked a medieval, Gothic European castle.[38]

The Serail and the Menchiyyeh ('Public Garden') are the work of the gifted Armenian-Lebanese architect, Bechara Affendi. He was also the builder of another architectural icon, the Police and Internal Security Headquarters, which had graced the city's centre for about a century and a half. Miraculously, the building was spared the devastation of the protracted rounds of heavy fighting only to be unfortunately demolished in the early 1990s to make way for the square's massive reconstruction project. This elegant building housed at subsequent intervals the Ottoman Bank, Khedivial Hotel and the headquarters of post and telegraph services.

Train station (1895)

In 1863 the Beirut–Damascus road (originally planned in 1851) was completed by a French company, thereby strengthening the link with Damascus and the territory beyond Mount Lebanon and the coast. This tolled caravan route extended from the Bourj Square in a valley between the Ashrafiyeh area and the western regions of Moussaytbeh and Mazraa. Under Daw D Pasha (1861–8) the streets of Beirut were widened and macadamised to accommodate the carriages of the French Damascus Road Company. Greek Orthodox merchants were, it seems, in a position to benefit most from the improving regional economic role of Beirut.

In 1866, the Syrian Protestant College, renamed the American University of Beirut in 1920, was founded in a desolate mulberry plantation west of the city walls. Its location in that compelling coastal stretch came to play a pivotal role in redirecting the pattern of the city's urban growth. Of equal importance was its impact on attracting and sustaining the emergence of a professional, confessionally mixed, fairly open and liberal urban middle-class.[39] Seventeen years later, in 1883, French missionaries from the Jesuit Order of St Joseph established an institute for higher education on the eastern elevations beyond the city walls. The relentless competition between the Anglo-Saxon and Francophone cultural legacies of these two inveterate institutions was pivotal in reinforcing the cultural pluralism, cosmopolitan lifestyles and ideological predispositions receptive to experimentation and change. For approximately a century, the two institutions – until national and other colleges and universities started to offer alternate venues for higher education – served as the exclusive reservoirs from which the country's professional, intellectual and political elites were drawn.

So compelling was the sight of these cultural and educational institutions that they stood out as the most visible and imposing urban edifices on the city's emerging skyline. Indeed, any panoramic view of the urban-scape of Beirut – from the 1860s onwards – readily reveals the prominence of these institutions. In many respects they had preceded and prefigured the assertion of religious, commercial and recreational structures that overwhelmed the city space in subsequent decades. The elegance of most of these buildings was largely the outcome of less than a handful of local architects who made appealing efforts to reconcile Anglo-Saxon and French elements of design with the local vernacular. In addition to the sprawling campuses of the SPC and USJ, the following stood out: the German School of Deaconesses (1862), the American School for Girls (1866), the College of Notre Dame de Nazareth (1869), the Sisters of St Charles Borromeus and the British Syrian Mission (1911).

In 1890 a French company was awarded the commission to expand Beirut's harbour facilities and to construct a jetty parallel to the coast. In 1895, another imposing structure, Beirut's train station, was completed by a British-Ottoman company. Also the last two decades of the nineteenth century coincided with a marked construction boom, particularly among the urban bourgeoisie (mostly returnees from Egypt), eager to build their ostentatious townhouses and exclusive villas on the outskirts of the city. The eclectic style of the Petite Serail served, it seems, as a pacesetter in inspiring a few of the noted

Syrian Protestant College (SPC)

American seminary for girls

Université Saint-Joseph (USJ)

Sisters of St Charles

German school

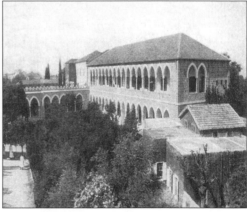

British Syrian mission

local architects, such as Yusuf Aftimos and Bishara Deeb, to built the villas of the Sursuqs, Mudauwars, Fara'uns and the like in Zuqaq al-Blatt, Gemmayze and Rumayel.

Three other commanding structures – a clock tower, a department store and a vocational school – all novel additions to the urban-scape and emblems of urban modernity, played a decisive role in shaping and redirecting the urban growth of the city at the turn of the century. The imposing clock tower, built in 1898 by Sultan Abdulhamid, was largely a response to repeated and earnest requests by the Wali of Beirut (Rashid Bey) on behalf of the Muslims of Beirut. On 8 September 1897, he wrote the following letter to Sultan Abdulhamid at the Yildiz Palace in Istanbul:

> In the city of Beirut there are a number of foreign institutions that have established clocktowers with bells, all of them with a Western clock. There is no public clock for the Muslim population which shows times changed to Islamic times. And even the officials and users have to adapt to the foreign clocks. The Islamic people need urgently a public clock to link up with the rest of the empire. In order to build such a clocktower from municipal revenues, the administrative council has done research as to the location. An appropriate place in the vicinity of the government was found. There, the famous imperial barracks have a view in all directions. Since it is in such an elevated position, the vast square in front of the barracks was chosen as the proper place to represent the Sultan. Into the precious structure a large clock-bell with an unusual diameter will be installed at the top linked to the hanging clock. We thank the Sultan for graciously offering help in bringing about positive measures by honouring [us] with granting imperial authorization.[40]

The flattering tone of the letter notwithstanding, it conveyed a compelling urgency on behalf of the Muslims of Beirut. Given the preponderance of western clocks, the exalted Sultan was beseeched to offer the Muslim population the need to be oriented to 'Islamic times ...and to link up with the rest of the empire'. It is of interest to note, as in other such public projects, that the demand for and construction of the clock tower was largely the outcome of local initiative. It also predated other such ventures in the rest of the provinces of the Ottoman Empire. The planning, site location, design, building materials and workmanship were all the work of local engineers (again Aftimos and Deeb) and Greek Orthodox masons and artisans from Moussaytbeh.

The tower was built from a variety of local wood and marble: Jounieh limestone, Beiruti sandstone, Damascene basalt, and red stone from Dair al-Qamar. The obligatory Hamidian *tughra* was installed above the entrance. Inside its four-by-four metre square shaft, 125 steps in pioneering cast iron led up to the top. On the third floor a 300–kilogramme bell with a diameter of eighty-five centimetres was suspended. This floor contained four miniature neo-Orientalist balconies to which *mashrabiyya*-style doors led. Above the bell, four large clock-faces imported from Paris by the Ottoman embassy, two clock-faces with Arabic and two with Latin numerals, soberly heralded exact (but dual) city time.[41]

Ottoman clock tower (1890s)

Beirut at the time could already boast of a score of clocks and bells, all associated with either local Christian sects (The Maronite St Georges Cathedral) or foreign missionary institutions (College Hall of the Syrian Protestant College or St Joseph and the French Hospital). Juxtaposed against such parochial Christian and missionary icons, the new towering clock was intended as a transcendent and overarching symbol of regularity, discipline and rational order. Erected next to the Grand Serail atop the Qantari hill, the 25–metre high tower became the highest building in Beirut. It was also celebrated, like all other such inaugural events, with all the pomp and circumstance associated with such grandiose occasions. Louis Shaykhu who attended the ceremony recorded the following in al-Mashreq:

> The commanding tower was a fitting landmark of the Ottoman ethos of verticality and uniformity imposed on cities of the provinces to shape and structure the rhythm and daily routines of city life. It was also a lofty reminder of imperial goodwill and benevolence.
>
> The viewer on the roof can have a panoramic view of the whole city. Nothing would escape his eyes. His view stretches to the outskirts, as far as the coastal plains and to the border with Lebanon. The public laying of the first stone of the clock tower took place on 9 January 1897 – the birthday of the Sultan. The celebration was carried out in the presence of the high officials of the province, military rank and file and members of municipality. A military orchestra played a most delightful melody, and later a speech was delivered in Arabic and Ottoman calling upon the Sultan's resplendent and eternal nature, and the assembled crowd believed in these emotional exclamations. After the celebrations the governor general symbolically laid the first two stones with a silver hammer. At the end of the party, several photographs were taken.[42]

It is engaging to note that, doubtlessly, in response to the marked cultural and sectarian divisions within the city, the imposing clock tower was neo-Ottoman in style in more than one respect. Its architect, Yussef Aftimos – son-in-law of Bishara Affendi and the engineer of the Municipality – had successfully made creative and judicious use of this genre of eclecticism in many of the other civic and private buildings he constructed in the 1920s and 1930s. In this dramatic instance, the faces of the clock were made to reflect the religious demarcations already visible at the time. Hence, two of its faces gave the 'alla Franco' hour, while the other two gave the 'alla Turca' hour, which was adjusted to twelve o'clock at sunset![43]

Another unusual milestone is the Orosdi-Back department store, the first large-scale store of its kind in Beirut and, perhaps, the largest in the eastern Mediterranean. In retrospect, it stands out as a precursor, as early as 1888, of global franchises and the production of spatial enterprises for upscale and elite consumerism. Three global capitalists – Leon and Philippe Orosdi and Joseph Back – started to open branches of

Orosdi-Back (1880s)

their store in Paris, Istanbul, Alexandria, Cairo, Tunis and other cities in the Ottoman Empire. Beirut's branch was inaugurated, with much fanfare, on 1 September 1900 to coincide with the citywide commemoration of Sultan Abdulhamid's silver jubilee.[44] The logistical location of the store – at the intersection of the quay and the port's warehouses and custom offices – proved instrumental in several respects. It was a precursor to the expediting of Beirut's 'free zone' and '*entrepôt*' mentality. Hence, the store could import luxury items from Europe and then export them regionally as produced goods.

At the time, Beirut was just emerging as a port city with extensive connections with the hinterland. The Beirut–Damascus road was constructed, it should be recalled, by a French company in 1858, and a branch of the Ottoman Imperial Bank was established in 1905. The appeals of Beirut were more than just a reflection of its infrastructural and communication facilities. As suggested earlier, one could already discern the early manifestations of the *nahda* or cultural renaissance. For example, *Hadiqat al-Akhbar*, the first newspaper of the city, was published in 1858 and, within a decade or two, a large number of journals and periodicals surfaced in quick succession. By the turn of the century Beirut was already the uncontested economic, financial, intellectual and communication centre in the region.[45] More compelling for the purposes of this book, this was also the interlude when the concomitant transformations in lifestyle and the 'Occidentalisation' of public manners and fashions was taking place.[46]

Naturally, the foresighted entrepreneurs must have anticipated the pivotal and speculative character of its spatial location. At the hub of this interplay of local, regional and international forces, it was bound to exploit and facilitate such propitious windfalls. As an elite store, it took advantage of the transit and '*entrepôt*' features of its setting and became an appealing site for local, regional and international customers: more so once the newly constructed railway line (DHP), serving the Syrian interior, became a transit stop for Muslim pilgrims to Mecca as well.

Three of its spatial and architectural elements are worth noting. As a private enterprise, and since local architects were not involved in its design, no effort was made to blend the outward façade of the store with the prevailing architectural style. Other than its monumental and ostentatious character, it had very few Ottoman traces. Nor did it incorporate any features of the local vernacular. Hence, it stood out in sharp contrast to its surroundings. Its building material, the colour of the two-storey façade and the triple-domed, grey rooftops seemed out of sync with the conventional sandstone and red-tiled roofs of adjacent *khans*, *qaysariyyas* and *wikalas*.[47] Furthermore, it was also innovative as a '*magazine des nouveautés*', which was fashionable at the time as a European marketing gambit. Indeed, in Paris it took the form of an 'Oriental bazaar' which was reproduced in world exhibitions.[48] Hence, for the first time, the gadgetry of modern consumerism and marketing (elevators, in-house telephones, window displays and layout of merchandise, etc) appeared in Beirut and became a pacesetter for other such features. Finally, and most importantly, by reclaiming the landfill upon which it was built, Orosdi-Back played a significant role in the 'gentrification' of that as yet undeveloped stretch of the cityscape. The Port Company, with a speculative eye for real estate, introduced measures to attract such urban development. A score of notable urban bourgeoisies, such as Badawis and Tabits, quick to respond to the demand for office space, constructed buildings on the wharf and leased them out as business establishments. This early instance of gentrification predated by over a century developments that were to become pivotal in Beirut's spatial reproduction.

While Orosdi-Back facilitated the gentrification of the harbour and adjoining districts, the Sanayeh complex extended the urban sprawl westward into the relative wasteland of Ramlat al-Zarif. To a considerable extent, the Sanayeh vocational school project was a by-product of the same local initiative that had led to the construction of the clock tower on the Qantari hill. Mobilised largely by Sunni Muslim notables and the Maqasid Benevolent Association, their intentions were two fold. First they were apprehensive about the inroads foreign missionary establishments had already made in rendering education more accessible to aspiring segments of the local population. Second, they were equally concerned about the retrograde and deficient system of traditional schooling and instruction propagated by the various *madrassas* and *kuttab* at that time. Hence, they sought to provide alternative venues designed to meet the nascent need for applied arts and practical skills demanded by the growing market for industrial crafts and commercial services. Once again, the governor general (Ali Pasha) dispatched a memorandum to Yildiz Palace in Istanbul on behalf of the local groups.

As in other Ottoman public projects, the imperial powers in Istanbul, buoyed up by portraying themselves as champions of modernisation, scientific and interconfessional education, heralded the project with their noted fanfare and proclivity for a photo opportunity. In September 1905, on the Sultan's coronation anniversary, the governor ceremonially laid the corner stone for the envisioned complex. As seen in the staged photo marking the momentous event, concerted efforts were clearly made to assemble such a massive cross-section of the city's population and beyond. Sultan Abdulhamid took an active personal interest in the project: arguably one of the largest urban development undertakings during his reign.

More than the gentrification of the port area, the Sanayeh complex had a transforming impact on the character and future pattern of the urban fabric the city was to witness. The site itself, Ramlet al-Zarif, was a formidable and desolate stretch of sand dunes. Until it was tamed by the project, it was always perceived as a source of dread, a hazard to public health and orderly trade relations. Redressing the damage and allaying the public fear generated by the periodic visitation of such treacherous sandstorms and wind erosion, had aroused considerable public concern, as seen by the attention some of the leading periodicals and newspapers, such as *Lisan al-Hal, al Muqtataf* and *Thamarat al-Funm*, had devoted to such menaces. Indeed urban renewal projects and the establishment of public parks, scarce as they were, were always accompanied by periodic forestation projects. Of course, the pine forest planted by Amin Fakhr al-Din on the city's outskirts became a historic landmark and national treasure to be safeguarded and embellished.

It is in this multilayered context that the Sanayeh complex must be recognised.

Sanayeh (1905)

Intended initially as a project to meet the demand for practical and vocational schooling and to curb the growing dominance of foreign missionary education, it had other unintended consequences of far-reaching implications. Foremost, it became the first most visible instance of the triumph of purposive rational planning over the unwieldy elements of Beirut's natural habitat. As will be seen, this too became a precursor to other such recent efforts of reclamation and taming the scintillating but awesome ecological endowments of the cityscape. The Sanayeh public garden, again the first such venture in an otherwise vegetation-free urban setting, along with its adjoining grid of planned walkways, and a layout of aligned streets, became an appealing residential urban quarter.

The convergence of all the prime urban functions – education, sanitation, leisure, spiritual, benevolence and public welfare – as represented by the Sanayeh complex, its adjoining hospital, gated public garden and the eventual construction of religious edifices and other voluntary associations, managed to transform a foreboding wasteland into an edifying neighbourhood. In no time, it started to attract a confessionally-mixed group of middle-class families eager to enjoy such facilities. As in the harbour area, real-estate entrepreneurs stepped in to speculate in the elevated values of landed property. More, perhaps, than any other urban project, the Sanayeh complex – as a predominantly Ottoman-Muslim enclave – was vital in shaping and linking together virtually all the formative urban quarters of the city: Moussaitbeh in the south, Bashura and Basta in the east, Wadi Abou Jamil (the Jewish quarter) in the north, Ain El Mereisse and Ras Beirut in the west and other adjoining quarters such as the Qantari hill and Zuqaq Blat. It was also around this time, after the establishment of the Syrian Protestant College (SPC) in 1866, that other missionary groups – British, Italian, French, Scottish, etc – started to locate their premises in the area.

In the wake of the 1860 civil disturbances, as the pressures of urban growth became more noticeable, the Ottomans started to display a keen interest in urban planning, particularly in enlarging and extending public spaces and squares. Initially, and consistent with the Ottoman's proclivity for monumentality, a succession of public and social buildings was constructed, such as *khans* (trade hotels), *souks* (market streets), *sahats* (squares), cafés, shops, etc. Many of the new streets assumed regular gridiron patterns. Because of the active participation of the city's notables in such ventures, many of the markets acquired the names reflecting the involvement of those who had built them— Sursock, Ayyas, al-Sayyid, Bustros, Sayyur, etc – than the produce or product they had offered (Najjareen, al-Sagha, etc).

It was not, however, until the Municipal Council was established in 1878 that a series of specific urban policies was launched and implemented. Since the bulk of earlier Ottoman ventures had focused on the imposing Grand Serail, the clock tower, the military barracks and the hospital on the Qantari hill, their interest now shifted to the envisioned new administrative centre (the central *Saha* or *Sahl*) linking the port to the *intra muros* of the traditional enclave. The plan, in effect, meant opening up the old city with its labyrinthine quarters and cul-de-sacs and introducing new public spaces in the form of squares, parks, fountains, walks and pathways. The prominent engineer of the *wilaya*, Bishara Affendi, an Armenian Turk whose real name was Manuk Avedisian, was commissioned to design the project. As in his other architectural icons, the Sanayeh complex and the Ottoman Bank, Bishara Affendi made judicious efforts to incorporate elements inherent in European bourgeois public places without neglecting some of the avowed Ottoman motifs and expectations.

Outwardly, Beirut's centre started to display some of the 'trans-Mediterranean-inspired urban aesthetics' that brought it closer, in its physical aspects at least, to cities of the northern Mediterranean. In the words of May Davie:

> Beirut distanced itself from its archetype, the oriental city, which characterised the interior of geographical Syria, most notably Damascus. From the compact unit that sheltered specific elements of Arab communities of the Ottoman Empire, such as the *hammam* (public baths), the mosques, the *madrasa* (schools) and bazaars, the city evolved into a more open urban space, open both towards the sea and surrounding countryside and at the same time extending along the coast.[49]

In no way, however, did these outward changes mean that Beirut had turned its back on its local and vernacular architectural heritage. For example the 'Arabesque' Central-Hall House, with its triple-arched windows, red-tiled roof and elaborate facades, continued to punctuate the cityscape. Likewise, the new *aswaq* with their larger doorways, windows and wider streets, retained much of the traditional elements of intimate courtyards, vaulted archways and inward-looking buildings.

Altogether, *fin-de-siècle* Beirut was recognised and sought after as the uncontested capital of a prospering Ottoman *wilaya* which already had sidestepped all its maritime rivals, such as Akka, Haifa, Tyre, Sidon, Tripoli and Latakia. Even before the withdrawal of Ottoman forces in 1918, French influence was already widespread. It was then that the city was experiencing some of the early symptoms akin to Polanyi's 'great transformations': a marked expansion in banking, money-lending, speculation in international stocks and shares, speculative ventures in real estate, a sharp increase in transit trade and emigrants' remittances.[50] Through all this, French investors were walking away with the lion's share of concessions in railways, tramways, waterworks, port construction and communication.[51] Equally visible was the Occidentalisation of lifestyles.

The devastations of WWI, both material and human, were treacherous. Widespread famine, the allies' blockade and the perilous locust attacks on crops had wiped out one third of the population. The arrival of the first wave of Armenian refugees, fleeing Turkish massacres, compounded the dire conditions further. Azmi Bey, however, as Wali of Beirut, met the challenge head-on. He launched a series of urban infrastructural projects; he appropriated private property in the old city centre. With the assistance of a German team of urban consultants, he commenced the process of tearing down the city's medieval walls.

Shortly after the French entered Lebanon in 1918, they undertook a series of reconstruction projects intended to modernise the city. They were so eager, in fact, to launch these projects that they did not even wait until the formal proclamation of the State of Greater Lebanon in 1920 with Beirut as its capital. Spurred by the 'civilising mission' entrusted to it by the League of Nations, France was keen to put into effect notions of urban planning and spatial management they had applied in other of their protectorates in North Africa.

The calamitous post-war conditions must have left such an impression on the French that they also promptly launched a crash program of reconstruction and relief. The harbour was dredged of wartime wreckage. Concerned about the deplorable conditions of sanitation and public health, a comprehensive network of sewers was laid out. Likewise, health clinics were set up to attend to the needs of the enfeebled population. In the short span of two years, the number of hospitals tripled. Haut Commissariat statistics indicate that 10,000 children were hospitalised in Beirut in one year, while close to 140,000 adults received intensive care in emergency clinics.[52]

Most visible was the surge of infrastructural developments, part of the avowed efforts of the French to modernise the city. The inventory of the projects they undertook touched virtually all dimensions of public amenities: widening streets, paving the old network of dirt roads, land and lot parcelisation, replacing mule-driven carts by electric tramways and introducing a modern system of electric and water supply. Elegant streetlamps replaced the decrepit system of gaslights. Their modernisation efforts were considerably more ambitious since they implemented projects intended to transform Beirut into a modern communication and mass-media centre. The obsolete cable links with Cairo were replaced by a renovated system of transmitters which linked Beirut directly with the US and Europe. The French army built a makeshift aerodrome west of Beirut River, thereby establishing for the first time regional air links. Finally, intended as their mantle piece for their *'mission civilatrice'*, special efforts were made to transform Beirut into a broadcasting and media centre 'to disseminate French thinking [*rayonnement de la pensée française*] throughout the Middle East and to be vigilant to our language and all the manifestations of our culture'.[53]

Since some of the old notions of colonialism – those of imposing change on a *tabula rasa* or on a subdued and unresponsive local population – were no longer in vogue, the new Mandate opted for more reconciliatory policies calling for greater measures of collaboration with local groups. Wilfully or otherwise, they always found themselves in situations where they had to negotiate with local recalcitrant groups (mostly the upper bourgeoisie, clerics and a coterie of left-leaning ideological groups and liberal journalists) not too receptive to the prospect of seeing their personal, communal or public interests being undermined or threatened by new plans for urban renewal.

Their spatial interests and reconstruction programs converged on three sectors of the central city: the port, the city centre and the area north of the Petit Serail. Of the three, the reconstruction of the city centre – Foch, Allenby and today's Etoile and Maarad squares – was clearly the most compelling since it was intended as the mantle of colonial

Construction of Foch and Allenby (1880s–1920s)

planning in the Levant. Its striking star-shaped design, gallery-lined avenues and, above all, its manifest military undertones (wide streets conducive for the swift mobility of troops, policing and surveillance of the urban fabric) were a watershed in more than one respect.

The plan necessitated the promulgation of a new land-code and cadastral system. It also facilitated the release of *awqaf* and other endowed property for urban use. These and other such transformative measures started to disfigure the earlier Ottoman and Arab modes of urban planning. For example, the entire southern part of the intramural area of the old town, with its labyrinthine, narrow alleyways, *souks* and quarters, gave way to radiating avenues with symmetrical blocks built on both sides. Expropriated plots were levelled and consolidated. The indemnification of previous landowners and shopkeepers, although earmarked, was not actually delivered until twenty years afterwards. Most visible were not only the new morphological patterns but also the names and public identities of new streets. They were all labelled, with little regard to local sentiment, after French military general and war heroes. The Municipal Council, suspended under the Ottomans, was revived. Much of the powers, however, were still controlled and jealously guarded by a coterie of French experts, supervisors and advisors. Many of the initial models for urban renewal, along with the massive urban works on the new infrastructure, were the outcome of French engineers and technocrats.[54]

What allayed the fractious and highly charged debate at the time was the presence of a fairly sizeable group of qualified, Western-trained architects, engineers and craftsmen who were eager to adapt the novel architectural forms and language to local situational exigencies. Given the technical expertise and grounded experience of this group, the Mandate authorities would have been remiss had they overlooked or bypassed them.

Indeed, the French made judicious use of such local expertise often to legitimise or, more appropriately, to camouflage and dress up their 'colonial' impositions or intentions. Virtually all the public buildings constructed carried an Oriental-style façade dubbed at the time as *'naw' sharqi'*. This neo-Oriental, Arabesque *'naw' sharqi'* style was very visible in the two most prominent architectural icons of the period: the municipality and parliament. They were, after all, the two new symbols of power that the Mandate wished to accentuate. The two leading local architects – Youssef Aftimos Affendi and Mardiros Altounian – were commissioned to design both. Aftimos's municipality and Altounian's parliament seem as though they were the product of the same architect. As prototypes of the *'naw' sharqi'*, they were a hybrid (at least in their façades) of the symmetry inherent in the crisp geometric lines of Western-inspired modern architecture within a stylised set of Mamluk and Oriental features.

The construction of these imposing edifices, along with the radiating wedges of the Etoile aligned with Art-Deco and Oriental-style public buildings, with shops on the ground floors and offices on the upper, were not imposed on a *tabula rasa*. They displaced much of what existed before: the *aswaq* of small traders, shopkeepers, artisans, street vendors and makeshift stalls. They all disappeared or were relocated in the adjoining areas of Abu Nasr, Mar Jirjis or al-Nourieh.

Municipality   *Parliament*

By and large, the response to the Etoile project was mixed. Clearly, those features which improved qualities of infrastructural amenities, traffic regulation, opening up the port area, the substantial increase in usable land and appreciation of commercial and business opportunities were all favourably received. Also the massive projects drew upon the pool of native skills, particularly professional builders and craftsmen, and demanded a large number of daily workers. Altogether, it extended the magnitude of active participation to a large section of superfluous manpower and daily labour.

The opposition to the project was more vehement and came largely from three sources. First, owners of the *aswaq*, particularly those who dated back to the nineteenth century, such as Sursok, Abil Nasr, Hani and Raad. They saw in the project threatening prospects destined to undermine their economic well-being. Hence, a sizeable part of the merchant bourgeoisie and urban notable families (Sursok, Bustros, Tabet, Khayyat, Ayyas, Tueni, Sayyour) were just not predisposed to part with their ancestral property for the elusive promises of urban renewal avowed by the Mandate powers.

Second, an equally resistant group were the heads of religious orders *awqaf* and communal associations entrusted as guardians of places of worship. If implemented, at least three wedges of the eight-pointed star would have rammed three religious cathedrals of the three prominent sects: St Elie (Greek Catholic), St Georges (Greek Orthodox) and St Georges (Maronite). The Assaf Mosque would have also been victimised. The same misfortune would have beset another celebrated building: the Grand Theatre. This celebrated cultural edifice, built in 1930 by Youssef Aftimos, belonged to the Tabet family. Although members of the family, by virtue of their Francophile leanings, were close to the French High Commissioner, they still opted to resist the plan intended to extend Allenby Street in the direction of the southern suburbs of the city.[55] Otherwise, this architectural icon that was just beginning to grace the heart of the city as a most coveted and patronised cultural outlet, would have been sacrificed.

The most virulent and highly charged opposition was largely a reflection of broader divisive political culture and the worsening economic conditions that beleaguered the

Grand Théâtre   *Grand Théâtre (detail)*

country during the unsettling interlude of the two world wars. The polemics between the Arabist, nationalists, secular and other nascent political activists, on the one hand, and the residues of Francophone groups sympathetic to the Mandate on the other, delayed the ultimate approval of the plan until 1927. It was then that the Council of Ministers formally voted to accept the Etoile Project, dubbed at the time as '*Beyrouth en cinq ans*'.[56] Incidentally, it was this same plan that served as the basis for the Danger Plan of 1933.[57]

The opposition to the role of the Mandate in the urban renewal of Beirut was not entirely a reflection of the spatial restructuring and the accompanying consequences of defacing the pre-existing legacy of the old city. The French were quite exuberant about their '*mission civilatrice*' and seemed resolute in extending their Mandate to the symbolic and semiotic dimensions by incorporating elements of national and collective identity. Doubtlessly, the most graphic and indelible imprint they left on the visual and physical shape of the city was to be found in their efforts to de-Ottomanise the architectural and spatial character of Beirut. For example, the picturesque Palais des Pins, built by Azmi Bey as a private casino, was converted into their official residence. Interestingly, much of the redesign of the palace was transformed to mute Ottoman references and render them into French neo-Colonial style. They also displayed little regard for preserving some of the colourful and still functional relics that had sustained the fabric of the old city. The first to go were the traditional *aswaq* – *al-Haddadin* (blacksmiths), *al-Khammarin* (wine and coffee shops), *al-Tujjar* (merchants) were converted into Foch and Allenby. This proclivity to designate streets after military generals and officers was wilfully subscribed to. This is how Gouraud, Picot and Climancau came into being. The Ottomans, at least in this respect, were a bit more timid and nuanced in comparison. The most they did was to replace the designations of *mahallahs* of the old quarters into *hayy* or *chari*.[58]

The quintessential design of the French star, a Haussmannian cultural transplant, had in the final analysis to be truncated. Since then what was intended as an archetype, a symbol of modernity and progress epitomised by its counterpart – the Place de l'Etoile of

Truncated Etoile

Paris – has remained mutilated in its transplanted setting. If anything, this is a reflection of the staying and resisting powers of the religious and merchant elite. Both had seen the plan as antithetical to their economic well-being, since they were the prominent property-holders of the most coveted spaces of real estate in the heart of the city.

What heightened the polemics further over the plan (judging by newspaper accounts it had become a hotly contested issue) was the changing political climate in the region and the accompanying circumstances that were beginning to undermine the standing of the French government, both in the Levant and back home. The Druze Revolt, the triumphal visit of Prince Feisal to Beirut, the resurgence of political descent among the disenfranchised groups of the population, particularly in the suburbs of Basta and Musaitbeh where Arabist and Syrian Nationalist sentiments were salient: these were enough to incite further opposition to the plan. French authorities tried in vain to mute the opposition by soliciting the support of traditional client groups, such as Maronites, Armenians and other Francophone sympathisers.[59]

Other critical voices – journalists, public figures and politicised groups – were also vociferous in their opposition to the plan. With such mounting criticism, which almost tipped the city in the ominous direction of civil unrest, the Mandate powers had no choice but to resort to their conventional arsenal of repressive measures: press censorship, arbitrary suspension of incriminated papers and the incarceration of suspected political activists.

To this day, the truncated Etoile – three, after all, of the eight wedges or avenues of the star could not be incorporated in the plan – is a compelling reminder of the failure of the Mandate powers to impose their Haussmannian grand design on Beirut. What was envisaged as a showcase of modernity and rational spatial management could not win over the participation of all the local stakeholders. One could extract from this episode another felicitous inference: that, despite Lebanon's fragmented political culture, contentious communities could suspend their differences in the face of imperial or Mandate projects perceived to undermine collective national interest. The experiences of the Ottomans and the French were symptomatic of the readiness of local agents to mobilise public protest to safeguard their interests.

In addition to the core of inventive, Western-trained architects and the early generations of 'civil engineers' and 'bétonniers', Beirut was at the time blessed with an equally gifted and resourceful group of self-trained craftsmen, masons and builders. In fact, much of the construction boom of the 1920s and 1940s may well be the outcome of such largely anonymous builders who had acquired their skills through apprenticeship rather than formal schooling. As will be noted later, professional education in architecture as such was still non-existent at the time.

The interlude between the two world wars, corresponding roughly to the French Mandate over Lebanon, witnessed the first substantial expansion of the city in virtually all directions: from north to south and from east to west. This was most visible in neighbourhoods adjoining the city centre: namely Achrafieh, Saifi, Rumayil, Bachoura,

Walk-ups

Museitbeh and Ras Beirut (mostly the coastline and Bliss street). Hamra, at the time, was still largely garden-farming, dotted with flat-roof farmhouses and a few suburban villas. Although substantial, the urban sprawl was still fairly moderate: approximately 1.5 kilometres from east to west and three kilometres from north to south.[60] Also, and perhaps more tellingly, the overall aesthetic character of the traditional architecture – triple-arched facades with their delicate wood scrolls, ornate balconies and red-tiled roofs – managed to survive.

Even the new apartment buildings and walk-ups retained much of the original form of the nineteenth-century bourgeois house, namely the central *dar* with its symmetrical layout of rooms radiating from it.[61] Speculation in real estate and land values had not as yet peaked to necessitate the sacrifice of such traditional icons. The advent of reinforced concrete, attributed to the American University of Beirut as early as 1900,[62] dealt an irredeemable blow to the authenticity and wholesomeness of Beirut's architecture. Such incursions became subsequently more irresistible with the advent of stucco (plaster), glass sheets and other prefabricated materials of construction.

The Endemic Failure of Successive Urban Planning Schemes

Beirut's encounters with swift urbanisation may also be seen in terms of the repeated but failed efforts of various political authorities to curb or regulate some of the adverse consequences of haphazard and unplanned urban growth. There was never a shortage of such efforts. Somehow, despite their good intentions, they generally failed to meet their avowed, often exuberant and high-sounding expectations.

The first of such efforts at introducing some measure of spatial control, by way of civic regulation of public hygiene, policing, quarantine ordinances and the like, were implemented early in the nineteenth century during Bechir II's eventful reign (1789–1840). It was not, however, until the first town council was set up after the municipal elections of 1868 that a recognisable and coherent effort at town planning was introduced. It was common for visitors and travellers at the time to bemoan the rampant danger, disorder and squalor of dark and dishevelled streets, the sorry state of public amenities and insecure labyrinthine quarters.

It should be remarked that this public concern for the production of space and urban management was not, as is often assumed, the exclusive outcome of imperial and centralised Ottoman state reforms or the Haut Commissariat of the French Mandate. The nascent urban bourgeoisie and a handful of notable families, nationalists and public intellectuals also played a decisive role in this emergent urban consciousness for public space.[63] This concern naturally coincided with the eventful transformations to which Beirut was being subjected as it evolved from a fairly insignificant maritime town, still enclosed within its compact medieval walls, to a provincial capital. It was during this interlude that one begins to see manifestations (typical of other port cities in the Eastern

Inauguration of port (1894)

Delahalle's design (1934)

Mediterranean) of the direct interplay between those three forces: the incursions of a world economy, Ottoman state reforms and local public-spirited notables. Hence in addition to the imperial architecture of Abdulhamid II, one also sees evidence of concrete legislation to safeguard public security, hygiene, sanitation and public morality. Swift urbanisation also brought with it many of the concomitant social problems associated with social dislocation and exposure to novel lifestyles, leisure and night entertainment.

Within such a context it is no surprise that the first municipal ordinances should be concerned with such prosaic and common-place matters as forbidding cattle and other domestic animals from being herded through narrow downtown streets on the way to the harbour. Other edicts addressed problems of gambling, prostitution, alcohol consumption and other nefarious activities associated with all places of public gathering such as casinos, beaches, circuses, bars and restaurants. The introduction of the 'Beirut Waterworks' in 1871, gas lighting in 1888 and the tramway in 1907 all fall within such contexts.

The decades between the two world wars were dense with activities of public and private construction. They were also marked by renewed efforts to introduce a modicum of urban planning and zoning. For example, in 1928 new property laws were enacted providing virtually unrestrained freedom over the use of private property. This was meant to annul the Ottoman edict that had restricted building on farmland. The Place de l'Etoile, the most visible instance of grandiose French urban planning, as we have seen was superimposed over the destroyed area of the old city. The Parliament building was constructed on one of the star-shaped Beaux-Arts grids encircling the square. This was intended to serve as a national symbolic setting where the seat of government was radiating its political primacy over the recently extended borders of greater Lebanon.[64] The other two eastern wedges of the l'Etoile, intended as a star-shaped design in the original scheme, are obstructed by the presence of three prominent religious edifices: Greek Orthodox and Greek Catholic churches and the historic Nourieh Shrine.[65]

Early in the 1930s, High Commissioner de Martel freed the Lebanese government of its burdensome debt – a sum of 32 million French francs – and channelled the much-needed funds instead into public-works projects, particularly the port, public buildings and road networks. In 1932, the first Master Plan for Beirut, the work of the French urban consultant Danger, was not approved by the government. The Plan had proposed major axes of circulation, building coefficients and land-use studies. It also recommended that neighbouring suburbs and villages be incorporated into future planning schemes. Rather than approving the plan, the government sought to legislate procedures for building permits and construction.

Another French architect and urban designer, M. Delahalle, presented a rather flamboyant and flashy design for the re-embellishment of downtown Beirut and the Bourj Square. The plan, perhaps inspired by Beirut's prehistoric Phoenician site, proposed opening up the Place des Canons to the harbour by devising a massive terraced space. Interestingly, the scheme had proposed the central square as the formal gateway to the city. The extravagant plan, gargantuan in dimensions and image, envisioned a monumental civic space opened towards the sea. If implemented, it would have diminished the Etoile, Foch, Allenby and Maarad and undermined their role as the linkage between the inner city, its commercial hub to the port.[66] Like its predecessor, the plan did not see the light of day.

During WWII, Beirut was miraculously spared what seemed at the time as imminent destruction. As Germany invaded France, all Mandated countries fell under the command of the Vichy government. Beirutis, fearing that the famine of WWI might well be repeated, started fleeing to surrounding mountain towns and villages. The earnest and persuasive pleading of President Alfred Naccache to declare Beirut an open city was heeded by the Vichy troops who were in control of the city at the time.

Another aborted Master Plan (this time by Michel Ecochard, a prominent French specialist on Middle Eastern urban planning) was introduced in 1944. Despite its drawbacks, the plan was the first attempt to incorporate the sprawling suburbs – from

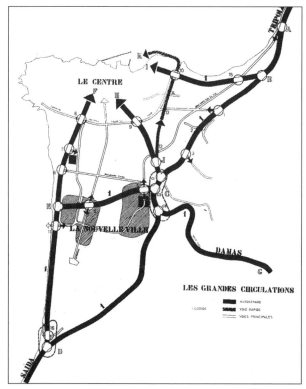

Ecochard's Master Plan (1963)

Nahr al-Mout in the north to Ouzai in the south – into the scheme. It also envisaged a second major axis within the city, running east to west, perpendicular to the Damascus Road. More substantive, it provided the first comprehensive study in land-use and zoning, proposing to distinguish between industry and commercial outlets from residential.[67]

The failure to implement some of Ecochard's proposals was compounded by the first influx of Palestinian refugees who initially settled in Beirut's southern outskirts. Eventually, they moved to refugee camps in Sabra, Shatila, Burj al-Barajneh in the southern suburbs and in Qarantina and Tel al-Zaatar in the north and northeast. By 1975, Palestinian refugees were estimated at 300,000. The Egli planning report of 1950, cognisant of the impending demographic pressures and mounting urbanisation, was the first plan to receive government approval. This was promptly followed by the Plan Directeur de Beyrouth (1951–4), which adopted most of the proposals of Ecochard and Egli.[68]

It should be noted here that in the wake of WWII, Lebanon, like other countries in the region, became the site for many foreign-inspired schemes for development and post-war reconstruction. Many of these schemes, often couched in the high-sounding tones of science and technology and propagated with much fanfare, remained unrealised blueprints. For example, the British private firm of Sir Alexander Gibb and Partners was commissioned in 1948 to conduct a major financial and economic survey. Soon afterwards, the United States Point IV Mission launched its comprehensive development programme to modernise the country's agriculture, transport, public health, housing and tourist sectors. Special emphasis was placed on the controversial Litani River Project. Among a string of other foreign advisors, the most notable perhaps were the Belgian economist, Paul Van Zeeland and Constantine Doxiadis, the Greek urban planner. Both, at least in their schemes, had perceived Beirut as the banking and financial centre and as a vibrant metropolis for the region. Given Doxiadis's background and public persona – 'flamboyant, hugely self-confident and a genius at self-promotion'[69] – he would not have considered the project of surveying the country's physical conditions and developing a housing program, had he not seen in this the prospects for rendering Beirut more receptive to assuming its ultimate standing as a cosmopolitan and bustling urban centre.

It is for such reasons that the experience of Doxiadis Associates, who were commissioned by the US Operations Mission and the Government of Lebanon in May 1957 to prepare a long-term 'Ekistics Programme' for Lebanon, is instructive in this regard. The massive survey Doxiadis undertook, doubtlessly unique in Lebanon's history, involved a comprehensive ekistics survey (both visual and analytical) of the entire country. Virtually nothing was spared. He employed novel quantitative and qualitative strategies to depict the spatial features of the built environment, its architectural character, housing types, public squares, *souks*, even intimate profiles of the facial expressions of common people. He also relied on personal notes, ethnographic material and tape-recorded impressions.[70]

Despite the formidable data it amassed, the survey fell short in producing any rigorous designs or grounded projects. The civil disturbances of 1958 might have been partly responsible for that. Altogether, it remained schematic in its proposals and perspectives, although some of these were subsequently incorporated in the Ecochard plans of 1963. Notwithstanding its shortcomings, it could still be considered as a promising experience since it provides positive proof of the potential of planning to operate independently of the political regimes that willed it.[71]

The building of the Camille Chamoun Cité Sportive to host the Mediterranean games (1956) and the completion of the new International Airport in Khaldeh both served to stretch the city limits further south beyond the boundaries of municipal Beirut. All subsequent attempts, particularly the stern planning policies enforced against laissez-faire urbanism during President Chihab's tenure in office (1958–64), failed to curb the incessant inflow of rural migration. To the credit of the Chihab regime, however, it was fully aware of the dire consequences of such dissonance between the schemes and their ultimate implementation. During Chihab's eventful tenure in office, the state, inspired by Western legal norms (via the introduction of planned development and spatial management) emerged as a centralised authority. '*Chehabism*' in fact, became a catch-all label for the regime's strong will to centralisation and reform. Spatial management and physical planning assumed prime importance. Added legislative interventions were made.[72] In 1963, the General Directorate of Urban Panning and the Higher Council for Urban Planning (HCUP) were created as advisory bodies to the president. The IRFED report, a comprehensive survey of the demographic, health, socio-economic, educational and cultural resources of the country, was published. Ecochard served as consultant to the general director of urban planning and, in that capacity, played a part in producing the second Master Plan: *Plan Directeur de Beyrouth et des Banlieues*. The plan called for the creation of a new modern city contiguous with the congested old town. It also provided a new detailed building code for the city, suburbs and the whole country.

Lebanon, and Beirut in particular, was never short on blueprints. The devil was always in the detail of implementation. Hence, there has always been a wasteful discrepancy between audacious and playful planning on the one hand and executive ineffectiveness on the other. This has plagued government bureaucracy for so long and has been a blatant source of administrative inefficiency. Some of the schemes for development are often so adventurous in their visions, they were destined to remain unrealised blueprints: victims of reckless and grandiose planning or short-sighted expediency. Examples of such disjunctions are legion. They are particularly visible in the failure of repeated urban schemes to curb some of the unsettling consequences of rural exodus and the unplanned and uncontrolled growth of Beirut into a primate city.[73]

The relentless inflow of displaced rural migrants into Beirut was compounded by two regional and global forces. First, the growth of agro-business brought about a significant decline in sharecropping: the traditional lifeline of Lebanese farming. While small farmers and sharecroppers constituted about 25 per cent of the active agricultural population in 1950, the proportion dropped sharply to no more than 5 per cent in 1970. Displaced farmers were either forced to migrate or suffer the status of being reduced to hired hands or wage labourers. Both were equally discouraging. Migrants became part of the swelling mass in the disreputable and pauperised 'misery belt' of Beirut's suburbs. Those compelled to become wage labourers had to suffer the indignities of competing with a cheap pool of itinerant labour, mostly Palestinian and Syrian refugees.

Secondly, because of incessant Israeli incursions, the growing insecurity of border villages generated waves of massive, involuntary, outward migration. Results of the only national manpower survey (undertaken in 1970) revealed that nearly one-fifth of Lebanon's rural population during the 1960s had migrated to Beirut's suburban fringe. The exodus from the south was as high as one-third.[74] Little wonder that by the early 1970s such displaced and disgruntled groups became easy fodder for any form of political radicalisation.

Altogether, the population of metropolitan Beirut had reached one million by 1970. This is approximately 45 per cent of the country's population concentrated into a surface area of barely 2 per cent. The last attempt to allay this imbalance before the outbreak of collective strife was in 1973. *The Livre Blanc* (the White Book) proposed a new master plan which addressed issues of decentralisation. By then, however, the envisioned plans were far too fickle and too late.

Several factors, embedded in Lebanon's socio-political culture, account for such endemic failure of repeated urban planning schemes. First, the process of rational urban planning has always been undermined by the persistence of clientelistic politics and other forms of patronage. These allow strategically placed individuals to control the distribution of benefits achieved through the manipulation of zoning laws and ordinances. Since good connections and political ties open many avenues for engaging in speculation associated with anticipated planning or rezoning schemes, even the ordinary citizen can secure favoured treatment of protection from the law. Second, the deep-seated weakness of state agencies and the consequent deficiency in civility and public consciousness – all of which have direct implications for urban planning – are exceptionally pronounced. The Lebanese state, compared to other forms of primary loyalties and communal allegiances, has always been an enfeebled and residual institution. Likewise, as a fragmented political culture, Lebanon has experienced a comparatively high incidence of repeated episodes of civil unrest and social disorder. The rampant chaos and lawlessness generated by such protracted episodes render any enforcement of law a vain and futile effort. Furthermore, when normlessness becomes so widespread, offences like the confiscation of property and the violation of construction and zoning ordinances become legitimate and forgivable transgressions.[75]

Finally, Lebanon's experience with urban planning reveals a curious but poignant paradox: a dissonance between the rather orderly and viable regulation of private space in homes, neighbourhoods and quarters matched by a mindless, almost total disregard for public space. In other words, the average Lebanese is so preoccupied with the internal comforts of his family and private domain that he shows little concern for public welfare and civic developments and becomes correspondingly more inclined to violate zoning ordinances. These dissonant attitudes towards the private and public spheres are clearly symptoms and sources of the deficiency in civility pervading society. They provide challenges and constraints that must be addressed in transforming the Bourj into a public sphere capable of harnessing and reconciling such redemptive elements.

The Architects' Legacy

The quality of any urban environment is also a reflection of the vision and resources available to the core of professional architects, planners and builders entrusted to safeguard the habitat and lived space. Lebanon's legacy in this regard is mixed. On the positive side, despite the shortage of architects, less than a handful of gifted practitioners until the mid-1950s managed to bequeath an admirable architectural heritage. As we have seen, no more than a trio of the 'founding fathers' of Lebanese architecture – Youssef Aftimos, Mardiros Altounian and Bechara Affendi – were largely responsible for some of

Youssef Aftimos – Barakat building

Youssef Aftimos – Municipality

Youssef Aftimos – Hamidiye Fountain

the most striking architectural icons of the period. For example, the Hamidiye Fountain, the Municipality, the esplanade of the Ottoman clock tower, the Grand Théâtre, the celebrated Petit Serail and its Menchiyyeh (public garden), the American College for Girls and the Barakat Building on the intersection of Damascus Street, as well as the Gergi Trad and Nsouli and Ladki buildings were all the work of Aftimos. A graduate of the Union College in 1891 in New York, he displayed his devotion for local and vernacular motifs very early in his career. Perhaps the most elegant in this regard is the inspiration he derived from the tenth- and eleventh-century Egyptian and Andalusian styles when he designed the Municipality of Beirut, which has been sensitively restored to pronounce such features. Aftimos's signal and eye-catching neo-Ottoman styles adorn most of his buildings during the 1920s and 1930s.

Mardiros Altounian was equally prolific and inventive. A graduate of the Beaux Arts School in Paris in 1918, he was an accomplished painter and sculptor. Growing up in France during WWI, the masterworks he was exposed to there must have left a lasting impression on his professional career. At a fairly young age he was commissioned to design the Parliament Building: a hemispheric horseshoe next to the Place de l'Etoile. He was visibly inspired – as can be seen in the triple arches and double openings – by the

Altounian – Clock tower

Altounian – St Paul

palaces and mansions of the feudal elite of the Chouf. His Oriental and neo-Moorish style was also striking in the Imam Abu Bakr Mosque facing the Municipality Building on Weygand Street. He also designed the Miguel Abed clock tower, the Armenian Orthodox Church and the elegant residences of villas of George Haimari, Omar Daouk and Chamille Edde. In these, as in other of his buildings, he stands out for initiating the transition from traditional to modern architecture.

Bechara Affendi, the oldest of the three (1841–1925), was largely self-taught and did not enjoy the benefits of any formal instruction in architecture. Yet he was privileged in being there and overseeing the beginnings of Beirut's landscape transformations. He was involved in the construction of Beirut–Damascus Road. He also supervised the construction of the Petit Serail (1884–88), the Sanayeh complex (1907) and the development of the Bourj Square in 1879.

This diminutive but gifted circle of pioneers served as mentors and role models to the younger generation of architects emerging at the time. Although in different ways, they all managed to forge an intuitive and symbiotic adaptation of some of the emerging modern and global architectural forms to local and vernacular exigencies. This could be seen first in the reproduction of neoclassicism and the Baroque and then eventually in Art Nouveau and Art-Deco elements. Many of the buildings around the Bourj, particularly Foch-Allenby and Etoile, grafted these features – notably, the use of wrought iron, ornamentation, bas-relief in floral themes, etc – over the oriental characteristics.

Baroque architecture in Lebanon has been traced by art historians to the five-year exile, between 1613 and 1618, of Emir Fakhreddine II in Tuscany. Florentine artists and craftsmen, who subsequently came to Lebanon, were commissioned by the Druze feudal chiefs to construct their elaborate palaces and mansions in such styles. Neo-Baroque features – such as marble, girders, red tiles from Marseilles, mouldings, wooden frames

Baroque architecture

for arcades, iron-works, etc – survived until the beginning of the twentieth century. The Ottoman Bank, the Orosdi-Back grand stores and the elaborately decorated villas of the upper bourgeoisie in the new and fairly exclusive neighbourhoods surrounding the Bourj, drew heavily from such salient European neo-Baroque, neo-Gothic and neoclassical styles. The elegant Sursock Museum (built in 1912 and restored recently) is a most exemplary prototype of such survival.

This playful adaptation implies that the founding fathers were not always enamoured with the faddish features of Western architecture. Nor were they obsessively captivated by some of the folkloric, decorative and nostalgic elements of traditional idioms. Instead, they made eclectic and judicious efforts to reconcile the two. Even when they were commissioned to undertake projects intended to celebrate Ottoman, colonial or other imported images or forms, these were almost always redefined locally. Hence, the resulting idioms were always a sensitive rendering or a symbiotic mélange of hybrid features which defied categorisation into fixed archetypes.

Such reproduction naturally became more problematic during the massive transformations the country was undergoing after WWII. Swift urbanisation, changes in the technology of construction materials and the influx of petrodollars for real-estate speculation generated problems beyond the control of architects and urban planners, despite their earnest intentions and concerted efforts to impose some measure of control over the forces beleaguering the spatial habitat.

Master crafstmen

It must be borne foremost in mind that architecture, as a professional discipline, was not as yet extant in Lebanon. In fact, it was not until WWII that formal architectural education was possible. Even then the type of instruction at both American University of Beirut (AUB) and University of St Joseph (USJ) were generally programmes in civil engineering. Hence, students were exposed only to the rudiments of architectural design and planning. In other words, there were no architects, in the individualistic sense, who were practitioners or gatekeepers of a recognised tradition.

What did exist, however, was a fairly large supply of master builders – *Mu'allem 'Amar* (masons) – who had intimate knowledge of the appropriate materials and processes of construction and potential users. Indeed, there was something close to a tripartite symbiotic relationship between this generation of master builders, the construction materials available at the time and the users. In other words, the forces of supply and demand complemented each other. Many of these craftsmen were patronised by the prosperous urban bourgeoisie families (Sursock, Bustros, Trad, Sayyour, Tabet, Tueni, etc) bent at the time on building their ornate palatial mansions in the nascent suburban quarters of Achrafiye, Minet El-Hosn, Zokak al-Blatt and Kantari. Resourceful apprentices were sent off to Italy to receive their tutelage by working under some of the prominent Italian architects. So accomplished were these local masters, including Wardini, Zoriek, Badrane, Bitar, etc, that they were often labelled by the status attributed to the place where they had received their apprenticeship (*Mu'allem Tuscani, Istanbuli*).

So meticulous were they about enhancing their 'masterly' credentials and reputation, designing their own makeshift catalogues, constructed by compiling all the ad hoc patterns they evolved over the years, they became almost akin to their own brand names. They were also keen on guarding their professional secrets, lest they become too ordinary and common. It is interesting to observe that they would not, for example, repeat the same design twice in the same neighbourhoods or quarters for at least two years.[76]

This complementary relationship could not accommodate or contain the forces playing havoc with the urban environment. The traditional craftsman was gradually becoming obsolete since he had no familiarity with, or intuitive feeling for, the new material. The user, on the other hand, could not resist the allures of modernity, particularly since the new technology promised a more effective exploitation of scarce resources, particularly residential space. The early dismaying manifestations of the degradation of the once-edifying spatial habitat were becoming increasingly visible. Raymond Ghosn, a budding architect at the time, had this to say:

> ... we see the elegant marble balconies on stone corbels and the graceful railings replaced, first by heavy reinforced concrete balconies and balustrades of all shapes and designs and later by deep square porches supported by reinforced concrete columns. The triple arcade motif is now overshadowed by this porch which is usually in poor proportion to the rest of the building. This was a basic change for which the master builder was not prepared. However, he now allowed himself all sorts of license in experimenting in designs for this porch. Since the restraint within which the master builder had operated in producing the traditional style was removed, he felt free to innovate, probably to please or rather impress a client.
>
> With the possibility of more floors to the building since now the building was supported by a skeleton of columns and beams and the walls were merely a filling in, by reducing the height of each of the two floors one can add a third floor for approximately the same total number of stair steps (important before the elevator came into use). So went the graceful proportion of the triple arcade. The pointed arch was truncated; pretty soon it became a rectangular transom above a straight lintel or some other immature or unstudied form. It was not long before the triple arcade was replaced by a single steel and glass door with wrought iron grilles for safety.[77]

The degradation of the spatial habitat was compounded further by the introduction of two inevitable features: the entry of the elevator into Beirut in 1940 and the staggering appreciation in real-estate values. Both, albeit in different magnitudes, had a far-reaching impact on the quality of the built environment. Among other things, they made possible the added intensification – both vertically and horizontally – of the exploitation of space.

Perhaps this is an over-drawn bleak portrait of Beirut's architecture at the time. Jad Tabet – an informed observer of that period, both because of his own work and intimate discussions he was privileged to have had with his father, Antoine Tabet – draws a more felicitous view by way of appreciating the spirit of what he considers a 'highly creative age ... where attempts were made to forge an architectural language which was not simply a degraded version of Western architectural modes ... despite the widespread use of standard commercial clichés, which have overwhelmed the architectural scene in Lebanon since the late '60s, and despite the present malaise, some of the architectural works produced during the '50s and '60s represented serious attempts to overcome the dilemma of choosing between "local traditions" and "imported modernity". Moreover, these attempts have more than a mere historical value. They offer interesting alternatives to the problem that seems to prevail today in the architectural debate everywhere in the Arab world, that of local identity versus globalisation.'[78]

The distinctive work of two other gifted pioneers, almost akin to true mavericks, reinforces this more sobering view. The architectural heritage they left behind is truly outstanding precisely because they attempted to formulate an architectural language more consistent with the emerging social, economic and technical conditions. When Lebanon received its independence in the early 1940s, the prevailing architectural style was unmistakably 'colonial'. Traditional forms were adopted, as Jad Tabet argues persuasively, without introducing any substantial changes to the conception of space and 'without dislodging the hold of previous building typologies'.[79] It should be remarked that the eclectic architectural styles salient during the 1920s and 1930s reflected, in part, the cultural and sectarian divisions within the city. With the demise of the Ottoman Empire, Western political alliances were eager to reinforce their patronage of local confessional communities. Hence, the cultural and socio-economic disparities were bound to become sharper. French-oriented Christians displayed their fondness, often with much abandon and *savoir faire*, for European lifestyles and consumerism. Ottoman-oriented Muslims, on the other hand, were still restless to part with their traditional proclivity for things Ottoman. Nowhere were such juxtapositions and cultural diversity as visible as in the architectural eclecticism of the period that was often a jarring mélange of 'upper bourgeois flamboyance and oriental exoticism'.[80] The ostentatious mansions and gated palaces of the late-nineteenth century mercantile elite, which continue to grace the neighbourhoods of Sursock, Joumblat, Gemmayze, Saifi, Zuqaq al-Blatt, Kantari, el-Zarif, etc are all living relics of that mixed heritage. Also, during the Mandate, French architects had virtual monopoly, given the scarcity of native talent at the time, over the nascent construction industry. For example, Lucien Carvo, a prominent French designer, moved from Damascus to Beirut in 1930 and established in no time a thriving practice. He may well be responsible for the design of many of these residences.[81] It is also this striking architectural eclecticism and stylistic pluralism which were selectively adopted and disseminated by the generation of master builders available at the time.

The point I am advancing is that this pioneering duo deftly and creatively broke away from this salient tradition. Farid Trad (1906–67) and Antoine Tabet (1905–64) were almost identical in age, professional schooling and career trajectory. Trad graduated from the celebrated Ecole des Arts et Metiers in Paris. Tabet, on the other hand, after earning a degree in engineering from the Ecole Supérieure d'Ingenieurs in Beirut, joined the studio of Auguste Perret in Paris, arguably one of the most prominent French architects.

Upon his return from Paris in 1931, and in association with his colleagues from Perret's studio, Tabet was commissioned to design and supervise the construction of Hotel St Georges. Perched on a splendid tip of Beirut's mythical bay (where St Georges slew that menacing dragon), this pristine, simplistic cube – with its rectangular frame enfolding an inner courtyard with surrounding guest rooms rendered more striking by overhanging balconies with unhindered views of the captivating sea and mountain – has been an ageless icon of the city's skyline. This same frank, sober simplicity – evident in the subtle placement of windowpanes and the rhythmic representation of horizontal and vertical elements – is visible in virtually all the architectural landmarks Tabet left us: the Ecole de la Sagesse (1937), the Union National Building (1952), the Mobile Office Building (1958) and the string of churches he designed.

Farid Trad displayed much of the same purified, simple and cubistic mélange of architectural elements. Of the two, Trad felt more at ease designing public buildings. Hence, as can be seen in his UNESCO Pavilion (1946) and Justice Palace (1959), he was more inclined to incorporate ceremonial and monumental elements, such as bold rectangular stone columns, floating cornices and the like. While Tabet worked closely within the classical rationalist tradition of Perret (indeed as his son, Jad, argues in his insightful analysis of his father's work, his buildings often seem like 'softer versions of Perret's prototypes'), Trad was more inspired by the Beaux-Arts school of the European tradition of civic monuments of the 1930s.[82] He was also recognised as one of the leading and, perhaps, first contributors to the use of concrete as an architectural medium. As a result, he was able to avoid symptoms of excessive ornamentation common at the time. He opted instead to embody notions of purity and rationality in most of his projects. Most noted was the Regent Hotel and the Dunia Cinema at the Bourj and a score of personal villas and residences, such as Villa Hitti on Clemenceau Street and Villa Choucair, next to the National Museum. In their later works – in the mid- to late-1950s – the intuitive and adaptive architects that they were, both started to abandon some of the classical elements and veer, instead, in the direction of 'abstract aestheticism'. This is visible in the way they incorporated prototypes and artifacts of the modern movement such as pilotis, *brise-soleils*, concrete struts and the like.[83]

It should be remarked, as several observers have noted, that colonial architecture in Beirut remained dominant until the early 1940s. Western-educated pioneers, along with the proclivity of other indigenous architects to collaborate with foreign colleagues, had expedited the introduction of an international and cosmopolitan style. Such manifestations were first visible in the works of Farid Trad and Antoine Tabet, particularly expressions in favour of rationalism and functionalism and the adoption of features such as glass, steel envelopes, wall-curtains and simple geometric forms with grid layouts.[84] These and other elements – perhaps most salient are reinforced concrete frameworks and slabs – played a substantial role in modifying Beirut's architecture in the 1950s.

Doubtlessly, the solid and diverse foreign professional training the first two generations of pioneers brought with them had done much to usher in this transition from colonial to modern architecture. With the exception of a few individuals, they were all recipients of either formal schooling or enjoyed the privilege of internships in the studios and workshops of prominent architects. The first generation were almost equally divided between French and American schooling: Joseph Aftimos, Bahjat Abdelnour, Ilyas Murr, Saleh and Fawzi Itani graduated from US universities (Union College of New York, MIT and Michigan respectively). Mardiros Altounian, Antoine Tabet, Farid Trad were, on the other hand, French-trained.

The second generation were also equally privileged in this regard. The following were US graduates: Bahij Makdisi (Michigan), Raymond Ghosn (MIT), Samir Khairallah (Berkeley) and George Riachi (Chicago). The rest were all French graduates: Pierre Neema (Beaux Arts), Henri Eddé (workshop of Marcel Lods, Paris), and Amin Bizri (ESA, Paris). George Rayyis (AA of London) and Assem Salem (Cambridge) were the first graduates of British universities.

Interestingly, Robert Saliba invokes the type of professional training this pioneering generation had received abroad to account for variations in their architectural styles.[85] In his view, for example, those who were schooled in the US were inclined to show more sympathetic concern for regional and local architectural heritage than graduates of French universities. The compelling Barakat building, designed by Aftimos in 1924, is a 'landmark of early transitional domestic architecture, with a hybrid structure integrating concrete with stone, and an "intermediate" architectural language neither Western revivalist nor Neo-Ottoman'.[86]

Beginning in the early-1950s, just as Tabet and Trad were in the twilight of their careers, Lebanon ushered in another generation of Western-trained architects. While the early mentors and pioneers remained, by and large, within a classical colonial tradition, this new generation – by virtue of their varied professional backgrounds along with the intensity of urbanisation and commercialisation Beirut was undergoing at the time – were more eclectic and cosmopolitan in their perspectives. They were caught, much like their European counterparts, 'between the dexterity of the contemporary world and the reliance on age-old traditions'.[87] Hence, they all, in one way or another, had to confront the nagging problem of how to render local technology more receptive to novel forms of design which departed from the reservoir of traditional crafts and skills.

Even those who did not have the benefit of Western education or training were keen to incorporate and blend into their work some striking foreign and cosmopolitan elements. Joseph Philippe Karam, arguably one of the most productive builders between 1950 and 1960, was very taken by Le Corbusier's syntax and language, particularly his modernistic avant-garde style. His excessive use of such elements, employed at times as aesthetic emblems and artifacts divorced from their function, was far from universally admired. Indeed, some of his excesses were often critically received by his colleagues. Still, one cannot overlook the impressive mark he had left on the spatial and visual image of Beirut's architectural landscape.

What is remarkable about this generation of architects, like their illustrious mentors, was their refusal to subscribe to one singular or essentialist perception of their work or the way they looked at the role of art, culture and their own national identity. Being the products of hybrid, pluralist and diverse political and socio-cultural settings, at a time when the paradigms of their own professional disciplines were being contested, they displayed a healthy affinity for experimentation and inventiveness without any inflexible or rigid disregard for local traditions.

Another striking attribute, which accounts for their pluralist leanings, as well as at times their unrestrained eagerness to incorporate novel expressions and styles, was their accommodating predisposition to seek collaborative projects with diverse partners. Indeed, many of them rarely worked alone. Some of their most prominent products were the outcome of such joint ventures, often drawing together multiple national identities and a diversity of architectural styles.

A cursory profile of the background, professional training and output of this second generation of architects reveals their hybridity and eclecticism and how adept some of them were in moulding forms and prototypes of stylistic expression and design which sought to forge a modern vocabulary without undermining the sensibilities of local mindsets and typologies. Like the pioneering duo Tabet and Trad, they too were not averse to collaborating with foreign colleagues or experimenting with new idioms.

The first two to enter this burgeoning scene were George Rayyes (1915–2003) and Theo Kanaan (1910–59). Rayyes was born in Haifa, Palestine, and received his professional training at the Bartlett School in London. He was also enrolled at the Architectural Association (AA), the renowned avant-garde school there. It was there that he met Theo Kanaan and evolved, from then on, an almost life-long association with him. Rayyes, however, dropped out in 1939 shortly before the outbreak of WWII. Interestingly, he never gave up on his desire for formal schooling and did, ultimately, earn his professional degree from ALBA in 1970 at the age of 60. It was in Palestine that they collaborated jointly (1939–48) on the construction of housing projects for the British Mandate authorities. Both of them left to settle in Beirut in 1948.

Early in his schooling, Rayyes was captivated by the life and works of Frank Lloyd Wright and had an equal passion for the Bauhaus. In many of his joint projects with Theo Kanaan he was keen on embodying a minimalist treatment of space and volume. This is manifest in the often simplistic representations of geometric lines to safeguard the uninterrupted free flow of movement. Despite the sudden and accidental death of Kanaan in Jarash at the age of 49, their partnership was very resourceful. Their vivid imprint became visible in the first building they were commissioned to build: the Arida Apartment Building in the Sanayeh quarter (1951). Departing clearly from any of the earlier classical expressions, the building was perhaps the first to begin articulating, as

Tabet argues, the idioms of modernity; namely 'simple geometric forms, sliding volumes and free-standing planes'.[88] Such features were further elaborated in the Pan Am Building in Beirut (1955), designed in association with Assem Salam, who had just returned to Lebanon. They left behind some other striking edifices: the Cinema Hamra, Sodeco Towers, the Hotel Excelsior and a score of private apartment houses and villas.

The second group to launch their work in Beirut in the early-1950s was also a striking instance of collaboration between four unusual architects: Karl Cheyer, Fritz Gotthelf, Bahij Makdisi and Wassek Adib. Cheyer, a Polish architect who had come to Lebanon after WWII, had worked closely with the German interior designer, Fritz Gotthelf, who he had met in Palestine. In Beirut they attracted two rather divergent Lebanese architects: Bahij Makdisi, a structural engineer, and Wassek Adib, who had been an associate of Umberto Turati, a prominent Italian architect. This most unusual professional quartet was successful, at a critical period in Beirut's urban growth, in introducing an authentic modernist style, a prototype of the abstracted rectilinear elements of the Bauhaus. To a considerable extent, they were responsible between 1950 and 1960 for popularising a form of avant-garde architecture which made creative use of the salient new techniques emerging at the time: namely, pure prismatic volumes, flat and light roofs with their fine flagstones.[89] Their firm produced the winning scheme for the headquarters and Alumni Club of the American University of Beirut (1953). Although subsequently dwarfed by the more imposing glass towers of Gefinor and the like, the Alumni Club remained for a while an elegant prototype of the abstracted rectilinear style of the Bauhaus. More striking in this respect was Cheyer's Horseshoe Building on Hamra Street (1958), which marked the conception of the first 'curtain wall' in Lebanon.[90] In quick succession, a score of such buildings, bearing similar styles, started to punctuate the urban-scape of the city and its suburbs: the Carlton Hotel, the Shell Building, Saroulla, Yamama, al-Thani, Eldorado, Ashi, Daouk, among others, stand out.

Although not in direct collaboration with local architects, a string of foreign architects were recruited, it must be recalled, to assist in the process of urban planning and construction under way during the post-Mandate period. In addition to the schemes of Danger (1932), Delahalle (1934), Ecochard (1943, 1963) and Egli (1990), the influence of foreign architects, mostly with eminent international standing, was considerable. Alfred Roth, Alvar Aalto, Oscar Niemeyer and André Woginski had a formidable legacy, both in terms of the architectural icons they left behind and their impact on informing, often shaping, the style and output of successive generations of local architects. Likewise, it was the partnership between Maurice Hindié and André Woginski that produced the Moscow Narodny Bank, the Library and the science faculty at the Lebanese University and the Ministry of Defence building.

One of the first returnees of the second generation was Assem Salam. Soon after he had completed his architectural education at Cambridge University, he had worked on the English new towns before returning to Lebanon in 1952 to establish his private practice and teach at the American University of Beirut (AUB). The trajectory of his career stands out because he was not the ordinary and conventional narrow-minded professional, obsessively concerned with the purely technical and marketable features of his craft. Early in his career he evinced a humanist and advocacy perspective by serving as a critical public voice to safeguard the built environment from further abuse. He was involved in teaching and collaborated with Raymond Ghosn in establishing the Faculty of Architecture at AUB.

His inclinations for broadening the advocacy component of architecture prompted him to be more publicly engaged. Hence, he did not shy away from participating in government councils, voluntary associations and other regional and global public ventures. He served successive terms on the Higher Council of Urban Planning (1964–78; 1995–9) and the Centre for Development and Research (CDR) when it was established in 1977. He was also elected president of the Order of Engineers and Architects of Beirut (1996–9) and chaired the Arab Federation of Architects (1998–2000). Given his keen and abiding concerns for protecting the country's habitat and architectural heritage, he was also one of the cofounders of APSAD, Lebanon's singular association for the protection of old sites and traditional architecture. With the establishment of Solidere in 1994, he emerged as one of its trenchant critics.

His own architectural heritage is rich, diverse and compelling in its impact. In his first project he collaborated, as we have seen, with George Rayyes and Theo Kanaan on the Pan Am Building in 1955. That its style echoes that of Le Corbusier is apparent in the plasticity of its imposing façades. Perhaps because he was at the prime of his career during the Chehabist regime (1958–64), Assem Salam was involved in the design of a score of government and institutional buildings. The following stand out: the Ministry of Tourism (1958), the Serail of Saida (1965), the Ministry of Information (1965) and the Brumana High School (1966). In these, as in other of his later projects – such as the Mosque at the 'Forêt de Pins' (1968), Gefinor Commercial Centre (1970) and the Verdun 2000 Commercial Centre (1992) – one sees a subtle, often nuanced, effort at reconciling the simplistic, geometric forms, grid layouts and postmodern stylistic expressions with more than just hints of Ottoman architecture. He is also credited for the restoration of a score of architectural landmarks.

While Assem Salam was expansive in his public role as an engaged architect, Pierre El Khoury was much more exclusive. Except for a brief stint as minister of public works (1983–4), the bulk of his creative energies were directed towards his architectural projects. His prolific output, let alone its diversity and refined aestheticism, is a compelling testimony to that. His professional portfolio includes over 200 projects, many of which were the outcome of intense international competition. He is also far from the twilight of his career. Indeed, some of his most recent projects are, arguably, the most inventive and interesting.

'Cheikh Pierre', as he is often referred to, in deference to his titled family lineage, was also privileged by his professional schooling at the Beaux Arts in Paris (1957) and the tutorship he had received at home. His father, Fouad El Khoury, was also a practising architect and, it seems, was part of that close circle of professionals André Leconte had drawn around him during his presence in Beirut.[91] This early exposure must have left an indelible mark on the young and impressionable Pierre, as did his training at the renowned studio of Gromort-Arretche in Paris. It is there that he reinforced his devotion to classical architecture and how to graft over it Mediterranean and Levantine elements and motifs. When tracing the conceptual genealogy of his work, Pierre always gives due credit to the tutelage and mentoring he had received at the atelier of that accomplished duo. Indeed, he attributes a healthy complementarity to them:

> Gromort, a famous author of treatises on geometry and Classical architecture, was steeped in architectural culture, whereas Arretche had a peasant's common sense. While the architecture of Pierre El Khoury is resolutely Modern, one finds in his work a skilful mix of what he learned with these two masters and his buildings combine composition, order and rhythm with a tactile sense of the setting.[92]

This sustained effort to reconcile the two traditions has been the most defining and constituent feature of his work. He started modestly by building his own private residence in Yarzé (1959), an exclusive, wooded suburb on the western slopes adjoining the Damascus motorway. This exquisitely modern residence, with sliding glazing, transparent partitions and patios reminiscent of Frank Lloyd Wright's celebrated Falling Water House in Mill Run, Pennsylvania, nestles in perfect harmony with its wooded site.

It is rather striking, if not anomalous, that El Khoury should launch his professional career in 1961 by winning bids to design diametrically opposed projects: convents and monasteries in Yarzé and Jazzine respectively and the penitentiary complex for the Roumieh Prison. As *asylums*, to borrow an expression from Erving Goffman, both prisons and convents are 'total' institutions which confine and strictly monitor the entry and exit of their inmates. The prison complex, perched on the hilly slopes of lower Roumieh, was a massive undertaking, designed with a team of specialists. It was composed of an interconnected set of structured triangles and hexagons.

So accomplished were his initial projects that his sudden acclaim generated a succession of other projects spanning the widest range possible: private residences, commercial centres, educational institutions, hotels, resorts and, of course, churches, cathedral and places of worship. Doubtlessly, the most spectacular and perhaps unrivalled in its size is the Basilica of Our Lady of Harissa, a monumental and daring structure that punctuates the sky atop the peak of the majestic mountain range overlooking Jounieh Bay. With the assistance of Noel Abouhamad, the basilica took the form of a luminous ceiling with sixty concrete shells varying in height from thirty to fifty metres.

El Khoury did not have any aversion to collaborating with other colleagues. Thus, the Lebanese Pavilion at the New York Fair (1963) was designed jointly with Assem Salam and Michel Harmouche; the Byblos Centre (1960) with Henri Eddé; extension of Beirut's Airport with Assaad Raad and the Sabbagh Centre with Alvar Aalto and Alfred Roth. He also had no hesitation in branching out beyond Lebanon. Like others of his colleagues during the oil boom in the Gulf, he also could not resist the challenge of partaking in these opportunities. He designed a score of prize winning international competition entries, most prominent among them the National Bank of Dubai (1970), the Muscat International Hotel (1974), the late King Faysal Palace in collaboration with Kenzo Tange (1975) and the Ministry of Foreign Affairs in Riadh (1979).

Disheartened by the neglect and destruction of old traditional houses and the abuse of the natural habitat, he took keen interest in the preservation of the country's architectural heritage. In addition to the houses he restored in Baadarane, Aley and Aramoun, he teamed up with Amin Bizri (1965) in the rehabilitation of the Amir Amin Palace in Beiteddine and its conversion it into a resort and conference centre. He was one of the founders of APSAD and was directly involved in proposing town-planning schemes for a score of towns and villages. He also participated in the post-war rehabilitation of urban districts adjoining the city's centre: namely, Saifi, Ghalgoul and the harbour.

One distinctive feature of Pierre El Khoury's career merits special recognition: perhaps more than his colleagues, he has always managed to attract and sustain a core of young and gifted architects with whom he collaborated. He was mentoring and generous in honing their talents and recognising their individual contributions. The following can be mentioned: Pierre Bassil, Joseph Faycal, Antoine Gemayel, Kamal Homsi, Jacques Abou Khaled, Semaan Kfoury and Joe Geitani. Indeed, a score of the recent 'postmodern' buildings which now stand out as distinctive landmarks in Beirut's contemporary architecture – the Economic and Social Commission for Western Asia (ESCWA) Office Building, BLOM headquarters, Dar an-Nahar, among others under construction – are all by-products of such a supportive professional setting. Although Khoury might not be at ease with the 'postmodern' label for his designs, they are, however, emblematic of a bourgeoning trend in the direction of 'monumental post modernity' in that they offer, as Arbid argues, an 'overstated high-tech exhibitionism ... and a trend towards hyper-futurism'.[93] At least, BLOM and the ESCWA headquarters, much more than others in their genre, do display spectacular elements by virtue of their aesthetically pleasing translucent and opaque features.

Pierre Neema, another resourceful member of this generation, graduated from the Ecole Nationale des Beaux Arts in Paris, a year after Pierre El Khoury (1958). Like El Khoury, he also benefitted from a supportive family background steeped in the arts and culture, particularly the circle of Lebanese architects in Cairo at the time.[94] His return to Lebanon in 1961 also coincided with the so-called 'golden age' of modern architecture, associated with the birth of modern state institutions during the Chehab era. Hence, like his other colleagues in this generation, his early career was marked by projects commissioned by the state: Ministry of Social Affairs (1963); military social housing in Fayadieh (1964); technical schools in Machgara (1965); Electricité du Liban (1966).

Pierre El Khoury – ESCWA   *Pierre El Khoury – Dat an-Nahar*

Early in his career, Neema evinced an admirable, often spectacular and eye-catching, refined aestheticism. This is most visible in his design of the Maison of Artisan in Aïn-El-Mreisseh (1963). As Gebran Yacoub puts it, this opaque and translucent structure is an 'expression of a domesticated modernity adapted to the local culture. Its structure was formed of bearing elements designed as an arborescent metal structure with four branches supporting a thin concrete slab. The unit is of elegant minimalism with its integral glazing, offering an unrestricted sight towards the horizon and the sea.'[95]

Neema did not shy away from teaming up with other architects, both local and foreign. As noted earlier, he had launched his professional career as a partner of Bahij Makdisi and Associates. Indeed, it was out of such collaborative ventures that he had won a score of his competitions. For example, his partnership with Antoine Chamaá led to first prize in the competition for the Greek Catholic church in Hamra shortly after his return to Lebanon in 1961. Likewise, it was his collaboration with Jacque Aractingi, Joseph Nassar and Jean-Noel Conan that resulted in the commission for the Bir-Hassan Government city. His partnership with Panaï Akl (a structural engineer) and Jacques Garcia (a decorator) proved to be even more beneficent. Most of the competitions he won during that initial interlude, between 1961 and 1973, before relocating in the Gulf were the outcome of this collaborative team.

Like many of his other colleagues, the oil boom along with civil unrest in Lebanon, had encouraged him to seek projects in Saudi Arabia, Algeria and Jordan. During that interlude much of his work was done in association with other more substantial construction and architectural firms and consulting companies emerging in Beirut at the time, such as the CETA Group, Arab Consult, ACE, CEO and Dar al-Handassa of Nazih Taleb.

His first major project and, perhaps, the most striking as a preamble for other successive works in the same genre and massive magnitude, was the SOFIL Centre in Achrafieh. Although the project was conceived in 1973, it was not completed until 1985. Its commanding composition as a set of terraces, with hanging gardens along with an interplay of glazed and solid bands, is rendered more exquisite because the centre of the block where the building is constructed is transformed into a lush garden, thereby associating the new construction to earlier existing structures. From then on, and often with the collaboration of M. Yapoudjian, Neema produced some of the most striking architectural icons in Beirut. They stand out both in terms of their monumentality and proclivity to harmonise modernity with salient elements of the local culture. The most accomplished of this genre are the Verdun Centre, Sadat Towers, the Chamber of Commerce and Industry and the Sehnaoui Building.

Much like Pierre El Khoury, some of his most daring and refined works have been the outcome of his more recent years. A few stand out in this regard: the Cap sur Ville complex in Aïn Saadeh (1995), the Rizk Hospital (1984 and 2000), the Gefinor Plaza Hotel in Hamra (2000) and the Tilal Building in Achrafieh (2001). Special recognition must also be made to the Grands Magazines Stores of ABC at Dbyeh (1989), also created in partnership with M. Yapoudjian, like all the above. Although built on a dense stretch of the northern motorway, this airtight and box-like metal structure stands out largely because of its unusual shape and opulent colours.

The versatility and resourcefulness of Neema are also evident in his landscape and restoration projects. He teamed up with Jacques Sgard, a French landscape designer, in re-planning the Pine Wood Forest (1993–5). To his credit, there are also a score of rehabilitation and restoration ventures, such as the French Cultural Centre, al Madina Theatre, the former French Embassy transformed into the Ecole Supérieure des Affaires (ESA) and the Presidential Palace at Baabdah. Like Assem Salam, his professional interests extended into teaching, in his case at the Department of Architecture at ALBA. He served as editor of *al-Mouhandess*, the mouthpiece of the Order of Engineers and Architects of Beirut, and was an active member of APSAD.

Samir Khairallah clearly belongs to this select core of architects. He shares many of the attributes that marked the careers of his other equally resourceful colleagues. Most importantly, he is a product of solid foreign education (UCLA, 1958) and was privileged to receive his apprenticeship at renowned studios and firms (William Wurster, Charles Eames and the BIW Architects in Richmond). He also had the same penchant for undertaking collaborative projects, often with reputable, high profile architects and firms. For example, in partnership with Paul Rudolph, he designed in 1973 the urban centre of the Fakhry Brothers. A year later, also with Rudolph, it was the TMA headquarters at Beirut's International Airport. The Meridian Hotels in Beirut and Jeddah were the product of his association with the Italian agency of Mileto and Associates. With Rafael Moneo he worked on the redesign of the traditional *souks* in downtown Beirut.

Khairallah was similarly keen on adapting some of the rational elements of modern architecture and contemporary material to the vernacular and local culture. Perhaps more than the trio of Salam, El Khoury and Neema, he belonged to a growing core of Lebanese architects (Khatib and Alami, Nazih Taleb, ACE, Dar al-Handassa, Laceco, etc) who sought the management of large-scale projects and the export of their expertise and technical know-how to other countries in the region. He also departed slightly from the salient career patterns of his colleagues in that he appeared to have a particular interest in designing and constructing institutional buildings and premises of universities, colleges, schools and associated facilities. There is hardly a campus in Lebanon – AUB, BUC, International College in Mechref, LAU – which is not dotted with his work.

Much like his other colleagues, some of his most refined and daring projects have been the outcome of his most recent years. A few stand out in this regard: the Cap sur Ville complex in Aïn Saadeh (1995), the Crown Plaza Hotel in Hamra (2000) and the Tilal Building in Achrafieh (2001). All these, among others under construction, display how adept he has become at incorporating judiciously some of the Hi-Tech elements of post modernism.

It should be noted that many of the third, and possibly fourth generation of Lebanese architects had been initiated into their career by apprenticeship in the offices of the pioneering pool of architrects.

Generally, these architects of the younger geneneration completed their professional training by the early 1970s and would have established their individual or group practices just as the country was about to lapse into protracted interludes of civil strife. Hence, more than their predecessors, they had to confront the disruptive circumstances of the war at an early and more vulnerable stage of their careers.

It is still fairly early to assess their full impact on the urban-scape and overall character of the built environment. Easily about half a dozen, however, stand out in view of their potential for further growth. In my view, they do not only sustain the hybridity and eclecticism of their predecessors, they also incorporate into their work more symptoms of Hi-Tech which were surfacing at the time. Hence, derivative features of flexibility, transparency, glass envelopes, aluminium and steel structures, the use of light and opaque material and other futuristic forms and 'images became more pronounced. Unfortunately, architectural Hi-Tech was being ushered into Lebanon during the early- and mid-1970s, at a time when the country was beset with strife and a sluggish economy. Hence, as a score of observers have noted, some of its manifestations departed from the restrained sobriety of existing forms and started to assume more of the dismaying features of contrived superficiality, pomposity and kitsch. The handful of architects I intend to dwell on, albeit too briefly, managed in my view to forge and articulate a more edifying synthesis of these dissonant elements.

The first to appear on this scene was Nabil Azar. He earned his degree from AUB in 1970, which incidentally he recalls fondly, particularly the mentoring he had received at the hands of Raymond Ghosn and Assem Salam. After collaborating briefly with Ghosn he founded his own firm, Builders Design Consultants, in 1973. The early rounds of strife in the country prompted him to transfer his work to the Gulf, where he stayed until 1990.

Upon his return he seemed eager to reclaim the credibility of his career and to validate his skills at partaking in the preponderant opportunities of post-war construction and rehabilitation. He quickly displayed some of the professional virtues of his mentors: versatility, eclecticism and a keenness to forge a symbiotic synthesis between some of the local traditions receptive to the contemporary modes demanded by high modernity.

After a few projects in partnership with Amin Bizri (the Islamic Hospital in Tripoli and the Justice Palace in Saida), he was commissioned by the Lebanese Parliament in 1992 to undertake three visible projects which served to enhance his professional credibility: the annex to the Parliament on Njemeh Square, the official residence of the parliament's speaker at Aïn El Tineh and the renovation of the parliament's chamber. In quick succession, he realised a score of institutional buildings (including the International College in Aïn Aar), hospitals (St Georges and Balamand), urban developments of public squares (Sassine and Abu Shahla), shopping malls (Salwan in Badaro), resort centres and seaside marinas (Jiyeh), private villas and residential apartments (Abela in Mkales) and low-rent complexes in Hadath. Likewise, and to his credit, he was heavily involved in restoration ventures, most notable the St Georges Cathedral in Nejmeh Square and the Protestant church in Zokak al Blatt.

Next to join was the duo of Farid Homsi and Pierre Bassil. Both are also AUB graduates (1971) and both did their apprenticeship with Pierre El Khoury (until 1973 for Bassil and 1974 for Homsi). Their first joint project (Baroud Chalet at Faqra in 1975) was a graphic preamble of what was to come. With its fairfaced concrete and open metal flooring, it portrayed many of the sensibilities of a refined modernist approach. Indeed, their most appealing projects were initially a score of such chalets and private villas in the mountain resorts and towns of Bikfaya, Faqra and Jdeideh. These, among other projects, embody the styles and expressions of noted architects like Le Corbusier and Mario Botta.[96] Perhaps their most spectacular projects are the Libano-Arabe Insurance Company in downtown Beirut (1991) and the Tois de Beyrouth high-rise in Mansourieh (1995–2000).

Two other architects who had completed their studies in the mid-1970s and had also suffered the unsettling circumstances of the war years deserve recognition: Samir Ghaoui and Ziad Akl. Ghaoui, a graduate of the National Institute of Fine Arts (INBA) in 1974, started his career with Maurice Hindie and André Wogenski on the Holiday Inn Hotel (1973–4). It was after he had established his individual practice in 1977 that he accomplished some of his most reputable projects: the ICN television headquarters in Sassine Square (1985), the Holiday Tower Centre 507 in Dbayeh (1988), the Moukarzel Centre in Mtaileb (1990), a residential compound in Serhal (1992) and the Sehnaoui office building in Sin el-Fil (1999). The ICN headquarters is particularly striking because of its luminous, crisp and clean-cut style, emblematic of the multifaceted architecture of glass structures.

In addition to his private practice, Ghaoui was involved in teaching at his Alma Mater (INBA) between 1974 and 1984. He served as vice president of the Beirut Order of Engineers (1998–9) and organised seminars on post-war reconstruction.

Ziad Akl has also produced, although in intermittent flashes thus far, a few promising works. Soon after he earned his postgraduate degree in regional and urban planning from the Ecole Nationale des Ponts et Chausées of Paris (1977), he established his own private practice. His work is striking because in his attempt to resolve the ubiquitous interplay between modernity and traditionalism, he is inclined at times to transcend modernity in favour of the local and vernacular. Perhaps most expressive in this regard is the Banque du Liban Building in Bikfaya (1985–8) and the sea resort of 'Dar Sur Mer' in Safra (1985–8). Both, incidentally, were done in collaboration with Nehmat Sfeir. The Bikfaya bank, an imposing modern, structure cascades over a traditional mountain house. Although dwarfed by the overwhelming structure, the traditional house still assumes a defiant centrality.

Through his firm ZAP (Ziad Akl and Partners), Akl collaborated with a number of partners in an effort to sustain this kind of bold but measured experimentation. The Delb Country Club in Bikfaya (1998), Holdal Company at Mkalles (2000) and the recent renovation of a five-star hotel in downtown Beirut, all provide evidence of such efforts. Incidentally, a few other members of this generation of young architects have already displayed similar expressive manifestations, most notably the Green Mall of Bechara El Bacha, the Mardini Centre (1990) by Louis Saadé and the Forum of Beirut (1996) by Elie Chehade and Mike Moussa.

We have in the making the harbingers of yet another promising circle of young architects groping to make a difference. Judging by the formative legacy they have already left, they seem destined to make an indelible mark on the country's built environment. They have all completed their professional education and training at prominent schools and their apprenticeship with noted – often world-class – architects by the mid- or late-1980s even the early-1990s. We are, in other words, dealing with a fairly young group of architects barely in their late thirties or forties. I wish to single out only a handful, again in the order in which they had commenced their professional practice: the ERGA group of Elie and Randa Gebrayel, Nabil Gholam, Bernard Khoury, Bawader Architects, Hashim Sarkis and George Arbid. Of course, one always runs the risk of the inevitable crimes of omission or commission in making such judgments. The selection is nonetheless the outcome of reviewing their published profiles and portfolios, interviews and discussions with a score of active professionals and my own judgmental impressions extracted from direct site visits.

The ERGA group is a project study firm, co-founded in 1982 by the husband/wife team of Elie and Randa Gebrayel. Both are graduates of INBA in 1980 and are among the few local architects who did not enjoy the privilege of foreign education or training. Three admirable examples of their work deserve recognition. The refined and measured use of Hi-Tech elements is made evident in their design of the Order of Doctors, the Badaro Trade Centre and the Faubourg Saint Jean Commercial Centre in Hazmieh. The design of the Mövenpick Hotel, stretching across the western slopes of Beirut's sea front, like the Order of Doctors next to Martyrs' Square, evinces a minimalist, simplistic style while seeking monumentality in its volume.

The Gebrayel duo have also been involved in restoration work. Most exemplary in this regard is their rehabilitation and expansion of the Trad Hospital on Clemenceau Street (1993). The construction of a new wing in modern style while preserving the red brick of the old 1930s building is elegant and harmonious. Doubtlessly their most successful and pacesetting is their participation in the reconstruction of the Saifi Village, the traditional urban quarter and carpenters' *souk* adjoining the eastern flanks of Martyrs' Square. The overall project, designed by Francois Spoery, a leading French architect, is a judicious blend of contemporary features while preserving more than just outward, cosmetic hints of nostalgia.

Nabil Gholam, a graduate of the Architecture School of Paris-Villemin (1986) and Columbia University (1988), is emerging as arguably one of the most productive of his generation. Soon after his graduation, he joined the workshop of Ricardo Bofill, a leading Catalan architect, which exposed him to global and international trends. Indeed, between 1987 and the establishment of his NG architectural and design office in Beirut in 1994, he had a resourceful and enriching career collaborating on major projects in Europe, China and the US. A few of those, incidentally, have won distinguished prizes and awards.

With his young and spirited team of associates, he built a score of hotels and residential compounds in Dubai and Saudi Arabia. In Lebanon, before he undertook some prominent and visible projects, all the outcome of international competitions, he displayed a genuine interest in restoration. He also devoted considerable attention to reclaiming and landscaping coastal and beach areas. To his credit is a score of marinas, yachting clubs, leisure and sports facilities. In the past few years his firm has been associated with a score of spectacular projects, often in association with world-class architects. Many are currently under construction: the Platinum Towers on Park Avenue overlooking the marina, Foschville, Block 94 and Saifi II adjoining Martyrs' Square.

Bernard Khoury, a graduate of the Rhodes Island School of Design (1991) and Harvard (1993), has shown considerable inventiveness and originality in his work. Before he completed his Masters at Harvard's Graduate School of Design, he was privileged to work with Jean Nouvel in France. Thus far, most of his projects, although diminutive and unpretentious, are ingenious, often cunning. His B 018 nightclub, a notorious popular haunt for the young, has become something of an eccentric architectural icon. So too is the Yabani restaurant. Another restaurant in Jemeyze, Centrale, is a restored building in which the makeshift scaffolding gives the appearance of a provisional and temporary structure in the throes of reconstruction. This same temporality, although more dramatic, characterises the City Centre Dome project currently under construction. The dishevelled remains of a once fashionable movie theatre, it stands today at the southwest end of Martyrs' Square, an eyesore from the city's belligerent past. Once restored, the 'Red Square', as it is currently labelled, will serve as a short-term cultural and entertainment centre.

Another promising group is Bawader Architects, established in 1992 by three AUB graduates: Muhammad Adra, Ikram Zaatari and Marwan Ghandour. The bulk of their joint efforts thus far have focused on the design and construction of nursery- and primary-school complexes in various neighbourhoods within the city and its suburbs. They have also rehabilitated a score of government hospitals in Saida and Baalbeck. Since the premises are mostly situated in fairly depressed areas, their elegant, rational and airy designs enhance both their own architectural appeal and the quality of their surrounding habitat.

Finally, Hashim Sarkis and George Arbid, both with Ph Ds from Harvard's Graduate School of Design, have opted to pursue more academic careers. Sarkis is currently the Agha Khan Professor of Islamic Architecture at Harvard while Arbid is at AUB. Of the two, Sarkis has had a decidedly more active and versatile practice. With hardly seven years in the field, and despite his demanding teaching and academic duties, he has already supervised the realisation of a score of unusual pacesetting projects, often in remote regions of Lebanon. Most noted are the following: the Fishermen Residential Complex in Tyr, the School of Aronomy in Mejdlaya, the Market and Centre for Young People in Zahle and Bab-el-Tabbaneh School in Tripoli. He has also participated in establishing the plan for the development of the University of Balamand in the Durah district and reconstruction of the public space of the Gefinor Shopping Centre. Most recently, his scheme for the International Ideas Competition for the Grand Axis and Martyrs' Square of Beirut was awarded third prize. Through his teaching and studies at Harvard's Graduate School of Design, he has been instrumental in exposing successive generations of students to direct fieldwork on the ground in various cities in the region. One of his students, in fact, has just won first place in that category for Beirut's Martyrs' Square competition.

THREE

The Spaces of Post-War Beirut

For almost two decades, Lebanon was besieged and beleaguered by every possible form of brutality and collective terror known to human history: from the cruelties of factional and religious bigotry to the massive devastations wrought by private militias and state-sponsored armies. They have all generated an endless carnage of innocent victims and exacted an immeasurable toll of human suffering. Even by the most moderate of estimates, the magnitude of such damage to human life and property is staggering. About 170,000 have perished, twice as many were wounded or disabled; close to two-thirds of the population experienced some form of dislocation or uprootedness from their homes and communities. By the fall of 1982, UN experts estimated that the country had sustained 12–15 billion dollars in damages: almost 2 billion dollars per year. Today more than one-third of the population is considered to be below the poverty line as a result of war and displacement.

For a small, dense and closely-knit society of about 3.5 million, occupying less than 4,000 square metres, such devastation is, understandably, very menacing. More damaging, perhaps, are some of the socio-psychological and moral concomitants of protracted hostility. The scars and scares of war have exacted a heavy psychic toll, manifested in pervasive post-traumatic-stress symptoms and nagging feelings of despair and hopelessness. In a culture generally averse to psychoanalytic counselling and therapy, these psychic disorders and fears are more debilitating. They are bound to remain masked and unrecognised and, hence, unattended to.

The demoralising consequences of the war are also visible in the vulgarisation and impoverishment of public life and the erosion of civility. Routine violence, chaos and fear only unravelled still further the frayed fabrics of the social order. It drew groups into the vortex of bellicose conflict and sowed a legacy of hate and bitterness. It is in this fundamental sense that Lebanon's pluralism, radicalisation of its communities and consequent collective violence have become pathological and uncivil. Rather than being a source of enrichment, variety and cultural diversity, the modicum of pluralism the country once enjoyed is now generating large residues of fear, paranoia, hostility and differential bonding

This chapter explores two striking symptoms of protracted and unappeased hostility. First, it will examine the manner by which the Beirutis, perhaps more than any other of their Lebanese compatriots, were trapped in the grim and inflexible processes of reinventing their spatial identities. Secondly, an attempt is made to explore the modes of adaptation they are employing to cope with such disquieting symptoms of disappearance. Our basic concern, of course, is to disclose the implications of such circumstances for the rehabilitative role the Bourj can play as a cosmopolitan public sphere receptive to the needs of groups.

The Reconstruction of Spatial Identities

The first striking and unsettling feature is the way in which the Lebanese, since the outbreak of the war in 1975, have been caught up in an unrelenting process of redefining their territorial identities. Indeed, as the fighting spread across virtually all regions in the country, few have been spared the anguish of uprootedness from their spatial moorings. The magnitude of such displacement is greater than is commonly recognised. Recent estimates suggest that more than half – possibly two-thirds – of the population have been subjected to some transient or permanent form of uprootedness from their homes and communities.

Throughout the war, in other words, the majority of the Lebanese were entrapped in a curious predicament: that painful task of negotiating, constructing and reconfirming a fluid and unsettled pattern of spatial identities. No sooner had they suffered the travails of dislocation by taking refuge in one community than they were again uprooted and compelled to negotiate yet another spatial identity or face the added humiliation of re-entry into their profoundly transformed communities. They became homeless, so to speak, in their own homes or furtive fugitives and outcasts in their communities.

The socio-psychological consequences of being dislodged from one's familiar and reliable landmarks, those of home and neighbourhood, can be quite shattering. Like other displaced groups, they become disoriented and distressed because the terrain has changed and because there is no longer a neighbourhood for them to live in and rely upon. 'When the landscape goes,' says Erikson, 'it destroys the past for those who are left: People have no sense of belonging anywhere.'[1] They lose the sense of control over their lives, their freedom and independence, their moorings to place and locality and, more damagingly, a sense of who they are.

Bereft of place, they become homeless in at least three existential senses. First, they suffer the angst of being dislodged from their most enduring attachments and familiar places. Second, they also suffer banishment and the stigma of being outcasts in their own neighbourhoods and homes. Finally, much like the truly exiled, they are impelled to reassemble a damaged identity and broken history. Imagining the old places, with all their nostalgic longings, serves only as a reprieve from the uncertainties and anxieties of the present.

Equally devastating has been the gradual destruction of Beirut's and, to a large extent, the country's common spaces. The first to go was Beirut's central business district that had served historically as the undisputed focal point and meeting place. Beirut without its 'Bourj,' as the city centre is popularly labelled, was unimaginable. Virtually all the vital public functions were centralised there; the Parliament, the municipal headquarters, financial and banking institutions, religious edifices, transportation terminals, traditional *souks*, shopping malls, entertainment activities, etc kept the pre war 'Bourj' in a sustained state of animation day and night. People of every walk of life and social standing came together there.

With decentralisation, other urban districts and regions in the country served as supplementary meeting grounds for common activities. They too drew together, albeit on seasonal and interim bases, groups from a wide cross-section of society, thereby nurturing outlets germane to coexistence and a pluralarity of lifestyles. Altogether, there were very few exclusive spaces beyond the reach of others. The social tissue, like all seemingly localised spaces, was fluid and permeable.

Alas, the war destroyed virtually all such common and porous spaces, just as it dismantled many of the intermediary and peripheral heterogeneous neighbourhoods that have mushroomed with increasing urbanisation in cities like Tripoli, Sidon and Zahleh. The war did not only destroy common spaces. It also encouraged the formation of separate, exclusive and self-sufficient spaces. Hence, the Christians of East Beirut need not now frequent West Beirut for its cultural and popular entertainment. Likewise, one can understand the reluctance of Muslims and other residents of West Beirut to visit resorts and similar alluring spots of the Christian suburbs. With internecine conflict, quarters within urban districts, just like towns and villages, were often splintered into smaller and more compact enclosures. Spaces within which people circulated and interacted shrunk still further. The socio-psychological predispositions that underlie this urge to huddle in insulated spaces is not too difficult to trace or account for.

Massive population shifts, particularly since they are accompanied by the reintegration of displaced groups into more homogeneous, self-contained and exclusive spaces, have also reinforced communal solidarity. Consequently, territorial and confessional identities, more so perhaps than at any other time, are beginning to converge. For example, 44 per cent of all villages and towns before the outbreak of hostilities included inhabitants of more than one sect. The sharp sectarian redistribution, as Salim Nasr has shown, has reshuffled this mixed composition.[2] While the proportion of Christians living in the southern regions of Mount Lebanon – Shouf, Aley, Upper Metn – was 55 per cent in

1975, it shrunk to about 5 per cent by the late-1980s. The same is true of West Beirut and its suburbs. Likewise, the proportion of Muslims living in the eastern suburbs of Beirut has also been reduced from 40 per cent to about 5 per cent over the same period.[3]

The war has also transformed the perception and use of space in a more compelling sense. When a 'playground' (as pre war Lebanon was legitimately labelled) turns into a 'battleground', inevitably this is accompanied by a dramatic turnover in land-use. Hashim Sarkis has demonstrated how space during episodes of civil strife develops its own logic and propels its own inhabitation.[4] He tells us that 'it precedes, resists, yields to, and survives those who assume it to be a neutral site for their control.' He also advances the view that 'inhabitants are more elusive in their relationships with places they inhabit. They move across given boundaries ... negotiate and renegotiate their spatial identities.' Much can be added to substantiate both these seemingly antithetical viewpoints.

The most graphic, of course, is the way spaces of war asserted their ferocious logic on virtually every nook and cranny of public and private space. Equally telling is the ingenuity of its besieged hostages in accommodating this menacing turnover in their spatial surroundings. Public thoroughfares, crossroads, bridges, hilltops, and other strategic intersections that served as links between communities were the first to be converted. They became 'Green Lines', treacherous barriers denying any crossover. Incidentally, the infamous 'Green Line' acquired its notorious label when shrubs and bushes sprouted from its tarmac after years of neglect. It is ironic that this great divide that rips the city in two was none other than the major throughway – the old Damascus Road – connecting Beirut to its hinterland and beyond. Likewise, major squares, traffic terminals and pedestrian shopping arcades, once the hub of gregarious activity and dense interaction, became a desolate 'no man's land': 'al-Mahawir al-taqlidiya' (traditional lines of confrontation) or 'khutut al-tamas' (lines of confrontation).

While prominent public spaces lost their identity, other rather ordinary crossings, junctures, hilltops, even shops, became dreaded landmarks. The war produced its own lexicon and iconography of places.[5] By virtue of their contingent location, these and other such inconsequential places and spaces became fearsome points of reference and demarcating lines, part of the deadly logistics of contested space.

Private space was not spared these tempestuous turnovers in land use. Indeed, the distinctions between private and public space were blurred and lost much of their conventional usages. Just as basements, rooftops and strategic openings in private homes became part of the logistics of combat, roadways were also 'domesticated' as family possessions, discarded furniture and bulky items spilled into the public domain to improvise barricades. Balconies, verandas, walk-ups, doorways and all the other open, airy and buoyant places the Lebanese craved and exploited with such ingenuity became dreaded spaces to be bolted and shielded. Conversely, dingy basements, tightly sealed corridors, attics and other normally neglected spaces became more coveted simply because they were out of the trajectory of snipers and shellfire. They became places of refuge.

Green Line/barricades

Of course, the symbolic meanings and uses of a 'house', 'home', or 'dwelling' space, as Maha Yahya has demonstrated, were also overhauled.[6] The most compelling is the way the family unit and its private spaces has been broadened to accommodate other functions, as disengaged and unemployed household members converted or relocated their business premises to their homes. The thriving informal war economy reinforced such efforts and rendered them more effective.

Perhaps most unsettling is the way the tempo of war has imposed its own perilous timeframes, dictating traffic flows, spaces to be used or avoided. Time, space, movement and interaction all became enveloped with contingency and uncertainty. Nothing was taken for granted any longer. People lived, so to speak, situationally. Short-term expediency replaced long-term planning. Everything had to be negotiated on the spur of the moment. The day-to-day routines, which once structured the use of space and time, played havoc with lives. Deficient communication and irregular and congested traffic rendered all forms of social interaction fortuitous and unpredictable. People were expected to accomplish much of their daily activities at unexpected hours, depending on

Domestication of public space

the merciless whims of fighters or the capricious cycles of violence. Beirutis became, as a result, astonishingly adept at making instant adaptations to such jarring modulations and precipitous shifts in the use of time and space.

Finally, it must be remarked that the post-war mood in Lebanon has generated its own pathologies and disheartening manifestations. Post-war interludes normally generate public moods of moderation and restraint. People are more inclined to curb their conventional impulses and become more self-controlled in the interests of reappraising and redirecting their future options. Rather than freeing them from their pre war excesses, the war has paradoxically induced the opposite reaction. It has unleashed appetites and inflamed people with insatiable desires for acquisitiveness and unearned privileges.

Mercantilism and its concomitant bourgeois values was always given a free reign in Lebanon. The outcome of such excessive commercialisation was already painfully obvious in the pre war years. With staggering increases in land values, commercial traffic in real estate became one of the most lucrative sources of private wealth. Hence, that ruthless plundering of the country's scenic natural habitat and the dehumanisation of its living space became starkly visible. With the absence of government authority, such excesses became more rampant. What had not been ravaged by war was eaten up by greedy developers and impetuous consumers. Hardly anything was spared. The once pristine coastline is littered with tawdry tourist attractions, kitsch resorts and private marinas as much as by the proliferation of slums and other unlawful makeshift shoddy tenements. The same ravenous defoliation has blighted the already shrinking greenbelts, public parks and terraced orchards. Even sidewalks and private backyards are stripped and defiled.

Rampant commercialism, greed and enfeebled state authority could not have produced so much damage on their own. These are exacerbated by the pathos of a ravenous post-war mentality. Victims, wracked for so long by the atrocities of human suffering, become insensitive to these seemingly benign and inconsequential concerns or transgressions. It is understandable how the moral and aesthetic restraints that normally control the growth of cities become dispensable virtues. They all seem much too remote when pitted against the post-war profligate mood overwhelming large portions of society. Victims of collective suffering normally have other, more rudimentary things on their mind. They rage with bitterness and long to make up for lost time and opportunity. The environment becomes an accessible surrogate target on which to vent their wrath. In a culture infused with a residue of unappeased hostility and mercantilism, violating the habitat is also very lucrative. Both greed and hostility find an expedient victim.

In such a free-for-all context, any concern for the aesthetic, human or cultural dimensions of living space is sure to be dismissed as superfluous or guileless. As a result, it is of little concern whether cities are ugly, whether they debase their inhabitants, whether they are aesthetically, spiritually or physically tolerable or whether they provide people with opportunities for authentic individuality, privacy and edifying human encounters.

What counts is that the unconditional access to land must satisfy two overriding claims: the insatiable appetite for profit among the bourgeoisie and the vengeful feeling of entitlement to unearned privileges among the disenfranchised.

By the time the authorities step in to restrain or recover such violations, as was to happen repeatedly in the pre war years, the efforts were always too little too late. By then, officials could only confirm the infringements and incorporate them into the legitimate zoning ordinances.

Unlawful constructions

New high-rise towers

The Geography of Fear and its By-Products

All wars, civil or otherwise, are atrocious. Lebanon's encounters with civil strife, I am suggesting, are particularly galling because its horrors were not anchored in any recognisable or coherent set of causes, nor did they resolve the issues that had sparked the initial hostilities. It is in this poignant sense that the war was altogether a wasteful and futile encounter with collective violence.

The muted anguish and unresolved hostilities of the war are now being compounded by all the ambivalences and uncertainties of post-war reconstruction and of the encroachment of conglomerate global capital as it contests the efforts of indigenous and local groups in reclaiming or reinventing their threatened spatial identities. What we are witnessing at the moment is, in fact, a multi layered negotiation or competition for the representation and ultimate control of Beirut's spatial collective identity. Much of Beirut's future image will largely be an outcome of such discrepant claims and representations. The contesting groups, such as funding and state agencies, planners, property shareholders, advocacy groups and voluntary associations and the concerned public, by virtue of their distinct composition and objectives, vary markedly in their proposed visions and strategies.

The ongoing competition and the public debate it has incited have also served to accentuate the fears of the public, particularly since the struggle is now intimately aligned with the intrusions of global capital, mass culture and consumerism. Hence, the fears of disappearance, erasure, marginalisation and displacement are assuming acute manifestations. The overriding reactions have much in common, in fact, with the three neuropsychological responses to fear and anxiety: namely, 'freeze', 'flight' and 'fight'. While the first two normally involve efforts to disengage and distance oneself from the sources of fear, the third is more combative since it involves a measure of direct involvement, negotiation and/or resisting the threats of erasure.[7] All three, in varying proportions, are visible today in Lebanon.

The first, and perhaps the most common, is a relic of the war. To survive all its cruelties, the Lebanese became deadened and numbed. Like other victims of collective suffering, they became desensitised and overwhelmed by muted anguish and pain. During the war, such callousness (often masquerading as resilience) served them well. It allowed them to survive but also to inflict and rationalise cruelties on the 'other'. By distancing themselves, or cutting themselves off from the 'other', the brutality of embattled communities became routine. People could engage in guilt-free violence and kill with impunity precisely because they had restricted contact with their defiled victims. To a large extent, it is 'the group boundaries', as Randall Collins tells us, 'that determine the extent of human sympathy; within these boundaries, humanity prevails; outside them, torture is inflicted without qualm'.[8]

There is a painful irony in this mode of response. That which enabled embattled groups and communities to survive the atrocities is clearly disabling them now as they are considering options for rearranging and sharing common spaces and forging unified national identities. Here, again, Collins is quick to remind us that 'the point is not to learn to live with the demons, but to take away their powers'.[9] The issue, here as well, converges on who is to mobilise or speak on behalf of those who have been rendered 'frozen': namely, disengaged, inactive and bereft of speech.

There is, after all, something in the character of intense pain, Elaine Scarry tells us, which is 'language destroying'. 'As the content of one's world disintegrates, so the content of one's language disintegrates ... world, self, and voice are lost, or nearly lost, through the intense pain'.[10] This is also a reflection of the fact that people in pain are ordinarily bereft of the resources of speech. It is not surprising that the language for pain should in such instances often be evoked by those who are not themselves in pain but by those who speak on behalf of those who are. Richard Rorty expresses the same thought. He too tells us that 'victims of cruelty, people, who are suffering, do not have much in the way of language. That is why there is no such thing as the "voice of the oppressed" or the "language of victims". The language the victims once used is not working anymore, and they are suffering too much to put new words together. So the job of putting their situation into language is going to have to be done for them by somebody else.'[11]

A second, more interesting and complex response is not purely one of 'flight' but also an effort to distance oneself from the atrocious residues of protracted strife and the disenchanting barbarism of the post-war era. This nostalgic retreat is a search for 're-enchantment' evident in the revival of heritage or the imagined nirvana of an idyllic past. Three manifestations of such escapist venues are becoming increasingly visible in various dimensions of daily life and popular culture: the reassertion of communal solidarities, nostalgic longings and the proliferation of kitsch.

As mentioned earlier, it is understandable why traumatised and threatened groups should seek shelter in their communal solidarities and cloistered spaces. Confessional sentiments and their supportive loyalties, even in times of relative peace and stability, have always been effective sources of social support and political mobilisation. But these are not, as Lebanon's fractious history amply demonstrates, unmixed blessings. While they cushion individuals and groups against the anomie and alienation of public life, they also heighten the density of communal hostility and enmity. Hence, more and more Lebanese are today brandishing their confessionalism, if we may invoke a dual metaphor, as both emblem and armour. It is an emblem because confessional identity has become the most viable medium for asserting presence and securing vital needs and benefits. Without it, groups are literally rootless, nameless and voiceless. One is not heard or recognised unless confessional allegiance is first disclosed. It is only when an individual is placed within a confessional context that his ideas and assertions are rendered meaningful or worthwhile. Confessionalism is also being used as armour, because it has become a shield against real or imagined threats. The more vulnerable the emblem, the thicker is the armour. Conversely, the thicker the armour, the more vulnerable and paranoid other communities become. It is precisely this dialectic between threatened communities and the urge to seek shelter in cloistered worlds that has plagued Lebanon for so long.

There is a curious irony here. Despite the many differences that divide the Lebanese, they are all in a sense homogenised by fear, grief and bafflement. Fear, as it were, is the tie that binds and holds them together. But it is also fear that keeps them apart. This 'geography of fear' is not sustained by walls or artificial barriers, as one observes in other comparable instances of ghettoisation of minorities and ethnic groups. Rather, it is sustained by the psychology of dread, hostile bonding and ideologies of enmity.

The implications of such heightened forms of spatial and communal solidarities for urban planning are clear. Expressed in more concrete terms, if urbanisation normally stands for variety, diversity, mix and openness, then what has been happening in Lebanon, at least in a majority of areas, is ghettoisation. In this sense the Lebanese are inverting what might be assumed to be the most typical course of evolution in social systems. How, where and when can such fairly 'closed' spaces become more 'open'? At the least, how can public spaces be made more malleable and accessible to divergent groups who continue to harbour residues of indifference or latent hostility towards each other? Clearly, any premature or imposed schemes that attempt to open up spaces for groups reluctant to mix and interact with others might be counterproductive.

Escape into a re-enchanted past has obviously a nostalgic tinge to it. This tinge, however, need not be seen as a pathological retreat into a delusionary past. It could well serve, as Bryan Turner has argued, as a redemptive form of heightened sensitivity, sympathetic awareness of human problems and, hence, it could be 'ethically uplifting'.[12] In this sense, it is less of a 'flight' and more of a catharsis for human suffering.

Finally, another mode of retreat or escape from the ugly memories of the war and the drabness or anxieties of the post-war is the proliferation of kitsch. While kitsch, as an expression of the appeals of popular arts and entertainment whose object is to 'astonish, scintillate, arouse and stir the passions',[13] its rampant allures in Lebanon are symptomatic of the need to forget and, hence, it feeds on collective amnesia and the pervasive urge for popular distractions. It is clearly not as benign or frivolous as it may appear. At the least it should not be dismissed lightly, for it has implications for the readiness of public to be drawn in and become actively and creatively engaged in processes or reconstruction and safeguarding the edifying beauty of their natural habitat and built environment.

It is not difficult to account for the allure of kitsch in post-war Lebanon. The need to forget and escape the atrocities and futility of a senseless war; the mindless hedonism and narcissism associated with an urge to make up for lost time; the dullness and trivialisation of everyday life; the cultural predispositions of the Lebanese for gregariousness, conviviality and fun-loving amusement have all contributed to its appeal. So has the ready access to the vectors of high technology and 'infotainment'. Lebanon is not spared the scintillations of such postmodern and global incursions. Indeed, bourgeois decadence, mediocrity and conspicuous consumption have compounded the public seductions of kitsch.

Its fundamental allure then is inherent in the ability of kitsch to offer effortless and easy access to the distractions of global entertainment. It is compatible with the public mood for lethargy, disengagement and uninterest. It is also in this sense that kitsch becomes a form of 'false consciousness', an ideological diversion: a novel opiate for aroused and unanchored masses. To the rest, particularly the large segments who have been uprooted from their familiar moorings, kitsch feeds on their hunger for nostalgia. Altogether, it is a form of collective deception since it is sustained by the demand for spurious replicas or the reproduction of objects and art forms whose original aesthetic meanings have been compromised. As Calinescu puts it, kitsch becomes 'the aesthetics of deception; for it centres around such questions as imitation, forgery, counterfeit. It is basically a form of lying. Beauty turns out to be easy to fabricate.'[14]

In Beirut the pathologies of kitsch display more ominous by-products. They do not only debase the aesthetic quality of high culture. Folk arts and vernacular architecture are also vulgarised. National symbols, historic and other cherished monuments become expendable trophies or vacuous media images. This frenzy for the prostitution of cherished cultural artifacts and the consumption of pseudo-art cannot be attributed merely to the impulse for status seeking and conspicuous consumption, potent as these predispositions are in Lebanon today. What constitutes the essence of kitsch, as Adorno, among others, reminds us, is its promise for 'easy catharsis'.[15] The object of kitsch, after all, is not to please, charm or refine our tastes and sensibilities. Rather, it promises easy and effortless access to cheap entertainment and scintillating distractions.

Here again the implications for urbanists and architects are crucial. How much can they accomplish in restraining or redirecting the distracting allures of kitsch into more redemptive and creative venues? This is not an easy task. Above all, it involves the incorporation or reconciliation of two seemingly opposing options: to tame and restrain the excessive manifestations of kitsch, while acting as sentinels who arouse the disengaged and uninterested by infusing their world with rejuvenated concern for edifying and embellishing the aesthetic quality of their built environment.

Providing outlets for the release of such creative energies should not be belittled or trivialised. As Nietzsche was keen on reminding us, an aesthetic solution through artistic creation could well serve as a powerful expression for releasing individuals from the constraints of nihilism and resentment. 'It is in art that we appear to realise fully our abilities and potential to break through the limitations of our own circumstances.'[16]

By far the most promising are the strategies various communities have been recently resorting to in resisting threats to their local heritage and identity. Here, responses to fear and uncertainty – whether generated by internal displacement, global capital or mass culture and consumerism – have reawakened and mobilised local groups to reclaim their contested spaces and eroded cultural identities. The emergent spaces reveal more than just residues or pockets of resistance. There are encouraging signs of so-called 'third spaces' or in-between cultures of hybridity, mixture and tolerance.

This is, after all, what Richard Sennett implied by 'cultures of resistance': that is, how a 'local spatial system retains many of its traditional institutions and utilises these to manipulate and control the extreme forces'.[17] Hence, many of the public spaces, more the work of spontaneity than design, are in fact spaces of bargaining and negotiation for national memory and indigenous re-emergence. More so than in other such instances of 'glocalisation', what we are witnessing in Lebanon today are manifestations of local groups becoming increasingly globalised and, conversely, global incursions being increasingly localised. In other words, we see symptoms of 'inward shifts' where loyalties are redirected towards renewed localism and sub-national groups and institutions. We also see 'outwards shifts', where loyalties and interests are being extended toward trans-national entities.[18]

This is, incidentally, a far cry from the portraits one can extract from recent writings on the spatial and cultural implications of this global/local dialectic. For example, in his polemical but engaging work on the interplay between 'Jihad' and 'McWorld', Benjamin Barber pits 'McWorld', as the universe of manufactured needs, mass consumption and mass infotainment against 'Jihad', a shorthand for the belligerent politics of religious, tribal and other forms of bigotry.[19] The former is driven by the cash nexus of greedy capital and the bland preferences of mass consumers; the latter is propelled by fierce tribal loyalties, rooted in exclusionary and parochial hatreds. McWorld, with all its promises of a world homogenised by global consumerism, is rapidly dissolving local

Architectural resistance

cultural identities. Jihad, by re-creating parochial loyalties, is fragmenting the world into tighter and smaller enclosures. Both are a threat to civil liberties, tolerance and genuine coexistence. 'Jihad pursues a bloody politics of identity, McWorld a bloodless economics of profit. Belonging by default to McWorld, everyone is a consumer; seeking a repository of identity, everyone belongs to some tribe. But no one is a citizen.'[20]

We see little of such sharp dichotomies and diametrical representations in post-war Lebanon. While many of the emergent spatial enclaves are cognisant and jealous of their indigenous identities, they are not averse to experiment with more global and ephemeral encounters and cultural products. Likewise, global expectations are being reshaped and rearranged to accommodate local needs and preferences. Expressed in the language of globalisation and postmodernity, the so-called 'world without borders', 'collapse of spatial boundaries' are not prerequisites for global encounters. At least this is not what has been transpiring in Lebanon. Indeed, as Martin Albrow argues, one of the key effects of globalisation on locality is that people 'can reside in one place and have their meaningful social relations almost entirely outside it and across the globe'. This, Albrow goes on to say, 'means that people use the locality as site and resource for social activities in widely different ways according to the extension of their sociosphere'.[21]

Recent case studies of three distinct sites in Beirut – Ain al-Mryseh, Gemmayze and the 'Elisar' project in Beirut's southern suburb – provide instructive and vivid support of how local groups and communities have been able to resist, avert and rearrange the powers of global agendas. Indeed, in all three instances, globalisation has contributed to the strengthening and consolidation of local ties and, thereby, reinforcing the claims of Persky and Weiwel when they speak of the 'growing localness of the global city' and the 'glocalisation' of urban structures.[22]

FOUR

Post-War Construction of Beirut's Central District

The story of Beirut's destruction, particularly the repeated devastation and looting of its centre, remains riddled with anomalies. The fiercest battles, displaying the most barbarous cruelties, took place there, as if the historic hub of the old city was both the most coveted and most maligned space. It had more than just logistical and economic values. To get hold of the centre clearly offered the historic opportunity to reclaim its contested identity and the prospects of redefining the outlines of its future and renewed national image.

Hence, it was not coincidental that the early rounds of fighting in 1975 and 1976 started for the control of the city's centre and then extended to the hotel districts, the south eastern suburbs and the creation of the infamous 'Green Line' along the Damascus Road, thereby dividing Beirut into two: the predominantly Muslim West Beirut and the predominantly Christian East Beirut. The social geography of the city drifted in the direction of exclusive and closed communities. In quick succession, all the Muslim enclaves in East Beirut – Karantina, Nabaa, Tel al-Zaatar – were destroyed. In a parallel fashion, the Ouzai coastline on the southern suburbs and private beaches were all overtaken by squatters. Similar tendencies encroached areas like Raouche and Hamra. One inevitable by-product of the early round of fighting was decentralisation. Secondary suburban districts and towns, on both sides of the divide, mushroomed in no time: Jdeideh, Dora, Zalka, Maamiltayn and Junieh to the east, Lailaki, Hayy al-Silloum and up to Saida on the southern sprawl.

The brief and deceptive lull in the intensity of fighting prompted the government in 1977 to establish the Council for Development and Reconstruction (CDR) to plan and administer the reconstruction of the devastated CBD (Central Business District). A French consulting firm, L'Atelier Parisien d'Urbanisme (APUR), was commissioned

Destruction of Central Business District (CBD)

to produce the master plan for reconstruction. The conceptual framework of APUR's plan was informed by five compelling considerations. 1) To maintain, where possible, the original urban tissue as well as the pre-existing tenure of property holding. 2) To encourage the legal owners and occupants of the CBD to return and reclaim their previous enterprises. 3) To facilitate the return of the CBD to its traditional role as a unifying and homogenising setting for the country's multi-confessional and communal composition. 4) To introduce the necessary infrastructural improvements to the CBD by way of expediting its rehabilitation. 5) To revitalise targetted areas which had been badly damaged through the establishment of conventional real-estate companies and other viable strategies of post-war reconstruction.[1]

Alas, the reconstruction was barely under way when it had to be suspended because of renewed fighting. The CBD, along with certain quarters of Ashrafiyeh, was subjected to further destruction. With the Israeli invasion of 1982, the CBD once again, along this time with the entire dense urban fabric between Martyrs' Square and Souk Sursock, was further damaged by a heavy barrage of targetted shelling and bombardment.

Eager to launch the process of reconstruction, Oger Liban, a private Lebanese-Saudi company, ventured to take on the immense project of reconstructing the CBD. Oger commissioned Dar al-Handassa in 1983 to prepare a master plan for the project. The resumption of another round of fighting, this time in the mountain regions, generated another influx of refugees to Beirut. The so-called 'Mountain War' provoked sedition against the government, which led to further destruction in the southern suburbs and areas of Ras Beirut.

In 1986 yet another French '*schéma directeur*' came into being. This time it was the joint collective product of CDR and the Higher Council of Urban Planning (HCUP), with APUR acting as principal consultant. The study proposed for the first time a master plan for the entire metropolitan district of Beirut, with four satellite commercial centres in Dora, Hazmieh, Lailaki and Khaldeh.

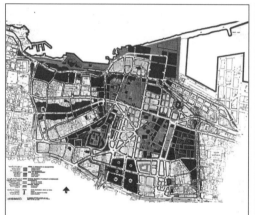

L'Atelier Parisien d'Urbanisme, master plan (1977)

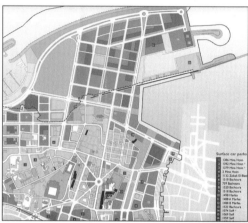

Schéma directeur (1986)

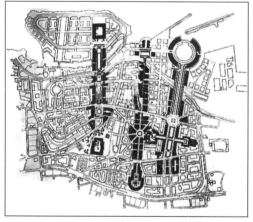

Dar al-Handassa (1983)

Henri Eddé (1991)

During the *de facto* division of the country into a two-state system between 1988 and 1990, the dislocation between various regions and sectors became sharper. So was the magnitude of anarchy as the belligerency of infighting among Christian factions and militias assumed internecine and turf wars. Much of the decentralised satellite suburbs of Jdeideh, Dora, Hadath and Hazmieh was destroyed.

The collapse of the two-state interlude in 1990 ushered in the first concerted efforts of post-war reconstruction. The head of Oger Liban in Beirut was appointed director of CBD. By 1991 a new master plan for the CBD, designed by Henri Eddé of Dar al-Handassa group, came into being. A decree of law for the creation of a private real-estate holding company (Solidere) to administer the reconstruction of the CBD was legislated.

This chapter begins by elucidating the rationale and philosophy of Solidere's Master Plan and the defining guidelines that inform its envisioned programme for the development, restoration and reconstruction of downtown Beirut. In appraising the overall quality of its accomplished projects and those under way, an effort is made to probe the obstacles it faced and the degree to which it has been able to realise its articulated vision.

No sooner was Solidere created than it was met with a public outcry. Voices of dissent, particularly against some of the financial, economic and legal implications of the total and uncontrolled privatisation of reconstruction, became more audible.[2] Public dissatisfaction extended to government departments entrusted to implement the plans, particularly those of HCUP and CBD. Within this contested setting, the Bechtel Corporation was commissioned to produce a strategy for reconstruction with the collaboration of Dar al-Handassa. The major thrust of the plan was to relocate activities within the centre in an effort to provide Beirut with a corporate international image. Cognisant of the disruptive implications of refugee displacement and rampant unlawful squatters, a new ministry for refugees was established to expedite the return of the displaced to their houses and communities.

The year 1992 was an eventful threshold in Beirut's post-war history. It was marked by two dissonant but related circumstances: first, the ominous influx of squatters and unanchored masses into the city centre and adjoining quarters; second, the more beneficent but poignant process of destruction of the already savaged and neglected buildings and cityscape. The urban design project for the city centre, the work of Dar al-Handassa, was approved with some modifications by the Lebanese Parliament. UNESCO was granted the privilege of excavating and documenting the archaeological heritage during the reconstruction period. The dramatic launch of the rebuilding of the centre by bulldozing the dishevelled relics of its historic core did not quell the contested and heated public debate over the city's collective memory and its envisioned future image. Like earlier such attempts at destroying or defacing past relics by the Ottomans and the French, the ventures were not accepted with passive resignation. Advocates and partisans on both sides had ample room to thrash out their polemical views and visions.

The destruction of Beirut Central District (BCD)

Since its incorporation on 5 May 1994, the Lebanese Company for Development and Reconstruction of Beirut's Central District, better known by its popular acronym Solidere, has swiftly emerged and consolidated itself as the most compelling and visible programme of urban reconstruction in Lebanon's history. Some observers go further to herald the venture as one of the largest contemporary urban development projects anywhere in the world.

The project covers approximately 1.8 million square metres (455 acres), this being the site of the traditional Bourj district of 1.2 square metres (296 acres) along with 159 acres of the reclaimed landfill from the sea. Consistent with its professed rationale, 225 acres will consist of public space, of which 146 acres are roads and close to 80 acres are public open space. In more explicit terms, this offers a mix of facilities totalling 4.69 million square metres. Altogether, this amounts to about 8 per cent of the surface area of greater metropolitan Beirut.

Solidere's uniqueness is not only an expression of its scale and magnitude. The company is more than just a land and real-estate developer. It also serves in three other vital capacities: as property-owner, manager and operator. It is entrusted with the responsibility for reconstruction and development of Beirut's Central District (BCD). As stated in Solidere's official memorandum of November 1993, the main features and objectives of the Master Plan are formidable. They are summarised as follows:

> ... links between 'traditional BCD' and reclaimed land; preservation of the historic core of the city between the Serail and Bourj Square; a new financial district mixed with entertainment and shopping facilities on the reclaimed land; reconstruction of the old souks; extension of the residential area to re-create the old distinctive 'Levantine cityscape'; creation of a seashore park overlooking a new marina near St Georges' Bay; extension of Beirut's famous public promenade; integration between BCD and the rest of the city; and limitation of the number of high-rise buildings.

The rationale or philosophy of the Master Plan is reiterated in Solidere's Annual Report of 2000:

> The plan respects the main natural features and topography of the site by maximising views of the sea and surrounding landscape; dwells on the formation of public spaces; remains faithful to the urban fabric through preserving and restoring historical urban elements; and ensures the harmonious integration of traditional and modern architecture. It accommodates a broad mix of land uses including business, government, residential, as well as cultural and recreational facilities.

One can easily extract from the above four defining elements or overarching concerns which underline Solidere's scheme: 1) To compliment and enrich Beirut's compelling natural habitat. 2) The newly created public spaces are to remain faithful to the city's urban fabric by preserving its historical features. 3) To ensure the harmonious possible mixture of land uses, business, government, residence, recreational and cultural facilities. 4) The overall land-use guidelines of the Master Plan comply with its avowed objectives of creating a vibrant and cosmopolitan central hub with a plurality of activities, yet remain malleable enough to be adjusted or rearranged in compliance with changing market conditions. Accordingly, the allocation of floor space (per 1,000 square metres) assumed the following distribution: residential (1,959), offices (1,582), commercial (563), cultural facilities and government offices (386) and hotels (200).

Doubtlessly, the most striking feature is that residential space is envisaged as the largest category of floor space. The anticipated timeframe of this massive program of development, restoration and reconstruction was envisaged to be about twenty-five years. The main infrastructural work, as seen below, will proceed in three phases.

Development and reconstruction plan of BCD

	Main infrastructure works	Main areas concerned	Built-up area in s qm
Phase 1 (1994-9)	All structural networks affecting the global project. Primary and secondary networks related to development areas. First line sea-protection, landfill treatment and west marina.	Etoile/Serail Souks	1,240,000
Phase 2 (2009-18)	Primary and secondary networks for the rest of traditional BCD and partly for the reclaimed lands. Second line of sea protection.	Remaining area of reclaimed land	2,060,000
Phase 3 (2009-18)	Remainder of primary and secondary networks for reclaimed land. Remainder of second line sea protection and east marina.		1,100,000

Source: Solidere

So far, despite unforeseen delays, Phase One has proceeded as planned. All infrastructure works in the traditional BCD, with substantive advances in land treatment, reclamation and marine works, including the western marina, have been executed. Along with the restoration of the historic core, substantive portions of the following residential areas have been completed: Zokak El Blatt, Saifi and the northern section of Wadi Abu Jamil (the Jewish quarter of pre war Beirut). Also the renovation or construction of large building complexes was finished, most notably the UN Plaza, the embassy complex, the Starco and Lazarieh office buildings. Work has also proceeded on parts of Phase Two, particularly in Wadi Abu Jamil, the Serail corridor, the hotel districts and areas adjoining Martyrs' Square and the completion of land treatment and reclamation of the waterfront.

Although envisaged as a central district, the overall character of the plan gives the impression of a fairly open and airy space. Indeed, approximately half of the total surface area (i.e. about 876,000 square metres) is accounted for as public space, of which about two-thirds are roads and the remaining third public open-space. Slightly more than half of the total area (i.e. 923,000 square metres) is allocated for developments including some 80,000 square metres for religious and state property. For a city that has chronically suffered from high densities, congested traffic and virtually little by way of sidewalks, public parks and gardens, the BCD seems airy, commodious and lush with green. Indeed the indelible impression one walks away with, after several intimate strolls throughout the area at different times of the day, is of an inviting and edifying place, both aesthetically pleasing and functional. More auspiciously, perhaps, it evokes the feeling that as a living environment it is a setting to which one can readily be committed and be creatively engaged in.

A striking feature in this regard, particularly by way of reclaiming the mixed and hybrid character of the pre war Bourj, is the incorporation of a residential population of 40,000 and a working population of 100,000. With this in mind, special regard is taken to provide space for car parks, gardens and courtyards. The reclaimed landfill alone will accommodate a variety of parks ranging in size from 100–square-kilometre gardens to a 72,000–square-metre public park.

Al-Omari Mosque

Omar Onsi garden

It is the aesthetic and refined architectural quality of the restoration that is so compelling and visible. Whatever reservations one might entertain about Solidere's overall plans and accomplishments, its restoration record must be exempt from such allegations, legitimate or otherwise. This became apparent with the completion of the Foch-Allenby and Maarad areas. The judicious blending of authenticity with progressive, often state-of-the-art, elements has become the hallmarks and guiding principles for all subsequent restorative projects.

The Recovery of Foch-Allenby and Etoile

Without doubt, the recovery of Foch-Allenby and Etoile, the historic and most edifying hub of Beirut's central business district, stands out as the most compelling achievement

Refined architectural restoration

of Solidere. The area is the mediating link or interface zone between the two distinctive features of Beirut as a Mediterranean city: namely, the sea and the hinterland. As such, it epitomises Beirut's dual role as port city and national capital. This is also an area that is suffused with a rich symbolic architectural history and more so since it has been subjected to earlier efforts of reconstruction and modernisation.

During the past century, in fact, one can easily detect emblematic signposts of its transformation from a walled medieval town to a maritime gateway, more recently displaying some of the formative features of a globalised and postmodern city. In many respects Beirut's evolution in this regard does not depart much from the four stages identified by Hans Meyer in his historical exploration of the prototypes of port-city developments.[3] For example, in its formative pre-industrial stage, it was no more than an 'entrepôt' port within an enclosed town. A caravan station at the city's eastern gate served as the main access point to regional trade routes. The old town, to a large extent, consisted of a port-related lower part (present day Foch-Allenby) and a bazaar-related upper part (today's Etoile). The main thoroughfare connecting the eastern and western gates (corresponding roughly to today's Weygond Street) is, as Beirut's archaeologists confirm, nothing but the Roman Decumanus: a remnant of the pre-classical Roman grid.

Second, between the mid-1880s and early 1900s, Beirut, much like other east Mediterranean port cities, started to grow largely in response to its ability to accommodate the global network of colonial mercantilism and the expansion of colonial trade. It was then that Beirut emerged as a satellite port-city through which raw materials were exported and manufactured products imported. Furthermore, it must be recalled, that it was also then that Beirut acquired the status of a provincial capital of the colonial administration of the Ottoman Empire. As Robert Saliba correctly argues, it was then that Beirut started to display all the manifestations associated with a dual city: a port and a capital city.[4] The former necessitated the modernisation and expansion of the port to accommodate increased freight traffic and steam-powered navigation. As such, between 1887 and 1893 a score of projects were launched to upgrade the harbour's facilities. For example, an Imperial Ottoman company, with European capital, undertook the construction of deeper and wider basins, larger warehouses and the creation of more mechanised loading facilities. By 1888, when Beirut became the capital of a provincial administrative unit (Wilaya) of the Ottoman Empire, it also benefitted from the extensive urban development projects initiated by the Ottoman authorities.

While the Ottomans focused largely on the interior and landward developments, the French were more oriented towards the harbour. By the turn of the twentieth century, the waterfront was fast becoming the prime setting for commercial and financial services. It was then that the port played host to some of the most monumental and picturesque buildings: the Orosdi-Back department store, the Imperial Ottoman Bank and the Custom House Offices. These and other waterfront developments made the harbour a showcase of maritime works and architecture by the turn of the century, displaying imported skills from the Pont-et-Chaussées and styles from the Beaux-Arts schools. The new jetty – already a popular visual icon in most photographic images of the period – became an appealing promenade site.[5] It was around this time that the city's townscape, particularly at the western flanks of the waterfront, started to attract hotels and entertainments outlets.

In 1920 the construction of the Foch-Allenby and Etoile, literally over the rubble of the medieval town, was intended, as we have seen, to celebrate Beirut as the showcase of France's colonial presence in the Levant. The two vertical arteries and parallel avenues (Foch and Allenby) were designed as the maritime gateways that linked the seaport to the hinterland. Appropriately, this was mediated through a central, prime, civic space shaped and named after the place de l'Etoile in Paris.

This opening of the traditional core of Beirut to the harbour is, doubtlessly, a defining milestone in its formation. It developed in two successive stages. Early in the 1920s, Foch-Allenby started to evolve largely as a wholesale district. By the 1930s, on the other hand, Etoile evolved into a retail district, along with new institutional and administrative services. In other words, within the short span of two decades, Beirut's dual identity as port and capital city was consolidated. Although the two coterminous areas retained some of their earlier defining boundaries, 'their urban fabric was transformed from a medieval organic pattern to a Beaux-Arts geometric pattern'.[6] Hence, shortly before independence, Beirut's spatial structure was a composite landscape of neo-Ottoman *souks* extending east and west of the Beaux-Arts-style of the Foch-Allenby and Etoile area. These were sandwiched between the two emerging but competing centres: the waterfront to the north and the Bourj to the south.

The third stage, corresponding to Meyers' typology, begins with Lebanon's independence in 1943 when this same dialectic between port and city continued to exhibit the same tendencies: namely, port expansion around the harbour and increasing functional specialisation around Etoile and beyond. The creation of the State of Israel in 1948 and the diversion of trade from Haifa's port to Beirut reinforced the intensification of this unplanned growth in both areas to accommodate the mounting demand for urban space. The sharp increase in maritime commercial traffic required the addition of a third basin in 1967, and a fourth was approved shortly before the outbreak of hostilities in 1975. Likewise, the consequent increase in free-zone traffic also resulted in fairly hasty and unplanned urban developments, particularly by way of warehousing for the storage and recycling of heavy and bulky merchandise. These carried with them the need to accommodate auxiliary urban functions accessible to waterfront daily and itinerant wage-labour. Hence, affordable and modest rooming houses, bars, cafés and places of entertainment for sailors, porters, truck drivers and the like had to be made available.

It was then that the entire region of the port and adjoining areas started to display many of the symptoms associated with urban blight and degeneration: congestion, unplanned and haphazard growth, dilapidation and the encroachment of disreputable and nefarious activities and services. Indeed, the public image of the port was far from

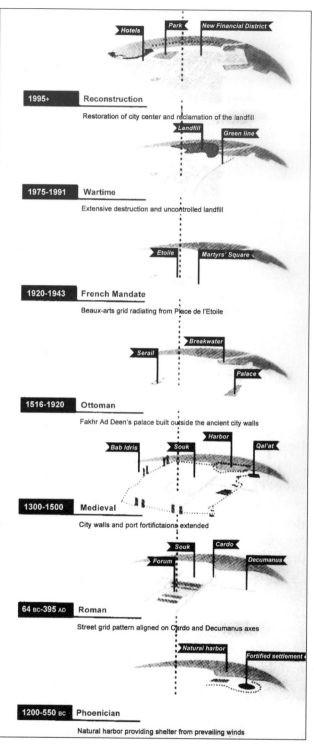

Hotels **Park** **New Financial District**

1995+ **Reconstruction**

Restoration of city center and reclamation of the landfill

Landfill **Green line**

1975-1991 **Wartime**

Extensive destruction and uncontrolled landfill

Etoile **Martyrs' Square**

1920-1943 **French Mandate**

Beaux-arts grid radiating from Place de l'Etoile

Breakwater **Serail** **Palace**

1516-1920 **Ottoman**

Fakhr Ad Deen's palace built outside the ancient city walls

Bab Idris **Souk** **Harbor** **Qal'at**

1300-1500 **Medieval**

City walls and port fortifictaions extended

Souk **Cardo** **Forum** **Decumanus**

64 BC-395 AD **Roman**

Street grid pattern aligned on Cardo and Decumanus axes

Natural harbor **Fortified settlement**

1200-550 BC **Phoenician**

Natural harbor providing shelter from prevailing winds

Layers of archaeological history

auspicious. It started to evoke dread: a place to be avoided. Although not to the same magnitude, the triple axis of Foch-Allenby, Etoile and Martyrs' Square was also subjected to the same forces of degeneration.

With the outbreak of hostilities in 1975, the entire central business district was the site of protracted rounds of street fighting. The port and the Bourj, in particular, were virtually devastated. Foch-Allenby and Etoile, however, were relatively spared. Hence, it is understandable that they should become of central and urgent concern in informing and spearheading the process of rehabilitation and reconstruction.

By any measure, the Foch-Allenby and Etoile area stands out as a very unusual urban cluster. Other than its rich and symbolic history, it epitomises a variety of architectural styles and traditions: Ottoman arcades and cornices, Venetian and Genoese arches and corbels, Islamic friezes and inscriptions and French Mandate portals. The Maarad Street and Nejmeh Square, site of the Parliament, deputies' offices and a few foreign embassies and consulates, are also equally rich with an imposing row of arcaded buildings with a blend of late Ottoman, French Mandate and Mediterranean-like architecture so typical of a Levantine cityscape.

The implementation on the ground of the restoration programme, sustained by exacting monitoring, has embellished and pronounced these edifying elements. High-quality craftsmanship, especially in stone-masonry, carpentry and iron-work, have all done much to reinforce these restorative sensibilities. All such schemes have been careful not to mar or violate the natural and topographical features of the site.

The Lebanese generally are very casual, often abusive, with regard to their built environment. They have what is akin to a built-in cultural aversion for any maintenance or special regard for upgrading the quality of their living space. Indeed, once constructed, public premises and private residences are prone to deteriorate quickly from neglect and misuse. This is, perhaps, one of the most disheartening sights throughout the country: how readily newly constructed buildings or landscaped ground on public roadways become dishevelled and suffer from lack of attention or regular maintenance. Aware of such realities, Solidere is investing considerable attention to property and service management to all its delivered buildings. Well-managed property is seen as an inherent added value destined to enhance the quality and appeal of the built environment. Its impact on the morale, productivity and well-being of workers and residents is also recognised.

Incidentally, this concern with the quality of the built habitat does not only assume an outward cosmetic dimension. All new buildings in the BCD have been designed to withstand natural and other disasters such as earthquakes, fires and other hazards. Solidere also undertakes the management operation and 24–hour maintenance of all premises. It provides site logistics services, including cleaning, safety, security and the operation and maintenance of electro-mechanical systems, traffic management during and after the construction process.[7]

This successful blending of the vernacular with the Hi-Tech can be readily seen in

Recovery of Foch-Allenby (before and after)

Recovery of Foch-Allenby (before and after)

Recovery of Foch-Allenby (before and after)

many of the restored and new structures. Most prominent among them are the new headquarters of the Audi Bank, the Atrium shopping centre, the UN plaza, the Saifi Village and *an-Nahar's* imposing new headquarters. The latter, among a few others under construction, are bound to emerge as architectural icons of elegance wedded to the panache of postmodern electronic technologies with some elements of the spectacle. So successful has Solidere been in encouraging such ventures, particularly in its penchant for refined execution and meticulous concerns for technical details of the highest order, that it is now serving as a template and role model for other such projects throughout Lebanon and elsewhere. Indeed, Solidere has become a byword for high-quality restoration and reconstruction.

The exquisite rehabilitation of Foch-Allenby and Etoile, particularly since it was accomplished with such fastidious attention to detail, has had a contagious effect. Adjoining areas and neighbourhoods could not resist this impulse to restore and embellish their premises. Municipal ordinances are now enforcing such requirements. Failure to face-lift and paint the exteriors of houses and apartments are subject to steep fines. Slowly, urban neighbourhoods and traditional quarters are being rehabilitated without defacing some of the quaint and elegant features of the vernacular architecture. A growing core of young and gifted Lebanese architects and designers, with evident sensibilities to render a judicious synthesis of traditional, contemporary and postmodern

Audi Bank   *Atrium*

elements, must be credited for some of the eye-catching and appealing gentrification projects which are beginning to punctuate the townscape of streets and alleyways adjoining the rehabilitated areas of the CBD.

Parting with legendary icons of the past does not always come easy. Ahwet al-Azaz of Gemmayzeh is a case in point. It is one of the last bastions of the 'glass' coffee houses which once graced the intersections and inner courtyards of the old town. In the end it could not resist the temptation to modernise. To the dismay of its veteran customers, it recently caved in to the competition from the legion of upscale and ritzy global chains such as Starbucks, Casper and Gambini, La Posta and the like. The Gemmayzeh coffee house was something of a landmark. In its heyday – during the Ottoman, colonial and post independence interludes – it evolved into a popular hangout for political advocates, intellectuals and journalists. Even customers from the lower ranks of the social hierarchy sought it as a sanctuary from the cares of daily life. As in other comparable sites in the old city, these normally run down, shabby and smoke-filled coffee houses were the exclusive preserves of men. They just wiled time away, sipping their eternal cups of coffee while playing cards or backgammon.

The demise and the rehabilitation of the old coffee houses is, perhaps, one the most striking and emblematic signs of the time. So embedded in the folklore of the city's popular culture, such coveted sanctuaries die hard. Indeed, they have resurfaced with a vengeance. The renovated Maarad Avenue, connecting Weygand with Etoile, is now lined with restaurants, bars, coffee houses and sidewalk cafés. Their over congested premises spill over into the cobbled pedestrian thoroughfare and inner courtyards. Indeed, they have virtually taken over this prime public space. At all times of the day, often way past the early hours of the morning, eager patrons indulge their *arghealeh*-smoking with such consummate abandon that the sweet perfumed scent of tobacco fills the air for miles around.

Solidere, in vain, has made efforts to restrain this overspill into, or appropriation

Overspill into pedestrian avenues

Overspill into pedestrian avenues

of, public spaces. They have successfully launched other attempts at safeguarding and enhancing the equitable access and diverse use of these spaces. For example, consistent with European customs, all roadways in the city centre are closed to traffic on weekends. Cyclists, rollerbladers, joggers and other sports enthusiasts have now state-of-the-art, well-tended and safe premises to pursue their favourite pastimes, such as basketball, tennis and volleyball. Even bungee-jumping, sponsored by Virgin Megastore, is available for the more spirited and adventurous.

Another striking addition, a colourful 'Balloon Landing Park', now graces the open grounds (and skies) of the rehabilitated hotel district aligned to the marina and waterfront esplanade. The site could not have been more appealing for such a post-war tourist venture. This was, after all, the scene of some of the heaviest and repeated episodes of fighting during the early rounds of the war. Given its commanding and strategic location, on the demarcation lines between East and West Beirut, warring factions fought fiercely for its control. They left the area a virtual ruin. To this day some of the damaged and potholed facades – such as the Holiday Inn – still stand out as stark reminders of this devastation. By a foreboding coincidence, it was also here that Hariri's motorcade was blown up on 14 March 2005, just three days, incidentally, after the inauguration of the project.

This seemingly benign addition adorns not only the historic and mythical bay where St Georges encountered the monstrous dragon, but it also shares the site with some of the most compelling architectural icons of the city's skyline: the Phoenicia Hotel, designed by Edward Durrell Stone; the Holiday Inn, co-designed by André Woyensky, Le Corbusier's office manager; the prize winning Yacht Harbour, designed by Steven Holl; and, of course, the St Georges Hotel designed by Antoine Tabet, one of Auguste Perret's disciples. Despite its appeal, the open grounds – perhaps because of prohibitively high land values – have remained relatively sparsely built. Indeed, many of the structures there – such as the sport facility, the Children's Science and Recreational Museum and other leisure-related playgrounds – are mostly leased on a temporary basis. It is interesting to note that one the auspicious by-products of the *Intifadah* in the wake of Hariri's assassination is that some of the lots and parcels in the area are beginning to attract the construction of high-rise ventures.

The Balloon Landing Park is the work of Hashim Sarkis and his design team at Harvard's Graduate School of Design. The client of the project (Round Concepts), envisioned the construction of commercial kiosks, a waiting area and a platform for an Aerophile 30: a tethered helium balloon which accommodates about fifteen passengers to a height of about 300 metres to capture a panoramic view of the city. The minimalist and translucent structure – both its exterior surface treatment and interior partitions of the kiosks – blend unobtrusively with the site. What stands out, of course, is the striking yellow balloon with a band of mixed colours.

Those who have been critical of some of Solidere's restoration projects, particularly its upscale quality, expressed fears that the historic hub of Beirut's centre will be reduced to an exclusive and elitist sanctuary for the upper bourgeoisie and those eager to flaunt

Weekend traffic

their conspicuous consumption. Such fears have been allayed lately in view of the diversity in style and affordability of commercial and entertainment outlets. A cross-section of society's status and socio-economic groups can be seen rubbing shoulders in dense and compact areas. If anything, the apprehensions might well be in the opposite

Balloon Landing Park

Children's Science and Recreational Museum

Artists on sidewalks

direction. Already, in fact, upper-class and prosperous groups seem uneasy that, given this irresistible encroachment of lower-class and unanchored groups into the area, it might become much too populist, common and ordinary. Hence, in anticipating, or proposing plans for, the envisioned reconstruction of the Bourj, such groups are predisposed to favour the establishment of cultural and artistic venues such as concert halls, theatres, galleries, museums and auditoriums to accommodate conference centres and forums for exhibits and intellectual debates.

Of course, Hariri's makeshift burial site has been elevated into a national shrine: by far the most venerated and widely sought public sphere. Since his assassination on 14 March 2005, the site and adjoining open grounds have been inundated with a relentless inflow of spellbound and expressive groups. The collective enthusiasm sparked by the astounding spectacle of memorials, public demonstrations and political mobilisation hosted there are bound, once again, to redefine the future identity of the Bourj and its public image. Already, the finalists of the second stage in the international competition for urban design ideas for Martyrs' Square have been instructed to incorporate into their proposed designs a Hariri memorial or monument adjacent to the imposing al-Amin Mosque. This will most certainly cast a momentous image of how the Bourj will be perceived and used in the future.

Saifi Village

The village, currently in the final stages of its development, is largely a restoration of a cluster of closely-knit traditional quarters converging along six narrow, winding streets and alleyways: Akl, Gouraud, Mhkalssiye, Debbas, Kanafani and Haddad. Although fairly compact in size, covering an area of not more than 7,400 square metres, it houses 136 residential flats and provides a total of 30,000 square metres of floor space.

In overall design and execution, the 'Village' epitomises Solidere's perspectives on the rehabilitation of traditional neighbourhoods. Meticulous care is taken to preserve the old city's spatial fabric with an effort to enhance the distinctive identity of these once intimate but spirited urban enclaves. Drawing on the scale and rhythm of the existing structures, the intrinsic character of the neighbourhood is not only preserved but it is made to exude an authentic feeling as though the houses were built at different time intervals. Some of the houses, it must be recalled, date back to the 1860s at the time the massive rural exodus (in the wake of civil unrest in Mount Lebanon) forced the population to spill beyond the city's medieval walls. Others were the turn-of-the-century suburban town houses and Art Nouveau villas or walk-ups.

The restoration process has enhanced and enriched these elements. The delicate care for detail and refined execution – the hallmarks of Solidere projects – are truly stunning. Soft pastel shades reflect the colour palette used on the restored buildings. The small-scaled cobblestone streets are made narrower by broadened and elevated sidewalks

Hariri shrine

aligned with rustic lampposts and flowerbeds. Discreet landscaping protects the enclaves from through-traffic. Most appealing, perhaps, are the inner courtyards connected by a network of landscaped walkways and quardrangled but open enclosures. Like other traditional neighbourhoods in Beirut, Saifi was characteristically mixed in land-use and largely self-sufficient. Residents generally worked and lived in the same quarter and attended to much of their public and civic needs in adjoining areas. Solidere has been keen to preserve these defining features. Hence, if the original units (mostly two-storied suburban villas or walk-ups) had commercial or vocational outlets on the first floors, these were retained. Strict zoning, however, consistent with the overall residential character of the 'Village', is rigidly defined and observed. Only nuisance and noise-free ventures are licensed. Virtually all the available space is already leased to art galleries, artisans, bookstores, wine shops, ateliers, studios, pharmacies, doctors' clinics, health clubs and the like. The 'Village' is thus user-friendly: active and vibrant in daytime and quiet at night.

Altogether, one is overwhelmed by the gentle and unobtrusive elegance and beauty of the symbiotic blending of traditional and state-of-the-art elements. Recycled basalt cobblestones and well-crafted masonry compliment the Hi-Tech street furniture, hardscaping and traffic signage. The 'Village', as a result, acquires a pastiche-like, almost picture-book, image. Although not fully inhabited at the moment, all the 136 units have either been sold, leased with the option to buy or rented. Already the Village resonates

Saifi Village

Saifi Village

with a sense of commitment to the serene comforts and security of an edifying living environment.

The sustained events and activities associated with the *Intifadah* spilled over into Saifi. As the village was declared a '*quartier d'art*' (artist quarter), its intimate courtyards and streets erupted with cultural energy. Many of the city's active artists, designers and curators have already taken up premises there. Virtually all the ground floor and shops – which are fitted out with special refractive glass doorways – are already occupied by art galleries, antique shops, design boutiques and artisan outlets of arts and crafts. The periodic shows, exhibits, book launches and opening ceremonies have done much to enhance the lived and interactive quality of the village. At least, it no longer seems like a placid picture-perfect but sterile and lifeless neighbourhood. Indeed, the traditional carpenters' *souk* has been reinvented into an upscale art district.

Three distinctive and unusual features of Saifi stand out. First, the relentless flow of culturally oriented and artistic ventures it continues to attract displays a formidable degree of inventiveness and, often, unabashed experimentation. Second, and perhaps more strikingly, these activities are virtually a monopoly of women. Women are now the undisputed cultural brokers, patrons or actual producers of this explosion in creative and artistic energy. They have been resourceful and enterprising in exploiting their extensive personal networks to reinforce the intensity of collective enthusiasm and mobilisation. Third, this surge in cultural and artistic expression is certainly related to the grassroot populist mobilisation sparked off by the *Intifadah*. As the Bourj, barely yards away, was acting as host to the boisterous dimensions of public protest, the seemingly exclusive grounds of the village offered a more soothing and aesthetically pleasing public sphere. This dialectical interplay between popular mobilisation and the proliferation of the arts has symbiotic and mutually reinforcing manifestations. Both are rendered richer and more profound in transforming symptoms of personal autonomy and well-being into instances of empowerment and structural change.

Four other defining features, destined to shape the collective identity and national image of future Beirut, deserve recognition: rebuilding the old *souks*, highlighting the city's archaeological troves, the waterfront projects and the restoration and embellishment of religious edifices.

The Souks

The public image of pre war Bourj, at least as retained and conjured up in the collective memory of veteran Beirutis, is invariably associated with its traditional *souks*. They continue to be invoked with considerable nostalgia, bordering at times on reverie. In recent years, largely because the *souks* were totally destroyed and levelled, the public debate regarding their rehabilitation has been understandably overheated. The controversy has often assumed testy and acrimonious tones. Those critical of Solidere's scheme continue

Quartier des arts

to maintain that much of the old *souks*, although heavily damaged by protracted rounds of heavy fighting, could have been preserved. At the least, such critics argue, Solidere could have been more sparing in retaining some of the distinctive traditional elements of the old *souks*. Public nostalgia revolves around the two most emblematic historic features of the city's centre: the Bourj and the Aswaq. The Bourj with its boisterous traffic hub and terminals, flanked by all the outlets for leisure, entertainment, popular culture, such as cinemas, bars, small hotels and rooming houses, sidewalk cafés and, of course, its infamous 'red light' district, was dubbed at the time as '*Karkhana*' or, derisively, '*Souk al Awadem*': that is, the 'chaste' or 'reputable' market. However, the city centre also stood for Aswaq (plural of *souk* or 'market'): the enclave of the three vertical narrow streets (Ayyas, Tawileh and Jamil) descending vertically from Weygand. This old, dense street grid with access gates, open squares and sheltered water fountains, was scaleable, colourful and accommodated a dazzling variety of outlets, ranging from the little mangy-looking shops with makeshift vending stalls to specialised stores and upmarket fashionable boutiques.

As in other restoration ventures, the new project intends to retain some of the traditional elements of the old *souks* but wedded to an innovative design by the renowned Spanish architect Rafael Moneo, which also meets the requirements of a modern commercial centre. In its entirety, the restored area will provide 100,000 square metres of commercial and leisure facilities serviced by a 2,500–space underground car park. Teams of international and local architects, commissioned through open competitions and tendering, have designed the various components of the projects, particularly the entertainment centre (consisting of a movie multiplex with three-dimensional and dome technology), gold *souk* and jewellers' premises, department store and multi-purpose building.

Although the master plan for the development of the *souks* was drawn in 1995, the work on the project was suspended over the past three years, pending the resolution of the regulatory permission process. Its much-awaited completion is bound to have a profound effect on reviving the *souks* as an open or vibrant public space, attracting perhaps a wider cross-section of shoppers and leisure seekers.

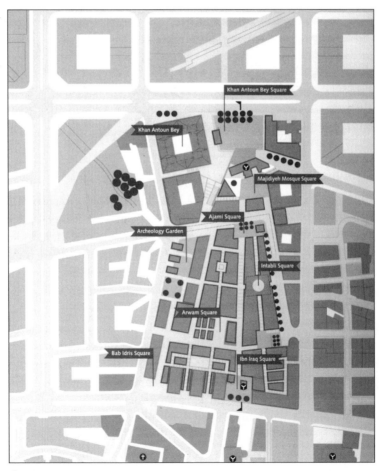

Aswaq

Open-air museums

An Open-Air Museum

Archaeological excavations and restoration in downtown Beirut, not unlike other sites rich with layers of history and contested cultural identities, have not been harmonious and unproblematic. The whole process of what and how much of this heritage should be unearthed and preserved is charged with profound and deep-seated emotions. What renders the experience in Lebanon more poignant is that it is reflective of the unappeased hostilities and reawakened segmental loyalties that continue to sustain the political and cultural divisions in post-war Lebanon.

It is also striking in that it has been a double-edged experience. Ugly as the war has been in its destructive manifestations and residues of grief, trauma and fear it has generated, it has also enabled the country to enrich its archaeological heritage. By 'bulldozing' such large portions of the old city centre, the war ironically provided access to the many of the hidden troves of ancient Beirut. The bane of the war has been a windfall to archaeologists. Indeed, as one leading Lebanese archaeologist maintained, the war has created the unique opportunity to excavate the largest urban site in the world (60,000 square metres). To date, no less than 136 urban lots with a total of 14,000 square metres have been excavated. This has naturally carried with it the exciting prospect of demystifying Beirut's 5,000 years of continuous history. In the process, the city centre of post-war Beirut is transformed into a beguiling open-air museum.[8]

But there is a darker side to this auspicious opportunity: it offers evidence of man's baser instincts and the antipathies groups continue to harbour to 'others', particularly their sacred monuments and spiritual artifacts. The most recent case in point is the restoration of the Greek Orthodox St Georges Cathedral, the oldest church in Beirut. Unlike its illustrious predecessor (the medieval Episcopal Monastery) which had been destroyed by earthquakes, St Georges, like a legion of other religious sanctuaries and monuments, was the victim of human avarice and bigotry. It was ransacked, burned and looted by unruly militias during the war. Ironically, the only icon that adorns the walls of the cathedral, albeit partially burned, was one depicting Judas Iscariot hanging himself for his betrayal of Christ!

Credit must go to Solidere, and a score of voluntary and advocacy groups must be applauded, particularly *an-Nahar* and its heritage page, who have aroused interest and launched campaigns to preserve such threatened legacies. In tangible support of such restorative efforts, Solidere has provided financial assistance to the score of teams working under the supervision of the Directorate General of Antiquities (DGA). During the last two years, research and excavation has proceeded on over twelve sites falling on public space. This has involved methodical documentation, digitisation and evaluation of findings.

Naturally, the keen interest of Solidere in preserving and highlighting the city's ancient history is not selfless. Cognisant of its inherent value, as a cultural, tourist and commercial asset, it has judiciously exploited such troves for enhancing the privileged

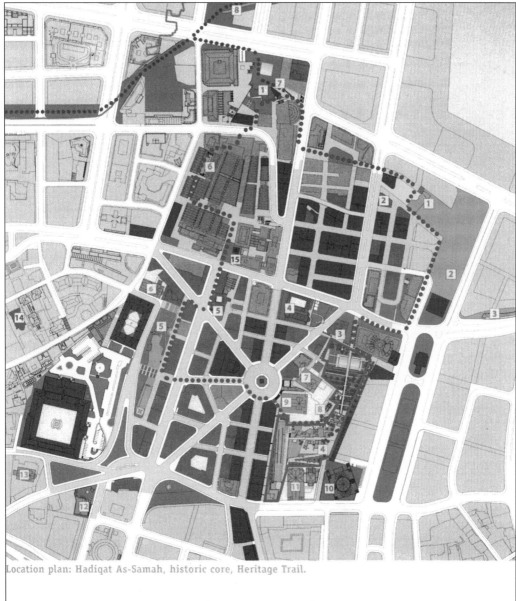

Location plan: Hadiqat As-Samah, historic core, Heritage Trail.

🗝 Hadiqat As-Samah	**1** Crusader Castle	**1** Majidiya Mosque	**9** St George Greek Orthodox Cathedral
•• Heritage Trail	**2** Ancient Tell	**2** Al Dabbagha Mosque	**10** Mohamad Al Amine Mosque
•• Other trails	**3** Phoenician City Wall	**3** Amir Assaf Mosque	**11** St George Maronite Cathedral
■ Heritage buildings	**4** Hadiqat As-Samah	**4** Al Omari Mosque	**12** Evangelical Church
■ Other retained buildings	**5** Roman Baths	**5** Amir Munzer Mosque	**13** St Nishan Armenian Church
■ New buildings in Historic Core	**6** Medieval Moat & City Wall	**6** Capuchin Church	**14** Maghen Abraham Synagogue
■ Site Museums	**7** Ottoman Quayside	**7** St Elie Greek Catholic Church	
	8 Ottoman Sea Wall	**8** Nouriya Chapel	

Garden of Forgiveness (location plan)

Garden of Forgiveness

appeals and national image of its project. Hence, archaeological sites and artifacts are being creatively incorporated into the fabric of the cityscape. For example, the Canaanite Tell and the Roman Cardo Maximus will form part of the public open space design. The exceptional interest of this Tell (about three hectares) is that it represents the site where the continuous urban history of Beirut is remarkably preserved from its inception in the third millennium bc, during the Early Bronze Age.

The Roman Cardo Maximus will also be preserved *in situ*. Following the Roman invasion, Beirut was built, as we are reminded by historians, over the urban grid of the Hellenistic City. Like other Roman colonies, the city was laid out in an orthogonal plan with two main axes: the Decumanus Maximus and the Cardo Maximus, intersecting at the main crossroad of the city and dividing it into the four quarters which prefigured much of the subsequent layout of modern Beirut.

One of the recent major discoveries from the Roman period is the north–south road paved with large slabs and stone plinths and stylobates for supporting columns. This has led to speculation that this might well be the Cardo Maximus, or one of the many other Cardos of the city.[9] This colonnaded road, by a beneficent historic coincidence, is located between the two St Georges Cathedrals: the Maronite and the Orthodox. Both are made more spectacular by this open archaeological grove in-between. Originally, the

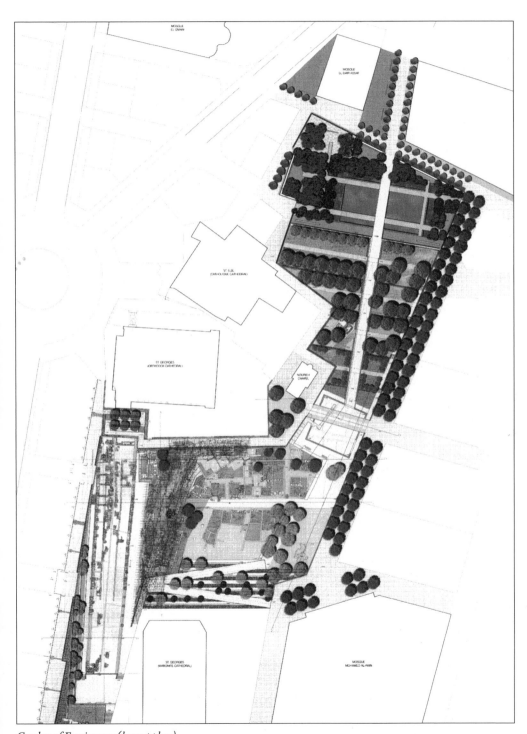

Garden of Forgiveness (layout plan)

Garden of Forgiveness (present site)

site was earmarked as an archaeological park. As of late it has been incorporated in the envisaged Hadiqat al-Samah (Garden of Forgiveness).

The idea for establishing the 'garden' as a sanctuary for introspection and healing owes much to the inspiration and vision of Alexandra Asseily. She was assiduous in articulating her vision and pursuing the necessary lobbying, with both local and international groups, to bring about its final approval. I am taking the liberty of extracting a few passages from her initial proposal to Solidere, from July 1998, by way of elucidating the vision and perspective of forgiveness as a key to reconstruction and rehabilitation:

> A garden in which people can gather strength and inspiration, a place for calm and gentle reflection. A garden for individual introspection, a sanctuary accessible to all. An edifying place, archetypal of Lebanon's flora, with flowing water, suitably covered by sun and shade, which nurtures sentiments of peace, joy, healing, blessing and humanity.
>
> The concept of forgiveness is an essential key to reconstruction and rehabilitation. Without it, the impressive physical projects under way may well be eclipsed by the same forces which razed their predecessors. Friends can live in the same shack and remain friends, but enemies, embittered by the cruelties of enmity and revenge, cannot share even a palace in the hope of becoming friends.
>
> Of all approaches sought to break the age-old cycle of violence and counter-violence so endemic to our country (and in particular to this very spot), none is more potent than forgiveness. Education, economic prosperity, social welfare and all efforts at integration do much to quell fears and clear misconceptions between different and segregated communities. However, even when successful, such efforts at best can only contain basic impulses. Unappeased hostility and vengeance, as the

chequered records of history painfully demonstrate, are almost always reawakened with heightened feelings of injustice and retribution. Forgiveness transcends the painful memories and grievances and redirects this energy into genuine avenues for peaceful coexistence.

Forgiveness is, in its essence, a spiritual force with boundless therapeutic virtues. It is espoused by all the great religions and countless great philosophers as the basis for goodness and well-being.

The Garden of Forgiveness is a wondrous and timely chance for the Lebanese to remind themselves about what is really important in their personal lives and collective identities in order to achieve a lasting cultural and political peace. It is a symbolic place which can reconcile past, present and future generations. It must be central and unencumbered.

The proposed site provides a truly momentous opportunity to bring together the visual, historical and spiritual features of the city and link them to the theme of forgiveness. Moreover, the location's symbolism provides a powerful context and argument for such a garden. The central district was always a meeting point for different communities and social strata in the country. In remaining open and un-built, it has not partaken in the segregation of the city. It can therefore offer the important neutral physical location with a multi-communal history that other parts of town cannot. From the garden, the destruction and reconstruction of the city can and must be reflected upon and re-examined. Otherwise, the memory of the war, like the harrowing events themselves, may well be trivialised and forgotten and hence, prone to be repeated.

By its very essence the Garden of Forgiveness must be a space open to all, not borne from or clouded by social, political, religious or financial special interests. Yet, by its very nature and through its own energy and design, it will play its own part in encouraging social reflection and integration (from below rather than from above). It should be a place of inclusion not exclusion. The foreign visitor will also be intimately drawn by the garden's universal appeal and emboldened by the values it espouses.

The garden of forgiveness here will be more than just a crucial lung at the heart of a big city. It will provide inspiration for the individual walking under its trees. People can therefore come to reconnect with their collective city memory, to learn about their heritage and each other. It can also be a site for re-enchantment with a damaged past, a place to reach out and embrace the 'other'. In this way, Beirut can reclaim its distinctive character as a mixed, hybrid and composite city.

If judiciously planned and landscaped, the garden could reinforce its geographic neutrality as a place for all religious and communal groups. Epigrams, aphorisms, reflective sayings and sobering thoughts, extracted from our rich spiritual and cultural heritage could be both cleansing and uplifting. The garden's location between the different churches and mosques will enhance the symbolism of bringing together.

At the very least the garden will offer a physical and conceptual link between these places of worship and reinforce a spirit of humanity. It will cultivate forgiveness as a universal concept and help all congregations to coexist in tolerance and mutual respect.

A multi-confessional space whose importance is held equally highly by different communities is not new to this spot. The Nourieh shrine has been witness to this for centuries.

As a transcending and neutral space, the Garden of Forgiveness will give a human face to reconstruction and lend character and soul to Beirut's centre. It will give all, irrespective of class or affiliation, reason to visit the centre for something other than business, shopping or outlets for popular culture and entertainment. As a public space it is desperately needed. Its motive and theme will be clear but each and everyone will draw something different from it. This is a unique opportunity. It will reconnect the Lebanese to their heritage, expose the past to dialogue and provide a bridge of hope to the future.[10]

The Garden of Forgiveness, given its scale and focal setting, will most likely evolve into a distinctive landmark and symbolic icon of future Beirut. A renowned British-American architectural firm, Gustafson Porter Ltd, won the international landscape design competition Solidere hosted in 1999. A joint team of archaeologists (Oxford and York Universities) provided technical assistance in the integration of the appropriate archaeological remains. The project has also won the support of the Prince Charles Foundation in the UK. The prince himself has been genuinely enthusiastic about the garden and sees it as an exportable model to be adopted in other comparable post-war settings. He has promised to assist in the international fund-raising campaign to be launched soon.

Buoyed by such international attention, Solidere is now keen on making the extra effort to incorporate this rich archaeological windfall into the public open-space design. For example, the Persian-Phoenician site will be integrated into the redesigned *souks*. A so-called 'Heritage Trail' will meander through the pedestrian zones where some of the striking archaeological sites are located, particularly the Roman baths and some of the religions edifices. Another noted French architect, Michel Macary, has been entrusted with designing the 'Trail' along with other sites such as the archaeological museum and the ancient Tell north of the Bourj.

Indeed, much of the vision of the Garden of Forgiveness in favour of creating a public space for healing, and harnessing collective energies into venues for peaceful coexistence, can be readily incorporated into the role envisaged for the Bourj. Only by reclaiming its distinctive character as a mixed, hybrid and composite public sphere will the Bourj once again be able to forge and reinforce such a beneficent collective image.

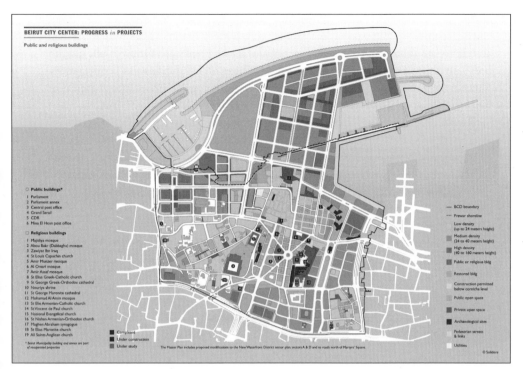

Heritage Trail

Waterfront and Marina Projects

Another eye-catching milestone, one that is also destined to restore one of Beirut's ancient images as a seafaring and Mediterranean centre and reshape its future skyline, is the substantial marine works Solidere launched early in 1994. This massive undertaking was intended to supplement Beirut's historic role as *'entrepôt'* and 'gateway' and to incorporate a new cornish system along the new waterfront to render the seaside drive more of a leisure and recreational zone. Constructing, however, a two-line defence system to protect the sixty hectares of reclaimed land was not an ordinary task. First, the environmental rehabilitation of the landfill necessitated a laborious process of land reclamation through biological, physical treatment and recycling of tons of refuse and war debris. More demandingly, the hydrological pressure of tidal waves, at that heady juncture of the Mediterranean, needed to be tamed. A conventional sea-defence system would have meant a twelve-metre high wall of steeply sloping interlocking rocks, both unaesthetic and inaccessible. Instead, the team of experts opted for a lagoon concept with an offshore undersea wall or artificial reef. Operating much like a coral reef, the structure will protect the inner lagoon and allow its active recreational use.[11]

The new waterfront district, reminiscent of other such recent international ventures – such as Baltimore, Sydney, Barcelona, etc – has truly overhauled the once maligned image of the old 'port' as a vilified, denigrated and, most certainly, an uninviting and inaccessible public space. The two picture-perfect marinas (east and west) will accommodate about 1,000 boats and yachts, along with breakwaters and a public quay to host a diversity of shopping, food kiosks and facilities for exhibitions and performances. These are naturally planned with the object of enhancing the international appeal of Beirut as a high-quality and fashionable tourist setting.

Two recent events, both timely and well-deserved accolades, reinforce such prospects in tangible ways. The overall project has been the recipient of a coveted international design award. More image-making, perhaps: Formula One, doubtlessly the world's most spectacular auto-racing event, has agreed to host one of their annual spectacles in downtown Beirut. If ever Beirut had fantasised about being the new 'Monaco' in the region, for good or ill, this is a furtive step in that direction.

Landfill and marina

Religious Edifices

Any consideration of the distinct archaeological and architectural heritage of downtown Beirut must recognise its unusually rich religious and spiritual legacy. Indeed, the old city centre might well boast of the largest number of religious edifices *per capita* in the world. Emblematic of the confessional pluralism coexisting in that dense and compact urban enclave, a total of seventeen religious premises are being restored or reconstructed. Of these, at least eight are currently functioning and are already drawing an incessant flow of regular worshipers.

Churches – and cathedrals, in particular – have also opened their sanctuaries to accommodate the growing demand for cultural activities, concerts, play-readings, recitals and the like. For example, Capucine St Louise (built in 1863) and the St Georges Greek Orthodox Cathedral (built in 1767) have been particularly active in hosting such events in their beautifully restored premises. Incidentally, mosques by religious edict are not permitted to use their premises for secular and cultural activities or for public gatherings other than prayer. Otherwise, like other religious edifices, all mosques in the city centre have been restored, refurbished, even extended, to claim adjoining landscape property. The Amir Assaf Mosque, facing the municipality, is perhaps the most prominent example. Indeed, all religious edifices, of all denominations, have become much more pronounced and visible. Thanks to the excessive use of electronic technologies, they have also become much more audible. Church bells, much like the *mua'zin's* calls for prayer, even the full services themselves, are vocalised loudly for all to hear. Efforts to persuade concerned authorities to take the necessary measures to control or mute this form of 'noise pollution' have been in vain.

The growing visibility and over-assertion of religious and confessional identities are largely a residue of years of unappeased hostility, compounded recently by the surge in global terror and its presumed association with Islamic radicalisation. Efforts can still be made to neutralise or redirect such profound sentiments, heightened by feelings of injustice and indignity, into more redemptive venues for tolerance and coexistence. Differences, religious or otherwise, may still be observed and celebrated without being indifferent to others.

Religious edifices: St Georges (before and after)

Religious edifices: Amir Assaf Mosque (before and after)

Religious edifices: al-Majidie (before and after)

Religious edifices: Armenian Catholic church (before and after)

FIVE

The Bourj as a Cosmopolitan Public Sphere

Despite its chequered history, the Bourj, more than its adjoining quarters and eventual outlying suburban districts, has always served as a vibrant and cosmopolitan 'melting pot' of diverse groups and socio-cultural transformations. While other neighbourhoods and districts of the expanding city attracted distinct sectarian, ethnic, class and ideological groups and communities – and eventually evolved into segregated and bounded urban enclosures – the Bourj always managed to remain a fairly open and homogenising space.

It is this openness and receptivity to new encounters, particularly foreign cultures, competing educational missions, European trade and an incessant inflow of goods, itinerant groups and borrowed ideologies that account for both its resonant pluralism and assimilating character. These three forces – pluralism, receptivity to change and tolerance to others – became the defining elements of Beirut's centre. It is also those features that accounted for its emergence and survival as a 'public sphere'. (I am employing the term here in its conventional sociological usage as propounded by Habermas and reformulated by a score of other contemporary scholars.)

Habermas, it must be recalled, traced the emergence of the public sphere back to the eighteenth century when various forums for public debate – clubs, coffee houses, newspapers and periodicals – proliferated. Much like other classical thinkers, he argued that these forms expedited the erosion of feudalism, which was legitimated by religion and custom rather than by agreements and consensus arrived at through public debate, open and unfettered discourse. As such, these emergent forms were of particular relevance and appeal to dislocated groups seeking to forge new identities and consolidate anchorage in the social fabric of the new social order. He went on to argue that such public spheres were given impetus by the extension of market economies and the resulting liberation of the individual from the constraints of feudal and other primordial ties of loyalty.

Newly liberated citizens, particularly the nascent bourgeoisie of property-holders, merchants and traders, among other new sectors in society, could now become active participants in advocacy groups and voluntary associations. At the least, they now had access to vectors through which they could mobilise their concerns about issues of governance and, possibly, participate in dissenting ideological groups to redress the dislocations and injustices in society. But that which enables can also disable. In a perspective that draws heavily on Max Weber's analysis of rationalisation, Habermas argued that the public sphere is threatened by some of the very forces that accounted for its expansion. In other words, as market economies become unstable, the state normally steps in to enforce greater measure of control. With the expansion of the powers of state into virtually all dimensions of social and everyday life, the public sphere is dwarfed. More dishearteningly, and much like other critical theorists, Habermas warns that the state can now seek to redefine problems as technical ones which can hence only be readdressed by technologies and administrative venues rather than by public debate, open discourse and argumentation.[1] Given these resolute and overwhelming constraints, the problem of resurrecting and safeguarding the enabling features of a public sphere becomes all the more vital in the context of post-war Beirut. Such prospects are considerably more compelling since they now involve resisting the impervious risks not only of an inept and unresponsive government bureaucracy but also of the distant forces of globalism and mass-consumerism. Within this context, this chapter explores two related dimensions. First, the genesis and evolution of the Bourj as a public sphere is elucidated. Second, an attempt is made to document and account for how it has managed over the years to reinvent its identity and public image.

Genesis and Emergence as a Public Sphere

The character and role the Bourj came to assume as a vibrant and cosmopolitan public sphere cannot, naturally, be appreciated without reference to its historic setting as an open and unbounded *maidan, sahl* or *sahat*. It evolved, after all, next to a walled and fortified urban sanctuary. This defining element survived throughout its history. However, it started to embellish and consolidate those features during the first half of the nineteenth century.

Partly because of its compact size and predominantly commercial character, the intermingling and collaboration between the various communities were both inevitable and vital for their coexistence and survival. Typical of a so-called 'merchant republic', traders and entrepreneurs of various communities were partners in private business ventures. They assisted each other in times of austerity and financial need. More importantly, they perceived themselves as members of an urban merchant elite, resisting the hostile elements that threatened their common economic interests.

In the old *souks* and bazaars flanking the Bourj, artisans and traders worked side by side. Spatial segregation and location of shops was occupational and not religious in character. Much like the spatial layout of residential quarters elsewhere in the burgeoning city beyond the Bourj, the bazaars and retail outlets were strikingly uniform in their architectural features. On the whole, social interaction was characterised by sentiments of goodwill and mutual tolerance and personal ties of intimacy, familiarity and trust. Such mutual cooperation was not confined to domestic and commercial relations. It spilled over into other spheres of public life. Christians and Muslims continued to meet together at official functions and served on the same committees, courts and mixed tribunals. For example, during the period of national struggle against Ottoman repression and centralisation of the Young Turks at the turn of the century, between 1880 and 1908, Christians and Muslims transcended their communal differences and participated collectively in underground political movements and secret societies.

Likewise, during the emancipatory struggle for independence and subsequent mass protest movements and demonstrations in support of labour unions, women's suffrage, Palestinian mobilisation and other dispossessed groups, the Bourj always served as a vector and rallying ground for giving 'voice' on behalf of neglected and marginalised segments of society. Student demonstrations, often with heightened confrontational strategies, reserved their most virulent expressions to the Bourj.

In the Mandate era, the resort to such public spheres became more pronounced. Elizabeth Thompson advances two plausible structural forces underlying this change.[2] First, the public underwent a massive expansion with the growth of transport and communication, public services such as schooling and health care, new entertainment venues such as cinemas and public parks and the publishing of newspapers and magazines. Second, the public was steadfastly emerging as a public sphere and primary political arena, particularly in the 1930s when the Parliament was shut down by the French for half a decade. Mass demonstrations, market closures, even street battles became the *modus operandi* of the nascent post-colonial political culture. Urban *zua'ma* and other urban notables mobilised their client groups in protest. Dissenting and subaltern movements and other excluded groups took to the street to voice their dissent. Turf battles with the French forces for control of urban space and the virtual public space (freedom of speech and media) became frequent.

The Bourj, largely because the Petit Serail, built in 1883, which served first as headquarters for the Ottoman postal service and later, from 1926 to 1950, became the official 'palace' for Lebanese presidents, was the ultimate destination of all public demonstrations. Public protests were legion in the 1940s, particularly demonstrations against poor living standards, inadequate distribution of flour and public-sector workers seeking better pay.

One interesting and unusual feature of the Bourj accounts for the role it played as meeting place for itinerant groups. At a time when transport, telephone, electronic and other virtual forms of communication were nonexistent, the outlets the Bourj devised for

Celebrations and processions (1920–44)

Celebrations and processions (1920–44)

Public demonstrations (1920–74)

Public demonstrations (1920–74)

such valued access were both inventive and functional. For example, the mushrooming hotels, pensions, *locandas* and residences were used as transit stops and meeting grounds. A nascent hotel industry, as early as the 1830s, was already developed to accommodate the growing stream of foreign travellers. Travellers to the interior always sought to stop in Beirut en route. Travelogues are ecstatic in their praise of the elegance of the hotels they encountered at the time. Some of the graceful hotels, especially the *locandas* and 'casinos' (with their terrace-cafés, patisseries and Levantine dragomen) built and managed first by Greeks, Maltese, Italians and then eventually native Lebanese, all came into being during the second half of the nineteenth century. The westward flanks, fronted on the Mediterranean and adjoining the old city (between the Zeitouneh quarter and Minet el Husn Bay) were particularly appealing for such growth. The most legendary were the Grand Hotel d'Orient (Bassoul's), Victoria, Casino Alphonse, Continental (Normandy), Universe and later, in 1930, the Hotel St Georges.

The upsurge in the number of hotels, restaurants and bars is almost similar to the

Hotels and locandas (America, Heliopolis and Carillon)

preponderance of these outlets today. In about five years, from 1923 to 1929, the number of hotels nearly doubled and continued to increase in the 1930s. The number of restaurants and bars also increased considerably in the same period: from twenty-one to thirty-two.[3]

Local groups, villagers frequenting the city to attend to their exigent needs, had their own chains of residences and pensions. Interestingly, some of these premises became associated with particular villages. For example, Hotel America became almost the exclusive preserve of visitors from Zahle. To groups in the throes of completing final arrangements or awaiting designated ocean liners for their anguishing departure from Lebanon, these hotels, such as Kawkab, America, Orient Palace, Victoria, Royal, etc, became settings charged with drama and emotional contagion.

Not only hotels but also bus and car terminals, transport agencies, especially coffee houses, served as meeting points for villagers. It was common for Beirut residents to deliver and receive their mail, messages and parcels of personal effects via such venues. To villagers seeking jobs, contacts and other city chores, these places became expedient stopgaps and surrogate homes and offices. Some coffee houses placed makeshift mailboxes for such purposes. Others became intimately associated with particular groups.[4]

This is, doubtlessly, the interlude in Beirut's urban history when displaced and uprooted groups – largely because of the quickening pace of urbanisation – felt the need to reconnect by seeking refuge in urban spaces amenable to such informal and associational contacts. Virtually all such collective public amenities were converted into public spheres. For example, at a time when recognised clubs, galleries, auditoriums and other formal public venues were still rare, coffee houses, restaurants and bars became expedient haunts for intellectuals, artists, poets, journalists and politicians. As early as the 1930s such places acquired notoriety precisely because they became meeting places for particular groups. Regular clients who patronised these places knew exactly what to expect, particularly since the outlets were intimately associated with popular figures and celebrities of the day. Coffee houses like Abou Afif, Republique and Parisienne were frequented by a close circle of poets of the likes of al-Akhtal al-Saghir, Elias Abou-Shabakeh, Amin Nakhleh and Said Akl. Singers, performers, songwriters, such as Assad Saba, al-Sibaaly, Zaki Nassif and the Rahbani Brothers, were drawn to the Roxy Bar and Hawi. Journalists and politicians were more likely to be found in Farouq, which later changed its name to Abd al-Nasir.[5] Even when regular public venues, such as the Lebanese Academy of Arts (ALBA), the Lebanese Cenacle and Dar al-Fan, established or relocated their premises close to the centre during the 1940s, these did not detract from the appeal or popularity of the traditional places.

This symbiotic coexistence between traditional outlets and the more specialised, commercial and corporate-like organisations continued throughout the post-independence period and beyond. Indeed, this proclivity to accommodate such 'third spaces'[6] was a distinctive attribute of the Bourj. The growth of secular and impersonal associations throughout the 1960s, and until the outbreak of civil hostilities in the mid-

1970s, did not displace the conventional shopkeepers, artisans and neighbourhood stores. They merely enriched the plurality and diversity of outlets. Hence, seemingly disparate groups felt equally at home: the villager and regular neighbourhood customer who was seeking familiarity and personal contacts and the itinerant visitor and tourist after novelty and adventure. In other words, both the footloose *flaneur* and the rooted conformist did not feel any dissonance in the spaces they were sharing.

Because of the protracted civil unrest and the unsettling political circumstances of the past decade, Lebanon lost one of its most coveted venues as an international public sphere. During much of the 1960s and 1970s, as political instability in adjacent regimes was at its height, Lebanon became especially appealing for hosting summits, international gatherings, multinational corporate meetings, academic conferences, symposia and cultural festivals. This has been restored lately. Indeed, its post-war setting, in view of its auspicious process of recovery, has become particularly inviting for such international gatherings. For example, in preparation for the Francophone and the Arab Summits in October 2002 and much like other such episodes, these became occasions to give Beirut

Coffee house

a quick and much-needed face-lift. Gutted buildings that still bore the pockmarks of war were spruced up and festooned with banners and draped with flags and colourful national logos of the twenty-two Arab states. Roads were freshly macadamised and landscaped; sidewalks, doorways, lampposts were spotless and emblazoned with fresh colours.

There was clearly more than banal cosmetics to the spectacles surrounding the eventful summits. Beirut was not just a showcase. Having suffered the deprecating image – often no more than an ugly metaphor for all the brutish 'Hobbsian' wars of self-destruction – Lebanon was, of course, eager to display its other, more benevolent image: that of a tolerant and cosmopolitan capital equipped to host, once again, peace conferences and forums for open and reconciliatory dialogue. A few optimistic observers harked back to earlier glories, to remind sceptics of how much the country had done in this respect on behalf of its bickering Arab states. One popular weekly magazine drew an analogy with the last such gathering Lebanon was privileged to host in 1956 in the wake of the Suez crisis. The Arab League summit at the time, presided over by President Camille Chamoun, denounced the joint Israeli, English and French incursions into Egypt. Just as that momentous summit had led to the Israeli withdrawal from Sinai, the magazine expressed the hope that the current summit might well mobilise global pressure to evict the Israeli forces out of the Gaza Strip and the West Bank.

Re-Inventing its Identity and Public Image

Throughout its chequered history, and largely because of the multicultural and pluralistic layers of ancient civilisations it sheltered, the Bourj had to reinvent itself repeatedly to accommodate the relentless succession of imperial occupations. The most intractable public label has, of course, been the Bourj – in reference to the imposing tower guarding its seafront ramparts.

Consistent with its ubiquitous and evolving national character, the popular labels and nomenclatures attributed to it have always been in flux and contested. It is rather telling that the first urban form the Bourj assumed was '*al Maidan*', one which prefigured some of the subsequent striking developments, particularly in its role as a collective common ground, a (public sphere) for itinerant and unanchored social groups. The *maidan* should not be dismissed as merely a fortuitous and insignificant interlude. As it evolved, it incorporated elements which account for the dual role it came to play and, hopefully, will continue to do so in yet another reinvented form: an open space – '*sahat*' – which is not a wilderness, a common ground which is not a home.

From its inception as an open, amorphous *maidan* (and this is how it was first labelled), the Bourj never served as a distinct enclosure or sanctuary. Rather, it acted as an open ground that exacted a measure of collective attachment. This is, after all, what the notion of *maidan*, in its Persian origins, conjures up. It came to be identified with images of plains, meadows, grounds or fields. In its Persian context it was primarily associated with pilgrims, traders and militias. As it found expression in other contexts, such as Cairo, Bombay, Ahmedabad, Calcutta, etc, it embraced many other elements and uses. Throughout, however, the idea of the *maidan* emerged as a result of human intervention directed not toward the addition of identity, events or character but rather towards keeping land free and indeterminate and therefore negotiable. Hence, it should not be confused with enclosed courtyards or cultivated parks. Nor is it a desolate wilderness, a dreary, parched stretch of land. Rather, as M. Mathur suggested, it is somewhere in-between; it is both nomadic and collective.[7] It is, in fact, close to what Ivan Illich calls 'commons', or:

> ... that part of the environment that lay beyond a person's own threshold and outside his own possession, but to which, however, that person had a recognised claim of usage – not to produce commodities but to provide for the subsistence of kin. Neither wilderness nor home is commons, but that part of the environment for which customary law exacts specific forms of community respect.[8]

A striking feature of the *maidan*, which is of particular relevance to the Bourj's emergence and metamorphosis, is its predisposition to embrace a diversity of cultures while containing measures of neutrality, anonymity and transcending attributes. As Mathur puts it:

> In cities of increasingly circumscribed social, racial, or economic enclaves, the *maidan* has come to both symbolise and provide neutral territory, a ground where people can gather on a common plane. It is a place that offers freedom without obligation. This ability to accommodate a diverse range of social and political structures makes the *maidan* an extremely significant space in the city. It is a place where people can touch the spirit of commonness.[9]

Given the scarcity and inevitable intensification and competition for the use of precious urban space, a realistic re-appropriation of a *maidan* in its original concept or form is naturally a remote likelihood in central Beirut. Its underlying spirit and sentiment are, however, still realisable. Indeed, because of the disappearance of many historical *maidans*, efforts are being made today to appropriate landscapes that lend themselves to both settled and nomadic or ephemeral elements. Hence, open spaces – 'sahls' and 'sahas' – made once again available for urban redevelopment are rare and challenging interludes for urban designers. Levelled and open spaces can once again offer rare opportunities to reclaim a measure of freedom and spontaneity within the enclosure of the city. All adjoining areas radiating from Beirut's centre are increasingly commodified, deliberately monitored and exploited in ways that are bound to discourage any spontaneous appropriation or unplanned development. Within such seemingly impervious constraints, where urbanists and landscape architects are seeking efforts to promote qualities of indeterminacy and

Visit of Willhelm II, 1898

open-mindedness, the Bourj offers such rare and coveted opportunities.

Naturally, as a reality, *al Maidan's* lifespan was short-lived. Gradually, and with signs of intermittent habitation, it started to acquire the interchanging labels of *sahat* or *sahl*: that is, an open plain. No sooner had itinerant groups started settling within the adjoining remains of the fortified medieval embankments, the Bourj became literally, '*sahat-al-sour*'. For a while – to this day in fact – old-timers, veteran taxi and service car drivers continue to employ the colloquial expression of '*as-Sour*'.

The first definitive change in its public identity occurred in 1772. The imperial Russian fleet, part of the Russian military expedition of 1772, had installed five massive pieces of artillery on its elevated fortifications. According to one source, the cannons were used to destroy much of the fortification of the old medieval walls.[10] Hence the appellation '*Place des Canons*' acquired its notoriety. By 1860, it was the imperial cannons of the French fleet that reinforced that label this time. Prior to that and for a brief interlude after 1850, when Beirut's centre was largely desolate, with only a few nomadic Bedouins from the interior who occupied one of its remaining fortified towers, it bore the designation of '*Sahat Bourj el Kachef*'.

When the French army entered Beirut in the wake of the 1860 civil disturbances, Poujoulat was quite impressed by the sight of this '300 by 150-metre square' with its multicoloured 'omnibus' which took passengers to the pine forest at fifteen-minute intervals. He was particularly impressed by the French character of the square with its stylish restaurants, cafés, shops and boutiques '*tenues par des Français*' which made their appearance shortly after the Crimean War.[11] With such preferential hints in favour of the 'Frenchness' of the square, its colonial manifestations were deliberately muted by successive Ottoman *walis*. Indeed, by the time Wilhelm II, the German Emperor, made his historic visit to Beirut in 1898, he had labelled it as the 'jewel in the crown of the Padishah'.[12]

Incidentally, the Emperor's visit, hailed as a milestone in German-Ottoman goodwill, was an occasion to dress up Beirut in its edifying and ceremonial best. Special

committees of Ottoman municipal authorities and the city's notables were established
to oversee the spectacles and reception prepared for the event. As municipal engineer,
Yusuf Aftimos was commissioned to decorate the square and adjacent roadways. Khalil
Sarkis, the noted editor of *Lisan al-Hal*, delegated officially to accompany the emperor,
reported the following on that historic day:

> The port company played an important role in the preparations, and the honourable
> municipality agreed [for once] with the gas company to line the throughways with gas
> lighting of the most beautiful kind. Along the entire path [of the Emperor's projected
> procession], the offices of the port company, the customs, the Khedival Lines and
> the adjacent mansions and all the official and unofficial Ottoman government offices
> were laid with cedar twigs, pine branches and splendid lighting. And especially Sahat
> al-Bourj was decorated by [the mufti] 'Abd al-Basit [al-Fakhuri] and the engineer
> Yusuf Efendi Aftimos with three arcs of the highest order, one on top of the other
> with a German and an Ottoman flag above.[13]

A crowd of 50,000, along with the city's entire student population who enjoyed a special
holiday to mark the occasion, had lined the streets along the designated route of the
procession. The emperor's guided tour of the spruced-up city ended in 'Sahat al-Bourj',
as it was called then:

> While refreshments were served, His Majesty feasted his eyes on the beautiful view
> of the city, the harbour, and the deep blue sea. In the other direction, he looked
> across a densely wooded plain up to the heights of Mount Lebanon ... the return
> trip resembled a triumphal procession. The route was flanked by countless people, all
> cheering endlessly. Night had already set in as the procession continued through the
> brightly illuminated city, across the Canon Square with its decorative public garden,
> and down to the harbour. Everywhere the streets, the windows, and balconies were
> lined with people, who were outdoing each other in expressing their joy.[14]

Long before Beirut became capital of the provincial Ottoman *Wilaya* in 1888, *Sahat
al-Bourj* was perceived as a potential visual corridor between its port and the traditional
city. In fact, as early as 1863, M. Stoecklin, consulting engineer for the port extension,
had this to say about its future prospects:

> It is not enough to build quays; these need to have convenient access to the city
> centre. This is where difficulties begin. Old downtown quarters neighbouring the
> port amount to a blind maze of dead ends, alleyways and covered passages through
> which it would only be possible to open an avenue at enormous cost ... But a more
> radical solution is possible: the extension of Martyrs' Square over its full length all
> the way to the waterfront.[15]

Imperial Ottoman authorities were adept at exploiting such recurrent rituals of ceremonial commemoration to reinforce the monumentality and visibility of their imposing architecture and public squares. In their initial and subsequent efforts at creating and regulating public spaces, *Sahat al-Bourj* had been a special target of such Ottomanisation. The first such efforts of regularisation, shortly after 1860, were predominantly infrastructural in character. The intention was to:

... level the inclination between the imperial barracks [*qishla*], *Sahat al-Sur* and *Sahlat al-Bourj*. A great earthen dam was built 'behind *al-Sur*' to ease the journey of the passengers of the Diligence service. They put together a great heap [*qantara*] of stones above Bab Ya'qub so that the carriages from above and the people from below may be free from worry on the way to the gate.[16]

	Piastres
Ayyas Brothers	2500
Yusuf al-Jadday	2000
As'ad Malhame	2000
Ra'ad and Hani	2000
Jurji Tueni	1750
Nikula Sursock	1500
Hanna Shakbur Trad	1130
Salim Tabet	1000
Bishara al-Khoury	500
Elias Sayyagha (Head Architect)	500
Saloum Bassul	500
Italian Consul	500
Abdel-Rahim Badran (Chamber of Commerce)	500
Christopher al-Rumi	250
Khalil Sarkis (Lisan-al-Hall)	227
Musa Freij	227
M. Aubin	227
M. Lafique (Beirut-Damascus Road)	227
Comte Perthuis (Beirut-Damascus Road)	227
Wakim al-Najjar	200
Omar Ramadan	"
Nicola Kimati	"
Elias Qutayta	"
Jirjis Sursock	"
Salim Shihab	"
Ahmad Ramadan (Municipal Inspector)	100
Said Jawish	"
Muhammad Badran	"

By 1863 the Beirut–Damascus road (originally planned in 1851) was completed, thereby strengthening the link with Damascus and territory beyond Mount Lebanon and the coast. The centrality of the Bourj was reinforced further. A tolled caravan route extended from Bourj in a valley between the Achrafiyeh area and the western regions of Moussaytbeh and Mazraa. Under Daw D Pasha (1861–8) the streets of Beirut were widened and macadamised to accommodate carriages of the French Damascus Road Company. Greek Orthodox merchants benefitted financially from the improving regional economic role of Beirut. In 1873, under Rustum Pasha, a public garden at Hazmieh was constructed on the outskirts of Beirut. Regular festivals and orchestral performances, from which commoners with ordinary native garb were excluded, were held on Sundays.

During the Mutesarrifate, the Municipal Council of Beirut launched a series of magisterial and eye-catching projects in 1879. It is interesting to note in this regard that, unlike other Ottoman provinces, private initiative and foreign capital contributed heavily to changing the urban landscape, particularly in the wake of the economic boom during the last decade or so of the nineteenth century. Initiated at that time, this form of private intervention or concern for the regulation of public space became, off and on, a recurrent feature. For example, as early as 1879, when Fakhry Bek launched his landscaping project of the public garden in the Bourj, about thirty families contributed to the effort. The newspaper *Lisan al-Hal* assumed leadership in supporting the campaign for the beautification of the *sahat*. Special feature-articles appeared, pronouncing and advocating the needs – planting of trees, lanterns, pathways, etc – virtues and appeals of a public garden in such a compelling central space. The paper also launched a subscription campaign and would list, by way of promotion, names, identities and the pledged sums of individual contributors. On 26 May 1879, the following list appeared in the pages of *Lisan al-Hal*:

The construction of the Petit Serail in 1883 naturally prodded municipal authorities to undertake the first landscape design for the open field or 'al-sahla' into its front, picturesque courtyard, as it were. An imposing octagonal kiosk with an ostentatious fountain lined with trees and shrubs and decorated with Ottoman-style architectural ornaments became the new landmark of Beirut's centre. It was also then that the nondescript open field or plain (*al-sahla*) was transformed into a fairly modern square (*al-saha*). By then the square had already attracted typical central urban functions and outlets: transport terminals, banks and government-controlled public enterprises. Public reactions, at least initially, were enthusiastic. The leading daily, *Lisan al-Hal* had this to say:

> The governor general has paved al-Bourj to make it the beauty spot it deserves to be as it is the entrance of the governor's palace and the Ottoman Bank and other administrative buildings as well as the garages of the railway company, the Tobacco Régie, the Beirut tramway, the gas company and the Lebanese tramway company.[17]

Al-Maidan (17th century)

Bourj al-Kashef (18th century)

Place des Canons (1890)

Le kiosque – Jardin Public (1890)

Place des Canons (1910)

Place des Canons (1925)

Place des Martyrs (1930s)

Bourj Square (1975)

Bourj Square (1984)

This 'Muntazah', as it was initially labelled, became the edifying centrepiece of the Bourj. Perhaps because of its novelty and the patrons it drew from a cross-section of the social fabric, the Bourj started to attract other outdoor cultural outlets for public entertainment. A music kiosk was built. From then on, the Bourj began to evolve into an urban hub or loop which drew in and around it a variety of activities ranging from official state and municipal bureaucracies, travel terminals, hotels, locandas, sidewalk cafés to business and retail stores, popular souks and other more seamy outlets such as brothels, bars, gambling joints and houses of assignation.

Soon, however, because of its novelty as a public garden, the Muntazah started to arouse public concerns about how to shelter it from abuse and neglect. Newspaper accounts of the period ran stories in opposition to the measures taken by the government to fence in the picturesque oval garden or to monitor and restrict public access to it. Others were proposing the destruction of the makeshift shops, stores and shabby, unkempt stalls which mushroomed around the well-tended oval and were, it seems, the source of much disorder and criminality.

Jurji Zeidan, in a poignant autobiographical sketch, tells how for eight years of his sheltered adolescence he was called upon to serve as bellhop in his father's locanda located in 1872 in one of the poor, unruly and rundown districts adjoining the Bourj. He recalled how he had to brace himself to cope, at such a tender age, with all the dreadful and aberrant manifestations pervading the area. He bemoaned his surroundings for being the tempting spot for derelicts, deviants and the unemployed, replete with drunkards, gamblers, prostitutes, tempestuous and shady characters.[18]

One might possibly view in this regard the emergence of Sahat al-Sur, located on the south western flanks of the old city, within this context. It became a natural outlet for the working-class neighbourhoods of Basta and Bashura. Migrant and daily workers would congregate early in the morning in the hopes of being recruited at one of the construction sites within the city. The installation of a new Ottoman telegraph office on the northern end of the sahat, next to the public hammam (Zahrat Suriyya), did not detract from its popular and local character. Unlike the comparatively more orderly and landscaped Bourj Square, al-Sur was unbounded and without any marked encircling footpaths or pavements. Hence, perhaps because of its intimate and unstructured character, it continued to be an attractive spot for lower-class coffee houses and other popular haunts. The construction of the tramway, between 1907 and 1909, connected al-Sur to other neighbourhoods of the expanding city: the port and Khan Antoun Bey to the north, Nahr Beirut to the east and Ras al-Nabá and beyond to the south.

Naturally, Sahat al-Sur was not planned or intended that way. Like other public squares, it acquired a life of its own, unrelated to its original intention. Converting the sahat into a public park dated back to 1869 when the newly established municipality appropriated and tore down, not without public outcry, all recently built popular shops and stores. Once again, on the occasion of celebrating Abdulhamid II's jubilee, on 1 September 1900, Sabil Sahat al-Sur, with an eight-metre tall white marble fountain, was inaugurated with the pomp and circumstance the Ottomans relished and admired. With the usual contrived crowds waving imperial banners and background military music, the governor turned on the water and ritualistically drank the first cup from the *sabil* pipes. Like the Qantari clock tower, it was designed by Yusif Aftimos. Two prominent local craftsmen contributed to the artistic embellishment of the fountain: Yusif al-Anid as sculptor and Muhammad al-Barbir as calligrapher to engrave the glittering commemorative plates on its pedestal.[19]

Clearly the Ottomans had special regard for public parks and squares. With an eye for monumentality and spatial visibility, such open spaces were not perceived for their edifying urbanist and aesthetic elements. Rather, their intention was to embody and promote the Hamidian personality cult and inspire a sense of public gratitude and awe to the benevolent sultan. Ironically, the very spaces and monuments intended to reinforce public loyalty and commitment worked to undermine Ottoman and imperial sovereignty. The public spaces became venues for public demonstrations and the mobilisation of anti-government protest. Somehow, Ottoman authorities never quite mastered the exacting requirements for managing the control of public spaces. Over the years, al-Bourj, in particular, was highly politicised and became a paramount political space for public processions and the mobilisation of public dissent on behalf of a variety of national issues and causes. Quite often the demonstrations transcended provincial and local concerns and addressed foreign issues.

For example, as early as 1908, when Austria had annexed Bosnia-Herzegovina, a group of Beiruti notables, intellectuals and public figures organised a street demonstration to protest Austria's violation of the Berlin Treaty.[20]

Another dramatic interlude or threshold in the metamorphosis of the Bourj was the succession of labels and changes in its identity it had to undergo under the Ottomans.

Prince Faysal visit (May 1919)

Two grieving women (1930)

Inaugurating the monument (6 May 1960)

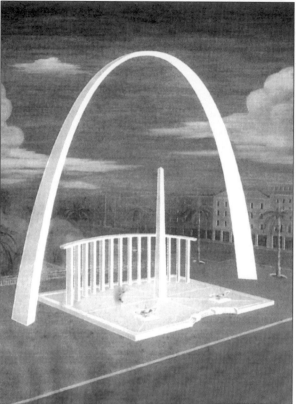

Abdul Baqi's maquette (1952)

First, it acquired the label of '*Sahat al-Ittihad*' or '*al-Hamidiyyah*' in reference to its Ottoman legacy, the former as an expression of the desired national unity under Ottoman sovereignty and the latter in commemoration of sultan Abdul Hamid. By the time Prince Faysal Ibn al-Husayn made his triumphant visit in May 1919, *Sahat el-Hamidiyyah* became '*Hadiqat al-Hurriyah*' ('freedom or liberation from Turkish oppression').

Freedom and liberation from Ottoman oppression did not, of course, lapse without exacting its heavy toll on a select group of recalcitrant nationalists. Beginning 21 August 1915, Jamal Pasha used the open square of the Bourj to execute, by public hanging, the first group of eleven martyrs. This was followed in 1916 by three other such nationally dreaded executions on 5 April, 6 May and 5 June respectively. Journalistic accounts of the day reveal widespread feelings of collective anguish, trepidation and pride.[21] In 1937, 6 May was declared a national memorial day. The commemoration of martyrs, given the repeated victimisation of innocent civilians with which the country has been beleaguered, is naturally a solemn and fitting commemoration.

Commissioning and securing a measure of public consensus on the design and ultimate installation of the memorial was fraught with problems and bitter controversy.

The first statue, the work of the prominent Lebanese sculptor Joseph Hoayek in 1930, depicted two grieving women ('*Deux Pleureuses*') – a Muslim and a Christian – lamenting the fate of their children. Because of its avowed sectarian motif, the statue became the target of intense and sustained disapproval. So rancorous was the objection that by 1952 the government announced an international competition for an alternate memorial. The winning design by a Lebanese architect, Sami Abdul Baqi, did not fare any better. It depicted a monumental arch enveloping an obelisk and an elliptic arcade of sixteen columns representing the number of martyrs. The project remained a celebrated but unrealised maquette.

Finally it was not until 6 May 1960 that the monument, the work of the Italian sculptor Mazacurati, was at last installed in an official ceremony presided by President Fuad Shihab and Prime Minister Saeb Salam. This too was not uncontested. Although its overall aesthetic and elegant quality was deemed admirable and refined, the monument was criticised for several shortcomings, particularly what was perceived as the 'un-Lebanese' features of its four celebrated figures. The theme is one of freedom and liberation, with a woman bearing a torch in one hand and enfolding a young man with the other. Two martyrs enshrine the base of the statue. The artist defended his choice by maintaining that he had wandered through various parts of the country and took reams of photographs to capture the defining facial and physical features of the archetypal or quintessential Lebanese. He argued that the most pronounced features have much in common with those prevalent in the southern regions of the Mediterranean.

The imposing statue continued to grace the central spot of *Sahat al-Shuhada* (Martyrs' Square), until the outbreak of the civil war. Repeated rounds of heavy street fighting scarred and defaced the statue with deep gaping dents and shrapnel holes. Mercifully, the statue was whisked away to a safe hideout at Kaslik University. Artists commissioned to rehabilitate the statue were successful, in my view, in retaining its war-scarred character: a fitting memorial of Lebanon's belligerent past. Although the statue was ready, it did not reclaim its rightful place in Martyrs' Square without a contentious, often embarrassing, tug-of-war between President Emile Lahhoud and Rafik Hariri, prime minister at the time. As major shareholder in Solidere, Hariri was naturally eager to see such a national icon restored to its historic place. Given Lahhoud's visceral animosity to whatever Hariri stood for, he resorted to his hackneyed and dubious alibis to procrastinate. Incidentally, the Hariri family, through Banque Mediterranée, owns around 8 per cent of Solidere. The remaining shares are divided among more than 6,000 shareholders. No individual or company is allowed to own more than 10 per cent of Solidere. With a market capitalisation of more than 1.6 billion dollars, Solidere is considered the largest firm in Lebanon.[22]

A momentous turn of fateful events, propelled by Hariri's brutal murder on 14 February 2005, transformed the Bourj once again into a spectacular public sphere for the mobilisation of collective enthusiasm, emancipatory movements and voices of dissent. The solemn funeral procession of Hariri was not just a stunning and hushed outpouring

Hizbullah demonstrations

Opposition demonstrations

of grief. It turned into a resounding collective protest, transcending all the fractious loyalties and divisions within society. The uprising had all the uplifting elements of a pure and spontaneous, consciousness-raising happening. Unlike other forms of protest, it was an emotionally charged rally, not a riot. As of this writing, it has remained peaceful and measured. After two months of sustained protest, often bringing together close to one million agitated individuals from every segment of society, not one episode of disorderly conduct has been reported. It has also, as we shall see, generated structural and behavioural changes vital for sustaining the grassroots movements and their auxiliary emancipatory by-products. Again, without access to the Bourj as a pliable and porous public sphere, virtually none of this would have taken place.

Although the labels and collective identities of Beirut's centre were in perpetual change and oscillated, for varying interludes, over a dozen such names, they can be meaningfully regrouped into four general categories. First, as a *maidan, sahl, sahat* or *muntazah* in reference to it as an open space; ranging from an untamed, wild, natural and organic plain or field to a fairly regulated, landscaped and bounded courtyard or public garden. Second, as *Place des Canons*, connoting its colonial legacy; either in view of the brief Russian presence during the Crimean War or of the extended hegemony of the French Mandate. Third, during the Ottoman period it witnessed at least four successive changes in its popular identity in reference to epochal events or political transformations – *sahat al-Itihad, al-Hamidiyyah, Hadiqat al-Hurriyah* – and finally as Martyrs' Square to commemorate martyrdom and, hence, the felicitous nationalist sentiment by way of celebrating the country's liberation from Ottoman control. Fourth, as a *bourj*, perhaps its most lasting and enduring label, in reference to the one remaining relic of its ancient medieval walled ramparts.

Regardless of its varying and shifting identities, however, it has displayed throughout its eventful history a proclivity to become a vibrant setting for marshalling inventive and collective voices of dissent. Such prospects, given Lebanon's Janus-like character, are always double-edged. Homogenising as public spaces may be, particularly when they become such spectacular vectors for the vindication of grievances and collective dissent, they also run the risk, in a fragmented political culture like Lebanon, of becoming sources for reawakening segmental and parochial identities.

This is precisely what transpired in Beirut in the wake of the epochal events sparked by Hariri's assassination. In retrospect, one cannot but marvel at the set of fortuitous circumstances that unleashed and consolidated the quickening and exhilarating turn of events. Had Hariri's family, for example, opted to bury him in Saida rather in the Bourj, the very setting identified with Solidere's formidable restorative venture, it is doubtful whether his stirring martyrdom would have generated such dramatic consequences.

As the Bourj was filled by voices of the opposition, demanding not only to unveil the truth shrouding Hariri's murder but also to safeguard Lebanon's freedom, autonomy and independence, the pro-government and pro-Syrian forces took over another public square, Riad el-Solh, to portray and celebrate diametrically polarised views. Although the unfolding events were of much greater magnitude, they were a replay of earlier episodes when the socio-cultural and political identity of the Bourj was starkly different from its adjoining neighbourhoods. By virtue of such differences, most pronounced during the Ottoman period and the French Mandate, the Bourj was largely a meeting place of the upper bourgeoisie and newly affluent social groups eager to display their proclivity for conspicuous consumption and snob appeal. The underclass and itinerant labourers were drawn to quarters like *al-Sour* (present-day Riad el-Solh), which for a while continued to be the favoured meeting ground for the disfranchised and deprived strata of society.

With the public commemoration of the thirtieth day of Hariri's murder, the Bourj was once again destined as a public sphere to play host to a popular uprising with all the formidable and emancipatory manifestations of genuine self-propelled peoples' power movement. If anything, this is another vivid instance of the intimate and reciprocal interplay between social and spatial structures. A particular spatial setting, by virtue of its historic socio-cultural identity, can become a source of collective participation and empowerment. Once transformed, and thereby invested with new meanings and loyalties, the setting itself can become a more persuasive vector for nurturing the civic and cosmopolitan virtues of conviviality, pluralism and tolerance.

SIX

Public Sphere as Playground

If one were to single out a defining element of the Bourj as a public sphere, then certainly what stands out are some of its playful, convivial and carefree attributes which reinforced its proclivity for experimentation and socio-cultural diversity. It is these attributes that generated greater prospects for aesthetic sensibilities germane to the proliferation of cultural and artistic expressions capable of transcending the rigidities of time and space. This is why, perhaps, as a metaphor, the Bourj as an urban setting approximates some of the redemptive features of a *playground*. As an ideal type, a playground conjures up images of an open space conducive to both personal, intimate and familiar ties, along with more fluid, protean and changeable encounters. Indeed, as we have seen, throughout its chequered history, the Bourj has always been adept at accommodating both elements: the 'sacred' and the 'profane'.

These seemingly dissonant elements are not as mutually exclusive as they appear. Just as one can understand and account for the resurgence of religious and parochial identities in post-war Beirut, one can likewise appreciate the seductive appeal of the Bourj as a secular space where groups can let down their guard and become freer in testing society's limits of tolerance. Their indulgence becomes a testing ground for assessing how far they can stray without inviting the censure and reprimand of their society. This is why, as suggested earlier, those seemingly polarised dichotomies – the sacred and profane, cosmopolitan and provincial, universal and particular, global and local – have been all along malleable and porous lines. Being dialectical in character, they reinforce and enrich each other.

It is this malleability and liminality which rendered it more receptive for fostering mass and popular culture, mass politics, popular entertainment and, as of late, global consumerism with all its disheartening manifestations of commodification, kitsch and the debasement of the threatened residues of high culture, fine and performing arts. Clearly, the proliferation of popular meeting spaces, most visible around the Bourj and adjoining areas, has been very conducive to fostering mass and popular culture. As we have seen, during the Ottoman and Mandate interludes, the Bourj – by virtue of its Petit Serail and its public square – was fully used for ceremonial functions, official and magisterial declarations and receptions for dignitaries. But it was also a *muntazah*: that is, a public garden.

Whatever the Mandate period saw by way of the emergence of distinctly bourgeois spaces and lifestyles, it also introduced a new mass culture. What was restricted to the elite in the late Ottoman period started to spread to middle and lower strata. By the mid-1920s, a new phase of capitalist penetration swept in a multitude of imported consumer goods and practices. By then, as Thompson indicates, even little girls in the mountains of Lebanon were already importing French dresses.[1] By the early 1940s a set of household inventories showed that average families were already enjoying the use of many imported or Western-style products: electric irons, imported dress shirts, toothbrushes, aspirin, electric lamps, telephones, packaged cookies, canned meat, tuna and sardines, chairs made of iron and wood and even gramophone records.

Electricity did not only make family soirées and charity balls more glamorous; it also expanded the horizons of the urban public with extended tramlines, radios and telephones. Electricity was introduced to Beirut before WWI. In less than a decade Beirut had already close to 1,000 subscribers. Telephones, long confined to military networks, spread gradually during the 1930s to homes, offices and public spaces. By 1935, there were already phone-booths at most busy intersections in Beirut.[2]

Venues for Self-Expression and Conviviality

Much like the Latin Quarter in Paris, Soho in London, or Greenwich Village in Lower Manhattan, the Bourj had many of the features – such as they were at the time – of an avant-garde and counterculture setting. Hence, groups with leanings to experiment with new ideas and lifestyles or to let off steam against some injustice in society were drawn to it. Intellectuals, journalists, poets, political aspirants, activists and ideological groups of all persuasions created their own venues for self-expression, conviviality and camaraderie. In the absence of sanctioned outlets, virtually any space – a private office or shop, a discarded portion of a house, an atelier or workshop, let alone the coffee house, the restaurant and the hotel lobby – could be readily converted into proxy meeting places.

The proliferation of such surrogate public spheres, which often assumed the form of an '*arrière boutique*' approximating Goffman's 'backstage', were legion, particularly during the 1930s and 1940s. Typically, such places would first emerge on a tentative, casual basis, involving no more than a small core of devoted friends consumed by a common passion or interest. Quite often a disquieting occurrence, a serendipitous event, would gradually extend the appeal and notoriety of the place. *Dar al-Makchouf*, a literary and publishing circle which emerged in the early-1930s, is a prototype of such a success story. Toufiq Youssef Aouad, an active member of its inner circle, singles it out for the vital role it played in 'transforming the literary arts, both poetry and prose, from a quagmire of rigidity and imitation to the new horizons of creativity and innovation'.[3] It was the brainchild of Cheikh Fuad Hubeish, who, it seems, initiated the venture in 1935 in its modest premises at *Sahat as-Sour.*

As implied by its Arabic derivative, *al-Makchouf* was intended first to expose, denude and demystify the more seamy and hidden foibles of society. Indeed, the first few issues of the paper had a sensational, sleazy slant, perhaps a few elements of a latter-day tabloid, since they dealt with matters of sexual and public demoralisation. Soon, however, its central foursome – Houbeish, Aouad, Khalil Takeiddine and Elias Abou Chabakeh – decided to transform the lowbrow paper into a credible literary and critical journal. Their driving force, as articulated by Aouad, was to open up the journal as a venue for the nascent creative energies of young writers and, perhaps more importantly in their regard, to revive the disaffected and disconnected literary circle of ten, *Usbat al 'Ashra*.[4] During WWII the *Usbat*, despite its modest premises and resources, became one of the leading presses in the Arab world. It is credited with introducing the novel genre of pictorial magazines to the publishing industry. Although its daily edition stopped in 1952, its publishing house survived until 1973, just before the outbreak of civil unrest.[5]

Two other graphic representations of such '*arrière-boutiques*' are worth noting. Oddly, both were pharmacies that became notorious sites for public protest and political mobilisation. At the back of the Baaklini drugstore, one of Lebanon's most prominent painters and sculptor, César Gemayel, had established his first makeshift art studio. Partitioned by a portable wooden screen, the studio became at night a spirited meeting place for political, intellectual and artistic debates. In one incident, recorded by Elias Abou Chabakeh,[6] tells of how he, César Gemayel and three other of their colleagues – Adib Mathhar, Badawi al-Jabal and Baaklini – launched on 13 January 1925 a public protest in support of the demand for the appointment of a national governor. Emerging from the atelier, the demonstration gathered momentum as it rendezvoused with the already agitated crowds gathered at *Ahwet al-Azaz*, another popular haunt. Interestingly, by the time César Gemayel established his more substantial professional studio for figurative arts at the Sagesse School, it too became an inventive setting for some unintended and formidable transformations. The Sagesse was headed at the time by Mgr Jean Maroun, known for his progressive and futuristic visions regarding the role of the performing and applied arts in higher education. Gemayel's atelier became a meeting place for prominent public figures like Hamid Franjieh, Jubran Tueni, Takeiddine Solh, Joseph Najjar and Farid Trad. It was then that the formative plans and guidelines for the establishment of ALBA (Academie Libanaise des Beaux Arts) were formulated.

The other more notorious pharmacy-cum-public sphere was that of Pierre Gemayel, at the time still a budding public figure known for his athleticism and enthusiasm for

César Gemayel in his studio

Sidewalk café

youth movements. He was already making preliminary efforts for the establishment of the Phalange party. The pharmacy was established in 1930 as the New Gemayel Pharmacy. Given his public leanings and ambitions, it carried the pretentious motto of '*al-Jayyid min al-Jadeed*' ('the good is from the new'). The pharmacy quickly emerged as a haunt for equally spirited and politically minded public figures like Takeiddine Solh, Henry Faroun, Houssein Sej'an, Zuheir Ussayran and Muhammad Choukeir. It is from the pharmacy, logistically located at the south eastern intersection of the Bourj, that Gemayel and his circle of colleagues launched a score of their public protests, most prominent being the anti-government demonstrations of 1937 and that of 1934 in condemnation of the detention of President Bishara El-Khoury and Riad El-Solh. By the time Gemayel retired from his professional career as pharmacist to devote his time to politics, his brother Gabriel, the head of the Lebanese Olympic Foundation, and his two sports-minded sons,

Amin and Bashir, took over the affairs of the pharmacy. It promptly reinvented itself to accommodate the interests of the new patrons of their sports-minded clients.

Often one outfit would display so much dexterity and inventiveness that it would eagerly give up and surrender its existing enterprise to catch new and more promising ventures.[7] The case of Carillon, a Francophone veteran coffee shop centrally located on the western side of the square, is a striking prototype of such versatility. Although it retained its original location, its name, the audience it drew and the programmes it sponsored underwent successive alterations to accommodate epochal political events, national and regional transformations and changes in socio-cultural realities, lifestyles and public tastes. Late in the 1930s, the exclusive and fashionable coffee shop became a rather popular public theatre: the Theatro Nadia. Until the mid-1940s it hosted a regular programme of theatre productions written and directed by local playwrights. It changed hands again to become a commercial establishment to take advantage of the emergent supply needs of the post-war era.

Its fairly large premises were appropriate for a storage warehouse for flour and other staple products. In another two years, by 1948, it was renovated to reclaim its earlier identity as a theatre house. 'Nadia' became 'Farouk', still at the heyday of his flamboyant reign in Egypt. Soon after the monarchy was abolished by the 1952 military coup of Abdel Nasser and his army officers, its name changed again to *Masrah al Tahrir* ('Liberation') and remained so until the eruption of the civil war in 1975.

Kawkab al-Charq, doubtlessly one of the post popular haunts in the Bourj, also epitomised the plurality and shifting venues such meeting grounds came to accommodate with such noted enterprise and virtuosity. *Al-Kawkab*, occupying a picturesque old building, was not just a hotel (*locanda*), but it also housed a nightclub and one of the most popular restaurants, *Abou Afif*. This too served as surrogate place of assignation and a choice rendezvous for groups from all sectors of society. Its resourceful proprietor,

Collapse of Kawkab al-Charq (1934)

always with an eye on extending the client base of his already congested premises, established the first public reading room in Beirut. The open and free library also drew an enthusiastic regular audience eager to exploit this novel and generous offer. Its notoriety became more demonstrable as it faced its accidental and disastrous collapse in 1934. While being subjected to extensive renovation, the shaky scaffolding of the entire structure broke down, burying forty casualties beneath its rubble and wounding three times as many. The collapse of *Kawkab*, given its popular standing, precipitated a heady political crisis between the major political factions of the day.[8]

Public Entertainment and Social Mobilisation

This same intensity in symptoms of social mobilisation and mass communication – more so since they were exacerbated by rapid and unrelenting urbanisation – were sustained throughout the 1950s and 1960s. It was also then that Beirut's image as a cosmopolitan, sophisticated, polyglot meeting place of world cultures was being established.

All the socio-cultural indicators, crude and refined, attest to this overriding reality. From the sharp increases in the flow of domestic and foreign mail, number of telephones and passenger vehicles to the more stupendous growth in the volume and diversity of media exposure (particularly TV, radio and movie attendance), all spoke of appreciable increases in degrees of physical and psychic mobility and high levels of consumption throughout the strata of society. On these and other related indices, Lebanon enjoyed disproportionately higher rates than those observed in adjoining Arab states. Shortly after independence, for example, Lebanon could already boast of over 8,000 passenger vehicles, or about seven per 1,000 people, which was considerably more than Syria, Jordan, Iraq and Egypt had in 1960. By then, Lebanon had leaped to 73,000 or close to forty cars per 1,000, compared to an average of four to six among those neighbouring Arab states.[9] By the early 1920s, Beirut had already three or four cinemas.

In the public imagination, and as seen in the personal memoirs and reflections of those in their early youth during the 1930s and 1940s, the Bourj is almost always associated with their memorable days when they were just discovering the novelty and marvels of the cinema as a form of entertainment. Some speak about it as though it were an irresistible addiction. Since in some circles protective parents were likely to harbour ethical concerns about its dubious impact, the forbidden fruit became, as it were, all the more seductive. For nearly half a century, after all, the Bourj continued to be the exclusive and uncontested preserve for movie-going. In other words, almost three or four generations of Lebanese youth must have been indelibly marked by the experience. The Bourj and the cinema became contiguous entities.

It should be noted that, unlike in other cities in the Levant, cinemas were not as socially and politically contested forms of public entertainment. They made their appearance first in traditional quarters, sharing makeshift tents with itinerant shadow-puppet shows (*karakoz*), picture shows (*sandouq al firje*) and, most notably, storytellers (*hakawatis*). For a while, such modern forms of mass entertainment did not displace the popularity of the *hakawatis*, who continued to draw their conventional devotees. At dusk, and not unlike the 'happy hour' for today's corporate set, the pressured and overwrought found soothing release on their way home in the conviviality, engaging humour and accomplished virtuosity of the celebrated *hakawati*. After his makeshift stage is assembled (no more than a high table or wooden platform), usually in a familiar cul-de-sac or intimate intersection in the old *souks*, he ascends the platform with his traditional garb, *tarboush* and proverbial stick, his sole prop which he rhythmically taps to sustain the enthralled attention of his audience. Gradually, the gathering, as coffee and *arghilehs* are served, turns into an amiable, often rambunctious, interactive performance.

The *hakawati* should not be trivialised or dismissed lightly as a passing or nostalgic interlude. It clearly served more than just an entertaining outlet. It epitomised the coveted virtues of conviviality and camaraderie as they were being eroded by the nascent spatial and socio-cultural realities associated with the dislocating forces of urbanisation. They also represent some of the features inherent in street theatre and modern-day sitcoms' In this sense as 'third spaces' they become precursors to formalised stage productions in theatres designed and built for such explicit purposes.

Gradually, movie houses were temporarily located in the upper floors of cafés, restaurants, merchant hostels (*khans*), *locandas* or congested residential compounds. This was the case, it seems, for some of the early cinemas. *Zahrat Suriyya* was the first projection theatre in Beirut, built in 1909. At the time, it was still primitive and elementary and only operated manually. It did not survive for too long. It was destroyed by fire in 1921 and then rebuilt as the Parisienne coffee house. Crystal (1913), Cosmographe (1919), and Chef d'Oeuvre (1919) were the first three movie houses specially built for that purpose. The last was converted in 1924 to the Royal. From then on, and in

Hakawati

a quickening succession, a string of movie theatres started to be built, mostly by local Lebanese architects.[10]

Most prominent, perhaps, was the Opera (1931), built by Bahjat Abd el-Nour, evidently inspired by features of classical Egyptian antiquity. The Opera stood out as a distinct architectural icon. For a while, it was emblematic of the new massive structures that eventually started to punctuate the square around the Bourj. So photogenic, it served as a majestic and picturesque backdrop for commemorating visits of foreign dignitaries. The triumphal visit of Charles de Gaulle in 1942 was one such spectacle. The Opera, incidentally, is the sole movie house that was restored and rehabilitated into a Virgin Store in 2000.

Given the stupendous popularity of the cinema as a popular pastime, in less than two decades, the Bourj and its outlying streets were virtually decked with movie theatres. Some like the trio – the Roxy, the Dunia and the Empire – were literally adjoining each other. The Roxy, designed by Elias Murr in 1932, introduced for the first times elements of Art Deco. This set the pattern to be emulated in the Dunia, the Empire and the Majestique, built approximately around the same time. As with other novel outlets of popular culture (cafés, bars, billiard lounges, brothels, etc), it was the Bourj that became the first permanent space for movie houses. Incidentally, because of their commodious premises and capacity to accommodate large audiences, cinemas were often used as lecture halls, auditoriums for French-sponsored charity events and other cultural venues and political mobilisation. For example, as early as 1925 the nascent Communist party held a meeting with workers in the Crystal cinema. In October of 1935, a group of students from Italian schools attended a showing of *Napoléon* at the Empire theatre. They all donned black shirts and yelled 'Long live Il Duce!' The provocation incited an affray between them and other students in the audience.[11]

The proliferation of movie theatres, many with such striking and monumental architecture, started to overwhelm the cityscape of the Bourj by the mid-1940s. Its identity and public image, in fact, became almost synonymous with cinemas. One's orientation and points of reference were almost always circumscribed in terms of the location of a particular movie house. By sheer number and the compact area within which they are located, their density is truly staggering. Perhaps it is unmatched elsewhere. By the early 1950s, just before cinemas started to decentralise in pursuit of greener pastures elsewhere, there were about twenty-five such outlets within the Bourj area alone.[12] Many of the cinemas, particularly these built during the French Mandate, were instrumental in introducing some of the contemporary architectural novelties – Art Nouveau and Art Deco – imported from across the Atlantic. The reproduction of such composite styles was visible in theatres like the Dunia, the Roxy and the Rivoli, among others. These dark theatres, reflecting Americanism with rigorous and refined lines and sometimes in monumental shape and volume, were also landmarks because they were the first instances of concrete being used.[13] Many, by the way, were designed by some of the leading architects of the day, such as Farid Trad (Dunia), Bahjat Abdel

Opera

Empire

Radio City

Rivoli

Destruction of Rivoli

Nour (Opera), Said Hjeil (Rivoli), George Araman and Giorgio Ricci (Capitol). All these works, with the exception of Opera, were demolished in 1993 to make way for the square's reconstruction. The variety of the premises, in terms of their aesthetic and socio-economic standards (first, second or third degrees), the programmes they offered (crime, comedy, western, romance, etc) and language (English, French, Arabic) compounded the number by extending the choice by its monetary affordability and the particular genre each of the houses specialised in.

During WWI German films had predominated in the three-to-four movie houses existing at the time.[14] After 1918, French and American silents started to prevail. Local favourites included Tarzan, police serials, westerns and the comedies of Charlie Chaplin and the French star Max Linder.[15] It was not, it seems, until the early 1930s that cinemas were equipped with projectors. Also, a measure of the popularity of cinema, most newspapers introduced regular movie columns.

Movie-going had become so popular for the youth that as early as 1931 students staged a march to the Bourj to demand more affordable tickets, just as they had earlier protested for cheaper tramway fares and electricity charges. If anything, this was symptomatic of how pervasive movie attendance had become. About the same time it began to arouse serious concern and public debate in the press. For example, in 1928 the Jesuit newspaper al-Bashir called for more stringent censorship, particularly with regard to their presumed corruptive impact on the young.

In a series of editorials, al-Bashir addressed issues of censorship and proposed the formation of such boards to prevent the demoralisation of youth by movie stars. A Catholic Youth Circle was establish and started, among other things, to urge families not to let their daughters go to the cinema alone. They proposed instead that the whole family could attend only the Circle's own, pre-censored films.[16] In 1933, a group of concerned mothers petitioned the Lebanese president to increase censorship. The French High Commissioner interfered to veto their demand, it seems.[17] By the time movies spread to other segments of society, Muslim leaders likewise started to demand an increasing measure of control over films perceived to be offensive to public morality. The Mufti, for example, strongly denounced the film Adam and Eve, which had been seen in Beirut earlier without any objection. He invoked Ottoman law to justify his opposition since, in his view, the film presented a demeaning portrayal of holy personages.[18]

It should be noted that the French authorities – High Commissioner de Martel at the time – did not always acquiesce to the demands for stricter censorship. Some of the particular episodes were so testy that they often provoked political crises. For example, when Maronite and Jesuit groups in Beirut protested in June 1934 against the showing of Rosier de Mme Husson (The Rosebush of Madame Husson), which had already received the seal of approval by French authorities, their protest was initially ignored. It was only when the Catholic clergy incited students to escalate their opposition by throwing stink bombs into the movie house where the film was showing, that the high commissioner promised to reconsider the censorship code in an effort to appease Catholic and Muslim concerns.[19]

So polemical had the issue of cinema and public morality become that Catholic students began publishing a special movie magazine, *L'Ecran*, which became their platform to vent concerns about how to shelter the young from the corrupting influence of films deemed offensive to public taste. For example, one of their demands was to have heads of households represented on the censorship board. The Maronite Patriarch, Antoine Arida, pronouncing himself guardian of public morality, went on in 1935 to demand the closure of all cinemas and houses of prostitution. He declared that 'it is France that perverts our people and introduces immorality to them'.[20] Muhi al-Din al-Nusuli, editor of *Bayrut* daily, went further in 1936, denouncing cinemas as seedy pockets of vulgarisation: 'they are favoured places of foreign women to seduce innocent Lebanese men and, thereby, corrupting their national loyalty'.[21]

L'Ecran did not remain passive at the time. As French authorities dallied in their promises, the periodical along with *L'Equipe* (a voluntary association of Catholic students in Beirut) developed their own advocacy strategies. *L'Ecran* started to provide their readers with its own assessment and rating of films. *L'Equipe* resorted to confrontational measures by often disrupting popular films perceived as damaging to public morality. For example, in January 1940, twelve members of this group were detained by police for protesting nudity in a film at the Rex theatre.[22]

Women's accessibility to the cinema also became, not unexpectedly, a contested issue. Initially, women were permitted to attend segregated movie houses. By the mid-1930s there were exclusive women-only screenings three or four times a week.[23] This is an interesting development since women were denied access to street theatres (*hakawatis*) or other performances in makeshift places like cafés and *khans*. Naturally, because regular movies were in enclosed spaces, it is understandable that they should be deemed more acceptable than outdoor and live performances. Actors on a screen cannot, after all, see the faces of women in the audiences!

The inference one may readily extract from this is that the Bourj – as in other venues of popular culture, socio-economic and political mobilisation – was the epicentre where such controversies were initiated and debated. Is this not what a public sphere is all about? Although no reliable surveys exist as yet to ascertain the actual magnitude of women's participation in such forms of popular entertainment, it is clear, because of the public debate the cinema had aroused at the time, that a fairly large portion of the upper and middle classes were already movie goers and that such opportunities were beginning to trickle down to lower-class groups. The comparative study of Prothro and Diab on changing family patterns in the Arab world, although done considerably later, still presented evidence from the sample of respondents to indicate that, indeed, some women had already been exposed to movies by the 1930s and that, by a decade later, all of them had.[24] It is in this sense, as Elizabeth Thompson correctly argues, that the issue becomes of particular significance. It allows us to consider its implications at three levels: colonial, class and gender.[25]

Mandate authorities, given their 'civilising mission', were naturally eager to use the beguiling allure of the cinema to disseminate and, hopefully, endear the diverse communities of Beirut to aspects of French culture and lifestyles. Its class context is also meaningful since this was also the period when the nascent bourgeoisie was groping to validate its commitment to some of the instrumental, utilitarian and consumer expectations of middle-class values. Finally, the subtle and contested gender implications were also unavoidable, since women in Beirut had already had a head start over their cohorts in other cities in the Arab world in grappling with issues of emancipation, justice, autonomy and equal access to avenues of participation in the public sphere. For example, we are told that by 1930 women in Beirut had already stopped seeking their husband's consent before leaving home. Hence, outdoor shopping in stores was no longer the exclusive chore or privilege of men.[26] A score of social historians have also confirmed that Christian Beirutis had generally adopted Parisian styles by 1914 and that if their Muslim compatriots continued to wear the veil, they were inclined to take them off when downtown and put them back on as they returned to their neighbourhoods.[27]

This is another revealing symptom of the emancipatory and liberating proclivities of the Bourj as a public sphere. It predisposed women to part with some of the confining elements of their local culture. By doing so, they were in effect crossing boundaries and negotiating more adaptive and fluid identities and lifestyles.

The Bourj's monopoly as an exclusive movie preserve started to decline by the late-1950s and early-1960s as movies started to relocate their premises to the new suburban quarters of Hamra, Verdan, Achrafieh, Sodeco and the like. The shift carried with it some distinct changes in both architectural style and scale. During the 1930s and 1940s there were, it must be recalled, less than a handful of architects to design the twenty-five movie theatres that once graced the Bourj's cityscape and shaped its public image. Lebanon is blessed today with an expansive generation of gifted and resourceful young architects. They are all proficient and skilled in the use of modern and postmodern architectural styles and their associated technologies. In no time the outlying suburbs of Beirut were, and continue to be, punctuated by a relentless stream of massive structures of centres accommodating often a set of six to eight theatres: Planet Abraj, Sodeco Square, the Concorde, the Dunes, the ABC, the Espace, the Galaxy, Sofil, the St Elie, etc.

For the moment, the Bourj and its adjoining CBD are without any movie houses. With the exception of Opera, which was spared the ravages of the civil war, the other twenty-four movie houses were either heavily destroyed during the fighting or bulldozed to clear the grounds for reconstruction. It is very unlikely that the square could once again attract the independent single units of old. If they are to resurface, they will most likely be part of the overbearing towers intent to celebrate monumentality. Indeed, a few such projects are currently being considered.

While the Bourj is no longer the epicentre that at the turn of the nineteenth century heralded the entry of the cinema into the entire region, Beirut and its suburbs have not been timid in this regard. Early in the 1950s, if measured by the number of movie seats *per capita*, Beirut was already living up to its reputation as the movie capital of the world.

Per-capita movie attendance was five per year. In another decade, it increased fivefold, a close second to Hong Kong.[28] During the same period, the number of movie theatres leaped from 48 to 170, an increment of twelve new houses per year. The accessibility of such theatres, rendered more appealing, as we have seen, by the variety of films, plush surroundings and low prices, only served to whet the proverbial appetite of Lebanese from all classes and age groups for this form of public entertainment. Indeed, before the advent of TV and home videos, anticipating, attending, and talking about movies already constituted the undisputed, most popular and most absorbing national pastime. Nothing as yet has transpired, despite the advent of other forms of public and home entertainment, to detract from the irresistible allure movie-going continues to elicit within virtually all groups in society.

The Commercialisation of Sexual Outlets

The public imagination of those who knew the Bourj existentially, before its beleaguering destruction during the civil war, was not only intimately associated with their initiation into the novel adventures of movie-going, street cafés, boisterous restaurants, bars, nightclubs and street demonstrations. The Bourj was also the *only* place where one could have been initiated into the shady and stigmatising world of prostitution. From its inception as an unregulated outlet for commercial sex, the Bourj has been notorious, even infamous, for sheltering the houses of ill repute; derisively and popularly known as *Souk al-Awadem* (literally, 'the Market of the Virtuous'!).

Initially, the area or *souk*, had no special identity. Historical records are not very definitive with regard to both its exact location or time of appearance. Some sources merely referred to '*Nazlet al-Pore*' or '*Khalf al-Bank*': in other words, 'the passage down to the port' or 'the area behind the Ottoman Bank'. Others maintain that it was located in *Souk al-Khammarine* ('the wine-sellers' market') between the Petit Serail and the port, east of the Muslim cemetery.[29] Actual dates as to when it started to be frequented by regular customers are also a bit hazy. One source traces this back to 1880.[30] Another, to 1895, after the enlargement of the port when some of the '*maisons de tolerance*', as they started to be called, had to move up in the direction of the city's growing commercial and administrative centre.

What is fairly certain, however, is that with the return of the French army in 1920, the number of prostitutes ('*al-mumsat*') increased to about 1,250: 400 of whom being Turkish, Greek, French, English and the remainder Palestinian, Syrian and Lebanese.[31] This sudden preponderance of prostitutes – and journalistic accounts of the day were already declaring it as the 'golden age' – aroused the concern of public health officials with regard to the transmission of venereal diseases. Indeed, the first measures were promulgated in 1921 to combat the outbreak of one such epidemic among French troops stationed there. Not only prostitutes, but dancers, singers and other so-called 'artists' were required to register with the local police. They had to carry identification cards, attend to their work in designated brothels and be subject to medical inspection twice a week. Special dispensaries or clinics were established within the district for that purpose. Those who absented themselves from such examinations were taken to court. Exit from the district was also closely monitored. For those who wished to abdicate their work, arrangements were made to have them live with a guardian.[32]

In 1931 the Ottomans introduced the first decree to recognise and regulate prostitution (*al-da'arah*) as a legal profession. The law defined a prostitute as any woman who submitted to sexual intercourse ('*irtikab al-fahsha*') in return for a monetary reward, overt or covert. It also distinguished between 'public houses' and other 'places of assignation' and declared all secret and unregulated prostitution illegal and subject to prosecution. Because of these restrictive measures, the number of registered prostitutes was reduced to 624, distributed among sixty-two houses. This is almost half the number the district was drawing during its heyday. Paradoxically, although depleted in number, the prostitutes and the district were becoming more visible and notorious. Like elsewhere in the Bourj, this was the period when all enterprises and entertainment ventures were becoming more commercially minded and attuned to novel modes of advertising, marketing and promotional design.

The enterprising '*patronas*' gave the maligned image of their tainted and damnable quarter, at least in the public imagination, the face-lift it needed to transform it into a more welcoming place. The prostitutes were identified with particular houses. They acquired 'brand names' which popularised the commodity they were marketing. Selling sex, in other words, was being increasingly commodified. With the advent of neon lights and other forms of imaging and public display, the district was festooned with decorative billboards advertising the 'stars' and celebrities of the house. To this day, regular habituates of the district, or those who made inquisitive but furtive sojourns into it, can still recollect the glittering names.[33] Sometimes the labels reflected a special personal attribute ('*Leila el Chacra*': 'the blonde'), or an identity of a particular place ('*Zbeidi al Mizranieh*') or a particular city ('*Hoda al-Halabie*') or a national identity ('*Hikmat al-Misrie*') or the 'French Antoinette' or the 'English Lucy'. The most interesting were those that bore their maternal identity: ('*Faride Im Abdou*').[34]

Of course, the most notorious was Marica Espiredone, the Greek emigrant who managed to cast her mythical shadow over the entire district for over half a century. Her epic rags-to-riches biography is riveting and has been told and retold scores of times. The little orphaned Greek girl, still in her early teens, disembarked at the port in 1912. She had nothing except a few pieces of currency tucked under her sparse garments and her nubile beauty, which instantly attracted the attention of a Turkish officer. Overwhelmed by her reception at the port, dense with fierce-looking and desirous Turkish soldiers and with no woman in sight, she had no choice but to accept the officer's offer to go home with him to assist his wife as a household help. From then on her story is a rerun of a most familiar theme in the recruitment and induction of prostitutes into the profession.

Red-light district (1960s)

Red-light district (1960s)

Already scarred and traumatised by an early initiation into sex by her mother's lover in Greece, Marica was a hapless victim of further such abuse in her new life in Beirut. In no time, the wife discovered her husband in bed with Marica. She was summarily dismissed and had to drift aimlessly in search of shelter. A handsome French officer, single this time, offered her the shelter she desperately needed. Again taken by her exceptional beauty, he lavished her first with loving attention and gifts. Soon, however, the relationship turned sour and violent. This time she ran away. After days and nights of roaming around the city in search of shelter she ended up on a sidewalk of the Medawar neighbourhood next to the Bourj. It is there that Maria al Halabieh, a prominent *patrona* and pimp, was instantly attracted by her potential, given her good looks and foreign accent.

From then, on her story departs markedly from the conventional and hackneyed prototypes of innocent and gullible young girls being taken in by city slickers who live off their earnings from prostituting their bodies. Marica was much too shrewd and enterprising to fall victim to such devious foils. In less than a year she became so popular and widely sought by prominent men who became her regular clients that she managed to break away from Maria's house and establish one on her own. Street-smart, savvy and quick-witted, she applied her business acumen to convert her house into a salon-like lounge – almost a drawing room – for the rich and famous. She recruited a team of resourceful and ruthless pimps and procurers who solicited prize recruits to meet the growing demand for her services. Her business was so lucrative that she was able to rent one of the most spacious and attractive buildings on Mutanabi Street: a three-storey walk-up suburban villa with Italian-style arches and elaborate balconies and balustrades.

With remarkable foresight and business sense, she went about mapping out the twelve rooms as though eager customers were purchasing sex as if it were any other ordinary commodity. Hence blondes, brunettes, lean girls or those more substantial in size and endowments and of different age groups etc were placed in separate, well-defined quarters. More appealingly, she converted part of the ground floor into a lounge and bar, thereby adding an aesthetic and non-mercenary dimension to her brothel. Indeed, during the 1940s and 1950s her house in that infamous quarter became a meeting place for the rich and famous. The memories of those who felt privileged being part of her intimate entourage are replete with nostalgic tales about the engaging and spirited discussions they conducted there, often unaware that this was also a public space associated with debauchery and the commercialisation of sexual encounters. They also spoke admiringly of her selfless generosity, benevolence for church-sponsored charity and concern for the poor and downtrodden.[35]

One could express this in more conceptual terms. Marica displayed very early in her career symptoms of a paradigm shift in the analysis of prostitution that was to become salient to the early 1990s. She was transforming herself from being merely a 'sex object' to a 'sex worker': from being a quintessentially passive and resigned victim of male domination and manipulation to being a wilful agent who actively constructed her work life.[36]

Marica

The fact that the red-light district, with all the sordid and disreputable activities it was attracting, was becoming so compelling and visible in the very heart of the nation's capital did not go unnoticed. By the late-1940s and early-1950s, judging by the extensive press coverage, the whole issue of legal prostitution was beginning to provoke public concern. The fact that the main street in the district was often named '*al-Mutanabi*', after one of the most celebrated Arab poets, compounded the outrage and contempt of the public even further. In their view, this was clearly not a fitting tribute to such a distinguished cultural legacy.

In their reactions to legalised brothels, moralists at the time harboured different ethical dispositions. Traditionalists, particularly heads of religious communities and sectarian associations, were inclined to regard prostitution as a necessary evil; a safety valve for the release of the superfluous sexual energies and untapped libidos of the virile, youthful segments of the population. In this regard, the prostitute protects the virtue of the family and the sanctity of marriage. If such outlets were unavailable, the purity and chastity of women would be, in their view, threatened. Others were more inclined to condemn prostitution because it involved the commodification of sexual intimacy, the confinement of women and the restriction of their freedom in prison-like sanctuaries.

By the early-1950s, it must be recalled, more and more countries were already closing their medically inspected brothels. The French, for example, who for many years were chief proponents of regulated prostitution, abolished it in 1946. Their famed '*maisons de tolerance*' were all outlawed. It was this system, by the way, under Napoleon I, which they brought over to Lebanon. In the US – with the exception of the state of Nevada – prostitution was, for all practical purposes, also made illegal. Likewise, Italy and Japan, among others, also closed their licensed houses in 1958. The British adopted perhaps the most realistic response. Rather than directing their attention to the futile efforts of suppressing prostitution, they were more concerned with preventing some of its harmful consequences and by-products. Although it was not licensed, prostitution in Britain was not illegal, and the Wolfenden Report of 1957 argued against making it so. As such, no prostitute was punished for what she is, but if she did something to promote her trade, such as street solicitation or advertising, then she was penalised.

A third group, while recognising the need for regulated brothels, were proposing their relocation to a less visible or prominent place. With the gradual liberalisation of sexual mores, more of the upper and middle strata of society were already enjoying greater access to more natural and humane outlets for sexual encounters. A fairly large number, however, for a variety of considerations, were still in need of licensed prostitutes. As long as such a demand persists – and it was not likely to disappear overnight in Lebanon – supply always has a way of meeting it: by fair means if possible, and foul means if necessary. Outlawing prostitution carried the risk, this group felt, of shutting off an expedient safety valve. In so doing, we could well be encouraging non-prostitution outlets as an underground and disguised activity: the profession will only change its form, and the prostitute her tactics. In most cities, for example, the few remaining brothels and houses of assignation were already becoming massage parlours, escort bureaus, Turkish baths and the like. The prostitute, through the help of pimps and procurers, was driven underground and forced to resort to clandestine means.

It is for such reasons that methods of dealing with prostitution were at the time undergoing a fundamental change. Historically, all such methods were steered in the direction of penalising or stigmatising the prostitute. By the early 1950s, at least in most Western societies, efforts were being made to legislate against third parties and to punish those who live off the earnings of prostitutes.

The prostitutes in the Bourj were already beginning to feel such pressures and were, hence, becoming legitimately anxious about their future prospects in the district. Manifestations of such changes had, in fact, appeared earlier and were, in part, associated with the regulative measures introduced by the UN in 1948. Alarmed by the proliferation of 'white slave' traffic and other forms of involuntary prostitution, the UN issued a declaration urging all member countries to abolish legalised prostitution. Lebanon concurred but requested a timeframe before they could comply with the intent of the prohibitive declaration. A decade elapsed before the Municipal Council of Beirut could issue their regulative decree of 1958. In it, the Council promised to suspend issuing any new licenses and to close any house after its *'patrona'* or proprietor retired or gave up the premises. Hence, by the 1950s the number of licensed houses was fixed at seventy-five, accommodating 207 prostitutes. Incidentally, the number of houses was determined by the number of permits issued. As such, there may well be more than one 'house' on the same floor, let alone the same building.

If and when clandestine streetwalkers were accosted, because of the UN decree they were issued a permit without being accommodated in the brothels. This rather unusual form of prostitution was defined as *'Mumis Sirriyeh'*: that is, as a secret but licensed prostitute. Although operating outside the red-light district, they were subject to municipal control and surveillance. By the mid-1960s these numbered about 175: an indication that there was still, despite the presumed liberalisation of sexual mores, an appreciable demand for commercial prostitution. The results of a rare empirical survey of legal prostitution in Lebanon, based on personal interviews with virtually all the sample of resident prostitutes in the red-light district at the time, are very revealing and instructive in this regard.[37]

First, the Bourj prostitutes were still comparatively active. The typical prostitute was investing around nine to ten hours per day in her work and was receiving, on average, almost one client per hour. Considering the perceptible increase in amateur and freelance prostitution, this fairly high estimate is clearly an indication that there was still a relatively substantial demand for the type of services the Bourj prostitute was offering at the time. For example, a comparable London prostitute was, around the same time, receiving not more than twenty to twenty-five clients per week; rendering her counterpart in the Bourj three times as busy.

Second, although Marica and her colleagues were fairly busy, around 85 per cent of

Red-light district destroyed

the prostitutes were already beginning to complain that their business had been declining. Clearly, their 'golden age' was a thing of the past, and they often evoked those days with considerable nostalgia and reverie. They were equally astute in attributing the decline in the volume of their business to three sources of societal competition: the preponderance of 'stereo-clubs' and bars, the car and the moral looseness and licentious predispositions of the so-called *bint 'ayleh* (well-bred family girl). With equal bitterness, they were also lamenting the decline in the socio-economic standing of their clients. Gone were the days when the elite of the upper bourgeoisie would drive into Mutanabbi Street with their mule-driven carriages or chauffeured limousines and their accompanying retinue of well-groomed and well-mannered men! These, along with a growing number of their counterparts in the new middle class, were already enjoying easier access, more natural, 'nobler' and adventurous outlets for satisfying their sexual urges. The proliferation of '*garçonieres*' and single men's apartments in Hamra and West Beirut were tangible evidence of such a relaxation in sexual lifestyles.

The destruction of the red-light district during the early rounds of fighting for control of the city's centre in 1975 and 1976, although it eradicated a few of the noteworthy architectural emblems in the neighbourhood, was altogether a propitious windfall. If judged by the quality of the industry and the expectations of those providing the services within it, there was little that could have been revived. The district was in the throes of its own tortuous demise. The prostitutes themselves were beginning to be aware that their life in a confined brothel was misbegotten and short-lived. They were also embittered by the alienating character of their work. Indeed, the bulk of the superannuated prostitutes still tending their declining trade were simply awaiting their imminent retirement and indemnification. Early in the 1960s the government was in fact already considering the prospects of moving the brothels to Sid al Bushriyyeh, a neighbourhood in the north eastern suburbs of Beirut. Clandestine prostitution, part of the early manifestation of the bourgeoning global sex industry, was already beginning to permeate society.

By then, and perhaps more so than other societies in the region, Beirut has not been spared some of the aberrant consequences of globalisation and mass consumerism. International migration has carried with it a dramatic change in the sex industry, particularly in the manner with which a growing number of consumers are now purchasing their sexual services and products. As in other societies, particularly those where tourism is likewise a viable sector, prostitution is now part and parcel of a thriving adult entertainment industry. The accessibility of X-rated videos, adult cable shows, computer pornography, adult magazines, even commercial telephone sex has, like elsewhere, invaded the inner sanctum of the home. In this respect, the globalisation of sexuality has paradoxically contributed to its privatisation. Porn, both in its 'soft' and 'hardcore' varieties existed in some of the run-down and dilapidated movie houses in Beirut during the war and shortly after. The past decade has, however, seen porn migrate from the movie houses to the privacy of the viewers' own living rooms. Little can be done to avert or control such an aggressive and tenacious invasion.

In tandem with such incursions, perhaps even because of them, clandestine prostitution in its various forms is now a thriving and income-generating industry. A recent study claims that the industry is worth an estimate of 140 million dollars annually and employs over 4,000 people.[38] As in other sectors of the post-war economy, its good fortunes are, it seems, part of the unintended fallout from 9/11. The market is clearly in an upscale mode, reminiscent of the heydays of the *maisons de tolerance* during Marica's notorious tenure in al-Mutanabi Street. The industry, with all its X-rated tourist attractions, caters now to a wealthier and more discerning set of clients demanding a level and variety of services comparable to those found in other capitals in the world notorious for jet-set prostitution, call-girl rackets and other nefarious outlets.

Taking advantage of a loophole in the country's public-health laws dating back to 1931, which penalises those who facilitate, encourage or live off acts of prostitution but not the prostitute herself, bevies of shrewd entrepreneurs emerged to exploit the potential inherent in such a laissez-faire setting. The most thriving part of this largely global industry is represented by the 'super nightclubs' that dot the coastline between Jounieh and Maameltein. There are somewhere between eighty and ninety such upscale joints in those tourist neighbourhoods. Each club is entitled to employ up to sixty hostesses, mostly girls from Eastern Europe or the former Soviet Union.[39] Others of lesser quality, and not as concentrated, can be spotted around Hamra, Ain Mreysseh, Mansourieh, Sin El File, Hazmieh and mountain resorts like Aley. To qualify as a 'super nightclub', the establishment must offer a cabaret and the hostesses are recruited as 'artistes' for six-month renewable periods. Only a few of the larger clubs provide such artistic performances or entertainment, however.

The main attraction is the opportunity to spend time with a girl of one's choice; the fee – ranging from 60 to a 100 dollars – depends on the quality of the drink and the time spent, not exceeding ninety minutes. The clubs are not bordellos, and the girls are not allowed to provide any sexual favours. Undercover policemen or Sureté Generale officers are expected to monitor the premises by making unannounced spot checks. In principle, customers are not permitted to leave with girls from the club. For a certain fee, however, a man is entitled to 'ask the girl out' during her 'off' hours, from one o'clock to seven o'clock. It is during these interludes that the girls tend to their trade. Depending on their personal appeal and resourcefulness, the business could be exceedingly lucrative, even though by the terms of their contract they are expected to share a stipulated portion of their earnings with the club proprietor and, often, the hotel manager for paying off security officers.[40]

The 'super nightclubs', generating an estimated 100 million dollars annually, is by far the most lucrative sector of the expanding sex industry in post-war Lebanon. Since the bulk of the workforce providing the services in this stigmatised profession are itinerant trans-nationals, some of the ethical reservations that traditional moralists continue to hold with regard to prostitution are partly allayed. Lebanon, however, like other countries involved in the illegal trafficking of women for sexual exploitation, has a questionable record on human rights which on occasion prompts the government to be more prohibitive in its restrictive measures.

Although not as visible or lucrative, the tourist sex industry has other outlets that cater to the eroticised needs of customers. Most prominent are massage parlours, often euphemistically labelled as anti-stress centres. Technically, the parlours are legal since licenses are usually sought for a hygienic 'treatment centre'. Under such a therapeutic guise, they openly advertise in the local press, and their premises are located in respectable residential or business quarters. They generate over 20 million dollars annually. Given their accomplished ethnic skills in this regard, most employees are Filipino or Asian women who attend to about seven customers per day. The session, lasting thirty to forty minutes, usually costs around 20 dollars – plus all the other additional services, up to 30 dollars – which are kept by the masseuse.

The three other conventional outlets, the closest to those offered by the traditional brothels, are the bar-girls, call-girls and freelancers. Together they generate another 20 million dollars annually. There are about two dozen such bars, recognisable by their traditional red lights, in the Hamra and Ain Mreysseh districts. They are usually managed by mature, enterprising *patronas* and employ about four women, mostly Egyptian and North African. The cost of a drink is no different from other ordinary bars. Unlike 'super nightclubs', the women are available – for about 50 dollars – for sexual encounters in a secluded modest room behind the bar or elsewhere in the premises. Since these establishments are unlicensed, the police have to be kept quiet and at a distance.

More upscale and glamorous are the rings of fearsomely popular Lebanese girls, often aspiring models, singers, dancers or those seeking marriage partners, who ply their trade in hotel lobbies, lounges and other fashionable resorts. The more ambitious advertise their 'escort' and other services in the many glossy magazines in the hope of being picked up by one of the agents who arrange, under a rich variety of proxies, regular weekend party charter flights between Beirut and the Gulf states.

The lowest on the totem pole of commodified sex, and the most accessible and affordable component, are the ordinary streetwalkers. They are generally Lebanese, Syrians and Africans who may be seen on highways, Raouche, Janah and popular intersections. Others might be domestic help moonlighting on their days off. As of late, many are frequenting cafés, bars and open meeting spaces of downtown Beirut: their original abode of old!

The Press as a Fourth Estate

Perhaps its most definitive expression as a public sphere is the role the Bourj played in nurturing the genesis and growth of journalism. The earliest Lebanese paper – *Hadiqat al-Akhbar* ('the Garden of News') was established in 1858 on the narrow and yet-unpaved street connecting the Bourj to the port. Just as the Bourj was the pacesetter in launching and accommodating the first movie houses, nightclubs, cabarets, bars, public reading rooms, brothels and public gardens, on a more enabling and vital level it can also boast of ushering in and sustaining Lebanon's credible image as a 'nation of journalists'. Although newspapers had appeared a little earlier in Egypt, Beirut has had the longest and most continuous press history in the Arab world.[41]

Because of their country's comparatively higher and earlier rates of literacy and exposure to liberal forms of Western education, the Lebanese have long displayed a distinct predilection and talent for establishing papers and periodicals sustained by an irresistible compulsion for reading them. Soon after *Hadiqat al-Akhbar* appeared, and in quick succession, the number of daily papers and periodicals increased exponentially. By the turn of the century there were already about forty such publications.[42]

This is certainly a dense volume of newsprint for a population of about 120,000. More importantly, they were also elitist in content and style, published by intellectuals with a literate and critical reading audience in mind. Since the commercial and service facilities were all at the time still concentrated around the city centre, the Bourj and adjacent neighbourhoods were home to virtually all the founding papers.

As in other dimensions of public life, the striking penchant the Lebanese showed for journalism was nurtured and cultivated within a network of family tradition. This intimate association between families and careers in journalism is of long standing. Families, more than ideological parties, advocacy groups or political platforms, have been the settings within which some of the most gifted journalists received their tutelage and commitments of journalistic careers. Illustrious families, such as Aql, Khazin, Taqla, Tueni, Zeidan, Sarruf, Gemayel, Tibi, Mukarzal, Awad, Taha, Nsouli and Machnouq, among others, have all produced successive generations of journalists. Fathers served as mentors and role models and often had direct impact on initiating scions into the venerable family tradition and in honing their skills and cultivating contacts.[43]

The critical, liberal foundation of Beirut's papers could not have fared well within the despotic and centralised reign of Sultan Abdul Hamid (1876–1909). Many Lebanese journalists were compelled to flee to Egypt to escape the strict and periodic censorship imposed by the Ottomans. There they joined the core of so-called 'Lebanese secularists', such as Yaqub Sarruf, Faris Nimr, Salim and Bishara Taqla, who already had a head start in launching some of the leading Arab journals and periodicals. Others sought refuge in the capitals of Europe from where they sustained their unsparing, often vitriolic, opposition to Ottoman despotism.

Those who stayed behind did not, however, restrain their critical stance. Like their expatriates, they were not just oppositional in their stance. They were instrumental in spearheading the surging sentiments in support of the Arab nationalist movement. They paid dearly for it. Sixteen out of twenty-one the martyrs hung on 6 May 1916 were

Al-Hayat

journalists.[44] Indeed, it is telling that so many journalists were martyred on their own turf, as it were: on the very ground which nurtured their voices of dissent, protest and liberation. Their acts of 'treason' were attributed to nothing more than stirring up public opinion against Ottoman despotism and for demanding freedom and independence. The Martyrs' Square and the National Holiday on 6 May have since remained a fitting memorial to their legendary and heroic acts of nationalist sacrifice.

During the French Mandate (1920–41), the penchant of the Lebanese to publish periodicals and newspapers was revived. Some forty papers and more than 300 specialised magazines devoted to literature, education, political satire, women's issues, religion and cinema, appeared during these two eventful decades. The French were liberal in granting licenses, but they were also prohibitive in imposing their restrictive measures on recalcitrant journalists. They were not sent to the gallows, but the French did, often arbitrarily, suspend a few of the intractable voices that had championed their country's territorial integrity and rights of self-determination at the time. For example, during its first six years, from 1933 to 1939, *an-Nahar* was suspended by the government no less than fifteen times because of its criticism of the Mandate powers and for its campaigns for constitutional government.[45]

Lebanon's independence was tenuously held together by the *Mithaq al-Watani* (National Covenant) of 1943, which was based on a delicate consociational arrangement which allowed various sectarian communities and interest groups with varied ideological leanings to sustain a modicum of coexistence and power-sharing. Such a pluralist political culture was naturally reflected in a fragmented, often contentious media. Despite its partisan character, the overall quality of the press, the diversity and scope of its coverage, made it particularly appealing to readers outside Lebanon. Indeed, a handful of its papers had a much wider circulation in various Arab capitals. Their critical exposure of the pitfalls of overcentralised regimes became a source of protracted interstate suspicions and hostility, particularly since political dissidents could easily use the relatively free and uncensored setting of the Lebanese press to lash back at the sources of their discontent and political dispossession.

Jealous of its freedom and independence, the Lebanese press was tenacious in resisting all measures to curtail or undermine its hard-won freedoms. Naturally, some papers could not resist being 'sponsored' or 'subsidised'. Given the stakes, some editors were known to be 'patronised', rented or bought – '*Ma'jurah*' – in return for more charitable and favourable presentations of the country's public image. Such realities notwithstanding, the leading papers were resolute in defying efforts at muffling or censoring their stories and editorials.

Their defiant predispositions were quite costly. *An-Nahar*, perhaps more than other papers, suffered more than its fair share of outright intimidation and punitive reprisals. For example, the year Ghassan Tueni took over the editorship of the paper, after his father's sudden death in 1948, he was summoned to court. From then on, virtually every year – in 1949, 1950, 1951 and 1952 – he ended up in prison serving terms of three months or more for writing what were deemed 'offensive' articles.

But their recalcitrance paid off. This was very evident in the role papers like *an-Nahar* and *al-Anba'* played in rousing and mobilising public discontent against some of the abusive and corrupt manifestations of Bishara al-Khoury's term in office (1943–52). Indeed, it was the sustained campaign of opposition launched by the press that ultimately led to the resignation of President Khoury in September 1952. This was the first open contest between the press and the first post-independence presidential term. *Al-Anba'*, the pro-socialist paper of Kamal Jumblat's progressive Socialist party, had published an editorial critical of Khoury's tenure. The paper was suspended and its editor jailed for fourteen months. Virtually all the other papers rushed to its defence by republishing the offending editorial. The government responded by suspending all thirteen papers. By then, the papers had no choice but to establish their own syndicate as a vehicle for self-protection and self-regulation. They also introduced ingenious forms of self-censure by blocking out officially censured passages.

Since the press had played a decisive role in ushering Camille Cham'oun into office in 1952, he returned the favour by lifting all restrictions and putting into effect more liberal publishing laws. The issuing of licenses for new publications became so permissive that in no time Beirut alone had fifty dailies sustained by sensational news and sponsored by public figures and entrepreneurs eager to get a share of the bourgeoning opportunities of the new government. The proliferation of newspapers became so excessive that the Syndicate supported legislation in 1953 to impose limits on such a free-for-all.[46] Ironically, Cham'oun's presidency, which was launched with such a liberal and permissive press climate, ended up, in the wake of the civil disorders of 1958, with a ban on the importation of some foreign publications, particularly Syrian and Egyptian, for the presumed adversarial role they were playing in supporting the rebels. Here again, the censored press, to display their defiance and independence, would opt to print blank spaces as a signal that they had been censored. Incidentally, this ingenious practice did not exist elsewhere in the Arab world.[47]

During Fuad Chehab's term (1958–64), the salient symptoms of pluralism and freedom of the press were sustained. The Press Law of 1962, which remained largely intact until the outbreak of hostilities in 1976, reinforced its liberalising intent. Restrictive edicts or prohibitive guidelines addressed two general caveats: to refrain from publishing news which endangered national security or unity or frontiers of the state and, second, news which denigrated a foreign head of state. From time to time, if a paper failed to observe the self-regulatory rules, the civil courts would hand out fines or prison sentences, most commonly for slandering the army or head of state or for revealing state secrets. One such episode occurred in 1973 when Ghassan Tueni, as editor of *an-Nahar*, along with his foreign editor, were arrested for printing the Algiers Arab League Conference secret resolutions.[48] Such episodes, however, were few and far between.

By 1975, the eve of the civil war, Lebanon had over 400 valid publication licenses. For a country of about three million, this is an incredible density of newsprint: perhaps the highest in the world. The majority were politically independent, although a small number might be associated with political groups. Indeed, so independent had the press become that it evolved into an autonomous institution, a 'Fourth Estate', along with the executive, legislative and judicial authorities. In addition to its much-vaunted independence, the press managed to retain its pluralistic and diverse orientations that might well reflect its various sponsors, religious or confessional affiliation and the views it held or propagated with regard to local, regional and international concerns. William Rugh, according to interviews he conducted with 'independent and qualified observers', made an effort to categorise the predominant orientations and readership of the twenty-one leading dailies in 1975.[49]

Naturally, the war had a decisive impact on the press. Although the major dailies continued to appear, some began to reflect the sharpened political and communal polarisation within society. Coverage became more constricted and localised, often confined to limited geographic areas and enclaves. Papers lacking support or patronage with any of the militias were compelled to shut down. Others reduced their size or relocated their premises outside Lebanon: a move which prefigured and facilitated their eventual globalisation by extending the networks of their circulation to reach the growing population of those in diaspora and other trans-national Arabs.

One of the most visible by-products of the war was the changing realignment and political orientations of the papers. As the political stakes of the regional patrons of local combatants and adversaries shifted, so did the orientations, political views and disparate agendas of their 'sponsored' papers. For example, it was generally assumed that al-Nida, al-Charq, al-Safir and al-Kifah had connections with, and probably received sponsorship from, Russia, Syria, Libya and Iraq, respectively. Likewise, al-Hayat was considered to have Saudi and right-wing Lebanese backing. Readers were also of the view that papers like al-Amal and al-Jarida must have had Lebanese nationalist financing, whereas al-Muharrir, al-Liwa, al-Anwar and Sawt al U'rubah were more likely to be patronised by Palestinians and Arab nationalists.[50]

As the magnitude and intensity of protracted violence escalated, it was extremely difficult for journalists or papers to maintain their neutrality or remain above the fray. For a while, the papers were immune to deliberate physical attacks. Eventually, however, a score of the more outspoken papers fell victim to direct assaults. Most appalling in this regard was when a large force of the Syrian-backed militia attacked the premises of al-Muharrir and Bayrout on 31 January 1976, and their two chief editors were killed.[51]

The socio-political transformation of the past two decades further reshuffled the standing, readership and orientation of some of the leading papers. Quite a few – al-Amal, al-Muharrir, Lisan al-Hal, al-Jarida – disappeared. A few others, relatively obscure – al-Diyar, al-Balad – rose to prominence.[52] Among the most prominent – an-Nahar, al-Safir, al-Anwar, and al-Diyar – the first continues to sustain its almost peerless and uncontested standing as the most influential and trusted paper, particularly by way of espousing its abiding philosophy for safeguarding republican institutions and basic civil liberties. This is in stark contrast to the abysmal quality of the subservient and nationalised

Arab press: either through direct state ownership or autocratic ideological regimes.

The success story of *an-Nahar* is most visible today in the commanding sight of its new premises. Altogether it is an adventurous, if not climactic, leap from the modest premises the newspaper initially occupied in the old *souks* of Beirut before the paper moved to Hamra in 1963. In 1933 Jubran Tueni Sr, a young struggling journalist at the time with virtually nothing by way of family capital or financial resources, moved into what was a fairly typical and unassuming suburban residence. The location of the premises, at the northern tip of Tawileh and Ayyas streets, compensated for its diminutive size, however. The intersection of the two traditional streets – Tawileh as a venue for fashionable upscale shopping and Ayyas as a popular commercial outlet – with Fakhry Bey Street was the most vibrant and coveted hub of the old *souks*. The first floor was occupied by the notorious Ajami restaurant, perhaps one of the most reputable haunts, almost a 24–hour hangout for political activists, intellectuals and journalists. For three decades those two inveterate 'institutions' – *an-Nahar* and the Ajami – managed to sustain a viable coexistence.

Because of its accessible and agreeable location and the political activism of its editor, particularly his advocacy in support of nationalist causes and political sovereignty, its modest premises became a meeting place for like-minded public figures and aspiring journalists. When Ghassan was called back from Harvard, where he was pursuing his graduate studies in political philosophy, after the sudden death of his father in 1948, he reinforced and developed those unusual attributes of his father's exceptional legacy. These were reinforced by a relentless stream of innovative, often adventurous, features: all pacesetters for upgrading the stature of non-political, literary, cultural and intellectual journalism. The following are worth identifying in passing, by way of elucidating *an-Nahar*'s distinguished legacy in this regard:

It established syndicated agreements with international newspapers such as *The Times* of London, news agencies like UPI, AP, Reuters, AFP, TASS and MENE and a network of roving and freelance correspondents.

Because of intense local competition, it also made an effort to enhance its readership through its 'file' pages of interviews, news analysis, inclusion of a wide spectrum of views and opinions and through its catchy and candid photographic images. It also introduced 'Extension 19', a special readers' service intended to give voice to those who bear legitimate grievances about government and bureaucratic inefficiency.

As early as 1968 it upgraded the quality of journalism by sponsoring and conducting public opinion polls and surveys on major and critical public issues. This necessitated establishing a special Research and Information Centre to assist in gathering the needed data.

In addition to its front-page editorial column, it introduced in 1971 a fully fledged editorial page where guest writers and special correspondents, along with noted documents or reports on regional and global issues are presented. Another appealing feature and pacesetter is its notorious eight-column wide political caricature, perhaps its most consulted and reproduced feature.

An-Nahar: original building (1934)

Most significant perhaps is the role the paper has played in cultivating and nurturing the much-needed culture of weekend reading. In addition to its twenty-six pages of regular daily newsprint, *an-Nahar* has introduced a score of supplements: *al-Mulhaq, Financial and Economic Reviews* and *Sports and Leisure*, its literary and intellectual supplement, has emerged as arguably one of the most widely read supplements of its type.[53]

It is at the technical and production level that *an-Nahar* has been most innovative and futuristic, almost always at the cutting-edge of new technologies and certainly ahead of its local and regional competitors. As early as 1974, it abandoned the lead and went into intertype production and processing. From then on it kept abreast of all the successive technological innovations in the industry. In 1984 it switched to linotype with the facility of being saved onto a floppy disk. By 1994 a Mac system was introduced with full layout applications. This was promptly followed in 1996 by *Naharnet* and *Nahar-online*, an electronic version of the paper. Again, in both these ventures, the paper was ahead of all others in the region. During the same year, PDF formatting as an independent downloading system was introduced. Another consequential first of the paper was its adoption of an HTML version as an interactive program.

Jubran Jr, who inherited the editorship of the paper from his illustrious father in 2000, will spearhead the paper into the twenty-first century. Judging by the monumental

El-Bourj bookstore

Japanese fountain

Rafic Ali Ahmad reading session

building recently completed, Jubran Jr appears to be reclaiming the roots of the paper with a vengeance, as it were: most certainly with all the magnificence and aplomb of advanced technology and the tested legacy of his gifted forebears. The site of the new building could not have been more compelling. It is perched on the old Phoenician wall on the south eastern tip of the Bourj. While it commands a panoramic view of Mt Lebanon, it is virtually nestled in the heart of the old city barely 100 yards away from the original premises.

Designed by Pierre El-Khoury, arguably one of Lebanon's most gifted architects, the building is a statement of magnificence and elegance. Like other recent El-Khoury icons that grace the city space, such as ESCWA, Bourj al Ghazzal and BLOM, it has dash and flamboyance but is also gentle and soft. The building itself spans some 20,000 square metres where half has been allocated for office space and 2,000 square metres for commercial use. A mere inventory of some of its more striking features sounds like a catalogue of the latest in Hi-Tech. For example, the building will be run by a computerised building management system (BMS), which controls everything from generators to air conditioning and fire security. There is also a 24–hour surveillance system with magnetic cards, plus seven intelligent elevators with a 25–second average peak waiting. All these and a legion of other gadgets are intended to provide absolute security along with an elegant and appealing working environment: for example, a high performance double glazing VEC system with low emission glass provides efficient sound and thermal protection. Likewise, the screen-printed glass on the façade, installed to withstand winds of 100 kilometres per hour, is also ideal for sun shading.[54]

The bistro-like restaurant-café, DT – for 'Downtown' – which graces its elegant entrance is a far cry from the boisterous but colourful Ajami of old. But DT is quickly emerging as a reputable joint for the corporate elite, journalists, public figures and other celebrities eager to be seen consorting with the rich and famous. While DT graces the eastern façade of the building, the El-Bourj bookshop is huddled on its western flank, facing the new shaded garden at the intersection of Weygand and Foch, with the two venerable but turgid ficus trees. The overbearing trees are cushioned by a soft, minimalist, Japanese-style pool. The gentle screen of overflowing water is a soothing and welcoming addition to an otherwise dense and boisterous street setting. Since its opening early in 2005, and thanks to the spirited efforts of its director, Chadia Tueni, its elegant and user-friendly premises have already become an inviting setting for hosting poetic recitals, one-man shows, spirited intellectual debate and book launches.

The Cosmopolitanism of a 'Merchant Republic'

Economic and social historians are keen to attribute Beirut's cosmopolitanism and tolerance of foreign cultures to its mercantile predisposition. Commerce, trade and the exchange of goods and services rest, after all, on the willingness to mix and interact in a

Banking district (1960s and now)

productive way with others. Throughout its history, Beirut has lived up to its image as being part of a 'Merchant Republic'. The Bourj, in particular, acted like an irresistible magnet for banks, credit houses and exchange outlets. Look how Charles Issawi in the mid-1960s depicts the profile of this emblematic prototype:

> Fabulous, yet perfectly authentic, stories are told of the transfer of gold from Mexico to India and China, of the shipment of copper from Franco's Spain to Stalin's Russia and of the sale of a huge consignment of toothbrushes from an Italian firm to a neighbouring one – and all directed from, and financed by, some mangy-looking business house in Beirut. In 1951, when Lebanon's gold trade was at its peak, it was estimated that 30 per cent of world gold traffic passed through the country.[55]

Like in virtually all other commercial and industrial enterprises, many of the early resourceful banking and financial houses were strictly family establishments bearing the family's pedigree, such as Haddad, Chiha, Safar, Sabbagh, Audi, etc. Kinship and family sentiments were not sources of lethargy and wasteful, nepotistic favouritism. Rather, they acted as a spur for inventiveness and fierce competition. Banks were so overwhelming in the life of the CBD that ultimately one of the most compelling avenues was named 'The Banks' Street'. As of late some of the successful banks are beginning to patronise the arts and other outreach cultural programmes to rehabilitate traditional artifacts and artisans.

Beirut's ebullient cosmopolitanism was not only reinforced by its Levantine mercantilism and tolerance for foreign incursions. By virtue of its location, composition and its historic role as a hybrid place of refuge for dissidents or a gateway for itinerant groups, Beirut has always been a fairly open and free space. Exit from, and entry into, society has been relatively easy. Indeed, the Bourj in particular became much too open at times, too hospitable and, hence, much too vulnerable to all the vicissitudes of internal and regional disturbances. Hence, its generative and positive attributes were often undermined by subversive elements with deplorable consequences. The Bourj became all too often no more than an expedient conduit, a transit point for the trafficking and recycling of displaced groups, goods, capital and ideas.

Naturally, such trafficking was not always of a desirable and lawful character. Inevitably, the capital – like much of the rest of the country – became notorious for smuggling, gunrunning, trading in drugs, the black-marketing of contraband products and other nefarious activities. Perhaps more damaging was the abandon with which dissident groups exploited this freedom to launch vilifying press campaigns and plots against repressive regimes in the region. This only served to arouse the suspicion and retributive strategies of the targeted states or groups against Lebanon. On both counts, Lebanon, and Beirut in particular, became unjustly victimised.

As a metaphor, a 'playground' conjures up images of an open, gregarious accommodating space, germane to felicitous inventiveness and experimentation but also vulnerable, as we have seen, to all the vicissitudes of excessive passions, heedless narcissism, complacency and indulgent egotism. In this sense it is a more neutral metaphor than the hackneyed labels for Beirut as a wondrous and privileged creation, as a 'Switzerland' or 'Paris' of the Middle East or worse, the more pejorative slurs it has been maligned with lately. 'Playground' neither adulates nor abnegates. It allows us instead to allude to and illuminate certain inescapable realities that cannot be wished away, whitewashed or mystified. It is also a more inclusive metaphor, thus enabling one to incorporate its everyday discursive and reflexive manifestations, which pervade virtually every dimension of society.

A playground, incidentally, is more than just a heuristic and analytical tool. It also has cathartic and redemptive features. By eliciting those latent and hidden longings for play, conviviality and adventure, a playground may well serve as an expressive and transcending outlet. It brings out all the '*homo ludens*' virtues of fair play, the exuberance of individual and competitive sports and the differential rewards for harnessed and accomplished feats of excellence. In this respect, a playground becomes an ideal site for cultivating the virtues of civility and commitment to the courtesies of the rules of the game. The very survival, after all, of a playground, particularly since it is associated with spaces where children can indulge in play, is predicated on the premise of monitoring and controlling the hazards of reckless and foolhardy impulse. When uncontained, a playground can easily slip into a free-for-all, raucous, rough-and-tumble public ground, as was the case in certain interludes of the Bourj's chequered history. It is then that lines demarcating civil and the uncivil, couth and uncouth behaviour, foul and fair play are blurred. Indeed, as the residues of protracted strife attest, fair becomes foul and foul fair.

The curative and healing aspects of a playground are naturally more pertinent in times of collective unrest and post-war stress and uncertainty. A boisterous political culture, suffused with factional and contentious rivalries, can find more than just momentary release in such outlets. Some of the enabling features of a playground – those of fair play, teamwork, equal recognition, and the sheer exuberance of doing one's thing without encroaching on the rights and spaces of 'others' – can all aid in the restoration of civility. At least, they need not be dismissed and trivialised.

Inordinate efforts and resources have been squandered on strategies of political and administrative reform and the broader issues of regional conflict and infrastructural reconstruction. Important as these are, they overlook some of the more human and socio-cultural issues of coping with pervasive fear and damaged national identities. It is also these areas that are amenable to individual intervention. Ordinary and otherwise passive and lethargic citizens are given opportunities to participate and become actively and meaningfully engaged in processes of reconstruction and rehabilitation. The Bourj as an open public sphere could very well become such an engaging and spirited place.

SEVEN

Future Prospects

The momentous events sparked by the assassination of Rafiq Hariri stand out as a critical watershed in Beirut's history. Once again, the city centre is in the throes of reinventing itself. No other area or space in Lebanon is more ideally situated to serve as an open and engaging public sphere than the Bourj. The chameleon-like receptivity of the Beirutis to adapt to new settings and to experiment with hybrid and cosmopolitan lifestyles must be restored and safeguarded.

By virtue of its openness and fluidity, the Bourj was not only receptive to accommodating a diversity of lifestyles and ideological trends, it has been akin to a gadfly. It seemed at its best when it was playing host to unconventional activities or unorthodox events that run against the grain and defy normative expectations. In this sense, it served as a safety value, a cultural broker, a playground or sanctuary to test society's limits of tolerance. By nurturing the momentous events in the wake of Rafik Hariri's tragic assassination on 14 February 2005, the Bourj has outdone itself this time.

Transforming this commanding site into such a sustained public sphere for political mobilisation, the Bourj was instrumental in inciting so much regional and global attention that it generated prompt redemptive diplomatic intervention. This is yet another decisive instance of how the Bourj has once again become the vector for dramatic and vital political transformations. Indeed, some observers have already heralded the momentous changes as ushering in the long-awaited birth of Lebanon's 'Second Republic'.

Until the unfolding of recent events, the Bourj seemed timid, often legitimately limited, in pursuing some of its public sphere activities. Given all the internal, regional and global uncertainties, it is understandable why the Lebanese were inclined to seek refuge either in religious and primordial affirmations or in the faddish and seductive appeals of mass culture and commodified consumerism. Both spatially and otherwise, these disheartening manifestations had become more pronounced in post-war Beirut. The Bourj is now more empowered in its envisaged rehabilitation to consider plans or programmes which could neutralise some of the adverse consequences of these two pervasive forms of false consciousness.

Such imminent considerations impose now urgent challenges on urban planning and design. It is imperative to consider strategies through which the redemptive, healing and enabling features of a common public sphere or playground can be nurtured and reinforced while safeguarding the Bourj from slipping into the 'dystopia' of a fashionable resort or a ritualised sanctuary for competing confessional communities groping to assert their public identities. Beirut's history in this regard, as alluded to earlier, has not been an unmixed blessing.

Also, much as in a playground, Beirutis displayed a proclivity for playfulness sparked by a mood of carefree and uncommitted activity; an almost sportive fancy with special fondness for jocular and humorous encounters. Here, as well, this pervasive playful mood is double-edged. It is a source of unflagging resourcefulness, sustained by a sense of experimentation and adventure. When unrestrained, however, it could quickly degenerate into restless expenditure of energy, mischievous activity and anarchy. Much too often a heedless element of play and unplanned activity permeated every fabric of society. The laissez-faire ethos in such a free-for-all milieu is clearly a relief to an inept government and a welcome to those adept at exploiting it.

The most edifying and enabling feature of a playground is doubtlessly its convivial and gregarious character. In part because of the survival of a large residue of primordial and intimate social networks, the Lebanese have long displayed a proclivity for festive, light-hearted and fun-loving encounters. If one were to single out a national pastime, the preoccupation of society with feasting, spontaneous social gatherings and companionship is clearly the most appealing and visible. Time and budget analysis reveals that an inordinate amount of time and resources are devoted to ceremonial activities, social visitation and frequent contacts with close circles of family and friends. Such contacts are invaluable sources of social and psychological support, particularly in times of public distress. As the public world becomes more savage, menacing and insecure, people are more inclined to seek and find refuge and identity in the reassuring comforts of family and community. So intense and encompassing are these attachments, that the average Lebanese recognises hardly any obligations and loyalties beyond them. Here lie many of the roots of deficient civility and the erosion of the broader loyalties to public welfare and national consciousness.

Once again, what enables at one level, disables at another. At the local and communal level, conviviality is a source of group solidarity and a venue for vital socio-psychological and economic supports. At the national and public level, however, they could easily degenerate into parochial and oppressive encounters. Compassion for, and almost obsessive preoccupation with and concern for, micro-interests coexist with – indeed, are a by-product of – the indifference for, and lack of interest in, others. Nowhere is this more apparent than in the disregard the Lebanese displays for public spaces or their lack of concern for national and broader issues. For example, societal problems such as child and family welfare, mental health, orphanages, the aged, delinquency, poverty, protection of the environment and habitat and concern for the threatened architectural, archaeological and cultural heritage – these and other such public issues are all articulated as parochial and segmented problems. Indeed, the character of voluntary associations, their membership, financial resources and organisational leadership continue to reflect sub-national loyalties. Even interest in competitive sports, normally the most benign and effectively neutral and transcending of human encounters, have been lately pulverised into bitter and acrimonious sectarian rivalries.

Finally, Lebanon is recognised and treated as a playground by the multitudes that perceive it and seek it as a popular resort. The country's captivating topography, scenic beauty, temperate climate, historic sites, colourful folklore, reinforced by an aggressive infrastructure of commercial, financial, medical and cultural facilities, have made it an all-year tourist attraction, a popular amusement centre and summer resort.

As a national industry, tourism and related services have always served to invigorate the Lebanese economy. Early in the 1950s it had already comprised the most important invisible export; earning more than half of the value of all exported merchandise.[1] Revenues from tourism grew four times in the period from 1968 to 1974, to provide 10 per cent of the gross domestic product.[2] By the outbreak of hostilities in 1975 it was contributing significantly (at least 40 million dollars annually) to GNP and thus offsetting the unfavourable trade balance. It opened up society further and enhanced the receptivity of isolated communities to diverse cultural contacts.

There was, however, a darker side to tourism and Lebanon's image as a resort centre. It exacerbated further the lopsidedness of the Lebanese economy by re-channelling vital resources into the largely unproductive sectors of the economy. The country was increasingly becoming a nation of services, middlemen, agents, idle *rentiers* and hotel keepers. Popular resorts invariably became tempting spots for venial and not-so-venial attractions. Lebanon was hardly a paragon of virtue in this regard. It had its fair share of houses of ill-repute, casinos, gambling parlours, nightclubs, discos, bars, escort bureaus and other abodes of wickedness.

More damaging perhaps was its blemishing impact on the country's national character. As a 'merchant republic', Lebanon became a country obsessed with, and too eager to please and serve, others, with all the cruel ironies that such ingratiation and servility often do to society's self-esteem. Artisans, villagers and farmers abandoned some of their venerated crafts, vocations and sources of traditional status to capitalise on the transient rewards of tourist-affiliated activities. Many became idle much of the year, awaiting the alluring promise of a quick and sizeable windfall generated by the influx of holidaymakers during the brief summer months. Others wallowed in aimless indolence.

Sparked by the ethics of a mercantile culture, it is easy to see how tourism could deepen further the inauspicious consequences of rampant commercialism and the vulgarisation of some of the cherished values and institutions. As a result, Beirut embodied at times the most lurid features of a bazaar and an amusement park, where the impulse for fun and profit are unabashedly released. Practically everything and anything becomes for sale or converted into a sleazy tourist attraction. Every entity and human capacity is conceived as a resource for the acquisition of profit or as a commodity to be exchanged for the highest bidder. This is most visible in the ruthless plunder of the country's scenic natural habitat and dehumanisation of much of its living space. Hardly anything is spared: shorelines, green belts, public parks and private backyards, suburban villas, historic sites and monuments ... they are all giving way to more intensive forms of exploitation to enhance their resort and fashionable attributes.

Throughout its long and chequered history, the Bourj has always been able to preserve some of the malleable elements of its local traditions without being indifferent to the incessant transformations and novel encounters it also had to accommodate. It is this receptivity to being eclectic and adaptive in its cross-cultural contacts that accounts for its survival as a cosmopolitan public sphere. Incidentally, there is consensus among scholars who have recently been revisiting the intellectual roots of cosmopolitanism – as a concept, mental predisposition, way of life or political project – that it is fundamentally shaped by ideals of citizenship and civil virtues which the potential cosmopolitan derives from the supportive networks of his small social groups and how these are transferred to broader forms of solidarity, autonomy and empowerment.[3] Here, again in other words, 'roots' could well serve as 'routes' or venues through which seemingly cloistered communities could retain their local and parochial attachments while being receptive to new cultural encounters.

The politics of civil society, as John Keane, John Friedman and Iris Young among others insist on reminding us, is emancipatory in at least two vital senses.[4] First, they enlarge the sphere of autonomy, particularly by providing public spaces based on trust, reciprocity and dialogue. Second, they provide venues for the mobilisation of multiple voices and, hence, political empowerment. Incidentally, Young here makes a useful distinction between *autonomy*, which is largely the sphere of the private, where groups can make decisions that affect primarily their own welfare without interference by others, and *political empowerment*, which calls for effective participation in all decisions that affect public welfare.[5]

Both are particularly relevant strategies at this critical watershed in Lebanon's history, caught between the throes of post-war rehabilitation and the disquieting manifestations of global and postmodern transformations. The promise of autonomy is inherent, after all, in this ability to encourage the active engagement and self-management of the myriad of local voluntary associations that have mushroomed during the past decade. Among other things, this calls for a dissenting and oppositional politics and the provision of venues for cultural resistance. Political empowerment, on the other hand, implies a shift from the essentially private and parochial concerns of civil society to the sphere of political community. Here politics become a struggle for inclusion, an opportunity for self-actualisation and a form of social justice that acknowledges the needs and priorities of different groups.

There is also another sense through which the concern for autonomy and empowerment can be particularly redemptive in Lebanon. Given the regional and global constraints, it is understandable why Lebanon might not be able to safeguard its national sovereignty or contain some of the global forces that undermine its political independence and economic well-being. At the socio-cultural and psychic level, however, the opportunities to participate in such voluntary outlets can do much to nurture some of the civil virtues that will reinforce prospects for greater measures of autonomy and empowerment.

Post-war interludes, particularly those coming in the wake of prolonged periods of civil disorder, anarchy and reckless bloodletting, normally generate moods of restraint, disengagement and moderation, War-weary people are inclined to curb their ordinary impulses and become more self-controlled in the interest of reassessing the legacy of their belligerent past and redefining their future options. Somehow, post-war Lebanon has witnessed the opposite reaction. Rather than releasing the Lebanese from their pre-war excesses, it has unleashed appetites and inflamed people with insatiable desires for extravagant consumerism, acquisitiveness and longing for immoderate forms of leisure and sterile recreational outlets. Some of the dismaying by-products of such mindless excesses, particularly those that continue to defile the country's habitat and living spaces, have become more egregious. Here as well, the active engagement in the burgeoning voluntary sector can be effective in resisting the forces of excessive commodification, government dysfunction, drain in public resources and corruption.

Concerted efforts must be made in this regard to shift or redirect the obsessive and effete interest of the Lebanese in the hedonistic and ephemeral pleasures of consumerism to more productive and resourceful outlets. Consumption is essentially a passive preoccupation when compared to the more productive and creative pursuits of doing things for oneself in association with others. This distinction is not as benign or self-evident as it may seem. Nor should it be belittled as a source of collective healing and rejuvenation. All productive activities, as John Friedman reminds us,[6] are inherently cooperative. Hence, any active engagement in a medley of activities – be it in sports, music, neighbourhood improvement, social welfare, human rights, programmes for continuing special education or participation in advocacy groups on behalf of the excluded and marginalised and, above all, cultural and artistic outlets – are all destined to become transformative, transcending experiences.

By transforming the private concerns of autonomy into sites of political empowerment, where issues of public concern are debated and addressed, such venues will also become the ultimate and most redemptive settings for the cultivation of civil virtues, participation in advocacy and grassroots movements and political mobilisation. It is in such hybrid and open spaces that this cultivation of civility will allow groups to appreciate their differences without being indifferent to others. Is this not, after all, what the virtues of tolerance are all about?

The Bourj is poised, once again, to reclaim its disinherited legacy. Indeed it has, and

Hariri's funeral procession (17 March 2005)

with such stunning and momentous consequences. The spectacle, thanks to an inventive and attentive global media, was relayed instantly throughout the world. The Bourj of Beirut became a household word and was privileged to enjoy more than just its proverbial fifteen minutes of fame.

The tragic assassination of Rafik Hariri – a rare and larger-than-life, charismatic public leader – inspired a stunning and spontaneous public protest of immense proportions. Outraged by the probable duplicity and/or involvement of the government and security agencies in the heinous crime, the Hariri family had, as we saw, the presence of mind to reject the offer of the government for a state funeral. They also did not consider the customary prospects of laying him to rest in Saida, the family's birthplace. Had they done so, it is very likely that none of the momentous manifestations of collective enthusiasm and the reawakening of national consciousness would have surfaced with such compelling and transformative consequences.

Instead, they opted for a site next to the imposing al-Amin Mosque he had bequeathed to the city in the centre of Martyrs' Square. The outpouring and contagious enthusiasm unleashed by the spontaneous and solemn funeral procession was unprecedented in

Lebanon's history. As the hushed and bereaved masses meandered through the streets and neighbourhoods of Beirut, the sombre procession turned into a resounding collective protest, transcending all the fractious loyalties and endemic divisions within society.

The pro-Syrian loyalists – largely Hizbullah, Amal and a bevy of left-wing parties and mercenaries who owe their political fortunes to Syria's obdurate tutelage over Lebanon – were visibly taken aback by the large crowds who were drawn to participate in Hariri's solemn and eye-catching funeral procession. In quick succession, they called for a public gathering to demonstrate their gratitude to Syria and to boastfully display the sheer numbers they can amass for the cause. Indeed, Hassan Nasrallah, the charismatic and fiery secretary general of Hizbullah, in a highly emotional and overcharged sermon, called upon the world to 'zoom in and out'. Since Hariri and seven of his fallen colleagues and aides were buried in the makeshift grave in Martyrs' Square, they graciously opted to host their gathering in the adjacent Riad el-Solh Square, southwest of the Bourj.

The 'battle of the airwaves', as it has been dubbed by the international media, should not be dismissed lightly as an image-making gimmick: a measure of the propensity of the two broad political coalitions to draw street crowds in support of their contentious positions. The battle to capture world attention prompted the opposition, mostly coalition groups demanding the long overdue withdrawal of Syrian forces and its notorious security agencies, to stage their own public demonstrations. If, by the rough tally of a head count, the first demonstration drew about 300,000, the second amassed an astounding million: most certainly twice the size of the first. More compelling, while the first was a stern, disciplined and over-staged demonstration composed of largely underprivileged groups from the southern suburbs – the South, Akkar and Beqaa – the second drew a much wider spectrum of participants. It also assumed a more celebratory, festive and joyous form.

Its carnival-like, popular and entertaining features notwithstanding, the uprising started to acquire many of the defining attributes of an emancipatory and revolutionary movement of collective protest. Leading figures of the opposition, many of whom were discovering and honing their rhetorical skills at public speaking, would appear around Hariri's grave to hold press conferences, articulate their demands and incite the expectant crowds to sustain their protest. In no time, the makeshift grave was transformed into a shrine and a solemn religious site for reciting the *Fateha* or observing a moment of silence. Foreign statesmen, diplomats, dignitaries and political aspirants sought the site for its photo opportunity, knowing only too well that their attendance was bound to be captured and transmitted by the attentive media.

It was then that it started to acquire one of the most defining attributes of a public sphere: an open and free-for-all forum for the articulation of the goals and platform of the *Intifadah*. These converged on four explicit demands: Syria's withdrawal from Lebanon, an international inquiry into former Prime Minister Rafik Hariri's assassination, the resignation of the Lebanese security chiefs and the holding of free and transparent elections without unnecessary delay. Some were also demanding the resignation of pro-Syrian president, Emile Lahoud. The demands became a ringing and emblematic slogan

EU delegation at Hariri's shrine

Secretary of the State Condoleeza Rice with Saad Hariri at the shrine.

14 March demonstration

on behalf of freedom, autonomy and independence. The three emotive words were appropriated by the young for their graffiti, placards and caustic political humour – even for their lyrics and rhymed verse.

At the risk of some exaggeration, the 'Independence *Intifadah*' might well turn into Lebanon's closest approximation to the historic Tennis Court Oath which ushered in the French Revolution. It must be recalled that on 20 June 1789, when representatives or deputies of the Third Estate were denied access to the conventional meeting hall at Versailles, they moved instead to a nearby tennis court. It is there that they took their historic oath never to separate until a written constitution had been established for France. In the face of such resolute solidarity, Louis XVI had no choice but to relent and ordered the nobility and the clergy to join with the Third Estate in the National Assembly.

In some comparable measures, although at the time of writing the by-products of the *Intifadah* are still limited to the resignation of Omar Karami's cabinet and the formation of an interim government with Nagib Mikati as prime minister, some of the long-term consequences could be much more substantial in their future implications. Indeed, some observers are already heralding the portents of a 'Second Republic'. It is, however, the popular enthusiasm that the uprising has sparked among the young which is the most promising. Thus far, they have experimented with every conceivable form of public protest: from those which call for participation in hardcore political and ideological parties to voluntary and welfare associations or other non-political performative and expressive cultural and artistic venues.

'Independence 05' tents

One of the most arresting is the tenacious group of protesters who, in defiance of municipal authorities, have built their makeshift 'tent city' in striking sky blue, the signal colours of the *Intifadah*. They are vowing to stay there until the '*haqiqa*' (the truth) regarding the identity of the criminals is revealed and when all the Syrian troops and secret agents are withdrawn. Their tone often seems scripted after characters in *Les Misérables*, but their defiant and resolute revolutionary bravado should not be belittled for its faddish gestures. Indeed, the collective frenzy was so maddening at times that had the Presidential Palace been within reach and not in the suburbs of Ba'abda, it would have been stormed much like the Bastille.

It is through the intensity and transcending quality inherent in such encounters that groups become receptive to the cultivation of new visions and identities. As Edward Said and Raymond Williams remind us, what we all need, particularly in times of thrust and dissonant transformations, is the construction of an emergent composite identity based on that shared common history – contradictions, antinomies and all. Clearly, such enabling states of mind and sensibilities are not the sole outcome of such transient mass encounters. The crucial role of a liberalising education, the humanities and arts in particular, with special interest in the 'other' is of profound significance. This is, naturally, a long-term agenda. In these, as in other voluntary activities of seemingly segmental and ephemeral public gatherings, efforts must be made to persuade threatened groups that validating one's identity should not – and need not be – accomplished at the expense of distancing oneself from the 'other'. Is this not, after all, one of the most enabling and defining attributes of a public sphere?

The lyrical message in Leonard Cohen's song, one of the epigrams that preface this book, is poignant and insightful. It also carries auspicious prospects for Lebanon's maligned political culture. Yes, the country has been riddled with 'cracks', both imposed and self-inflicted. They are not endemic or unredeemable pathologies, however. Ugly as the pitfalls, shortcomings and other derivative by-products of the 'cracks' have been at times, they should not be sources of morbid reflection or resignedly accepted as intractable aberrations.

The persisting manifestations of the cracks have become self-evident and fall within the same set of recurrent representations or misrepresentations of Lebanon as a fragmented political culture where confessional and sectarian loyalties have become so politicised that they obstruct the emergence of any transcending civic and secular agencies of collective mobilisation. Hence, the country remains beleaguered by the survival of neo-feudal, clientelistic and kinship ties, which shelter a moribund political elite willing and eager to serve as proxies for autocratic regimes and borrowed ideologies. The survival of such primordialism is also made accountable for the country's proverbial deficiency in civility and much of the displaced and protracted violence with which it has been beset.

A few of the inferences we can extract from an exploration of the social production of space and the healing and mediating role that central spaces like the Bourj have served as a cosmopolitan public sphere reinforces Leonard Cohen's prosaic but sagacious message. Pathological as they may seem at times, communal and other parochial solidarities need not continue to be sources of paranoia and hostility. They could be extended and enriched to incorporate other more secular and civic identities. If stripped of their bigotry and intolerance, they could also become the bases for more equitable and judicious forms of power-sharing and the articulation of new cultural identities. Here lies the hope, the only hope perhaps, for an optimal restructuring of Lebanon's pluralism.

This is not another elusive pipedream. Just as enmity has been socially constructed and culturally sanctioned, it can also be unlearned. Group loyalties can, after all, be restructured. Under the spur of visionary and enlightened leadership or during moments of resurgent collective enthusiasm as those aroused by Hariri's martyrdom, groups through a revitalised voluntary and advocacy sector can at least be re-socialised to perceive differences as manifestations of cultural diversity and enrichment: not as dreaded symptoms of distrust, fear and exclusion.

Just as the devastations of the war, barbarous as they were, rendered rehabilitation and reconstruction more feasible, Hariri's treacherous assassination became a source of new hope and revitalisation. At the very least, it has provided opportunities to forge new collective identities and transcending national loyalties. On a tangible and grounded level, it delivered a more reassuring message regarding how 'cracks' can be transformed into sources of 'light'. One such inference is of direct relevance to any post-war setting where ideologies of enmity, latent hostility and unappeased fear may be readily reawakened. What has transpired in Beirut in the wake of Hariri's assassination is a testimony that much can be done to assuage those still roused with latent fear. It was a realisation that groups need not be fully appreciative of the 'others' to be able to live with them. Some of the liveliest cities in the world are, after all, those that have managed to live with tolerable conflict among their diverse communities. Many in such places express violent aversions toward those with whom they do not identify. Yet they recognise such differences as given, something with which they must live.[7] Louis Wirth, in his classic essay 'Urbanism as Way of Life,' expressed this same reality when he declared that 'the juxtaposition of divergent personalities and modes of life tends to produce a relativistic perspective and a sense of toleration of differences.'[8]

Likewise, the Lebanese must also be reassured that their heightened territorial commitments are understandable and legitimate under the circumstances. But so is their need to break away. Being spatially anchored, as we have repeatedly observed, reinforces their need for shelter, security and solidarity. Like other territorialised groups, they become obsessed with boundary delineation and safeguarding their community against trespassers and interlopers. The need for wonder, exhilaration, exposure to new sensations, worldviews and the elevation of our appreciative sympathies – which are all enhanced through connectedness with strangers – are also equally vital for our sustenance. Witness the euphoria of children in an urban playground as they cut themselves off from the ties of family and home in play, or the excitement of visitors in a bustling city street. The village *makari* (itinerant merchant), as I have argued elsewhere,[9] played much the same role. He too broke away, crossed barriers and was a cultural broker of sorts, precisely because he exposed himself to new sensations and contacts. He had no aversion to strangers. He wandered away but always managed to return home. We need to revive and extend the ethos of the *makari* as the prototype of an idyllic national character. With all his folk eccentricities, he epitomises some of the enabling virtues of a 'traveller' and not a 'potentate'.

Edward Said employs this polar imagery to construct two archetypes for elucidating the interplay between identity, authority and freedom in an academic environment. In the ideal academy, Said tells us: 'we should regard knowledge as something for which to risk identity, and we should think of academic freedom as an invitation to give up on identity in the hope of understanding and perhaps even assuming more than one. We must always view the academy as a place to voyage in, owning none of it but at home everywhere in it.'[10] Are these not also the attributes or paradigms we should seek in restoring a city, or the places and institutions within it, to render them more permeable for this kind of voyaging?

The image of the traveller depends not on power but on motion, on a willingness to go into different worlds, use different idioms and understand a variety of disguises, masks and rhetorics. Travellers must suspend the claim of customary routine in order to live in new rhythms and rituals. Most of all, most unlike the potentate who must guard a place and defend its frontiers, the traveller *crosses over*, traverses territory and abandons fixed positions all the time.[11]

Ideally, this could well serve as the leitmotif of those entrusted with urban planning, cultural rehabilitation and political re-socialisation: that is, to create the conditions germane to this transformation of 'potentates' into 'travellers'. In the context of our concern with the transformative prospects of public spheres like central Beirut, this is a plea to keep them open. After all, the most constituent or defining element of a public sphere is inherent precisely in its ability to transform closed or cloistered spaces into more open ones and thereby to facilitate the voyaging, traversing, and crossing over. They should be, in other words, designed in such a way that people can move on when the need for communal support and shelter is no longer essential. Any form of confinement, in the long run, becomes a deprivation. Conversely, open urban spaces can also be rendered more congenial to cushion groups against the tempestuousness of city life or the threats of collective amnesia and the erosion of local and parochial identities.

The image of the Lebanese as a spatially anchored creature, compulsively huddling and defending his domains – in other words, the compact enclosures of family and neighbourhood – against potential trespassers, needs to be modified. He is also (or at least was until the war terrorised his public spaces) a creature of the outdoors. Urban planning and design can do much to restore the conviviality of such open spaces. Street life is emblematic of urban provocation and arousal precisely because one lets go, so to speak, and drops one's conventional reserves towards others. As Richard Sennett reminds us, as 'one goes to the edge of oneself, he sees, talks and thinks about what is outside ... By turning outward, he is aroused by the presence of strangers and arouses them.'[12] Sympathy in such instances becomes a condition of 'mutual concern and arousal as one loses the power of self-definition'. It is also in such instances that 'differences' are reinforced without sustaining 'indifference' to others.

Notes

Preface

1. Lynch, 1976.
2. Jameson, 1991.
3. Collins, 1995.
4. Collins, 1995: 34.
5. Jessup, 1910: 251.

Chapter One

1. Ragheb 1969, p. 110.
2. Sovani, 1969.
3. Hourani 1988: 7–8.
4. Chiha, 1966.
5. Cited in Gendzier, 1990: 35.
6. Salibi, 1988: 180.
7. See, for example, Gulick 1967; Khalaf and Kongstad, 1973; Khuri, 1975.
8. For further elaboration, see Khalaf, 2003.
9. See, for example, King 2003; Nasr and Voilet, 2003.
10. Roberston, 1992.
11. Ibid., 130.
12. King, 2003: 10.
13. It should be noted in this regard that its central dome is now forty-five metres in height. Its original five minarets were reduced to four and scaled down from seventy-five to fifty-five metres in height.
14. For further elaboration, see Short, 2001: 7–20.
15. Gellner, 1988.
16. MacCannell, 1989.
17. Jedlowski, 1990.
18. Connerton, 1989.
19. Ibid., 22.
20. Halbwachs, 1991.
21. Barber, 1996: 167.

22. Lowenthal, 2001: xi.

23. Ibid., xi.

24. Ibid.

25. Forty, 2001

26. Freud, 1969: 6.

27. De Certeau, 1984: 108.

28. Turner, 1987: 149.

29. Jarman, 2001: 171–95.

30. Forty, 2001:8.

31. See Forty, 2001: 7.

32. Quoted in Wolin, 1989: 37.

33. Hanssen and Genberg, 2002.

34. Ibid., 233.

35. Ibid., 234.

36. See Küchler, 2001: 53.

37. Yates, 1966.

38. Ibid., 99.

39. Young, 1993:3.

40. Danton, 1986: 152.

Chapter Two

1.   Badre, 2001: 17.

2.   Thomson, 1886: 47.

3.   Ibid., 48.

4.   Debbas, 1986.

5.   See Khalaf, 1997.

6.   Olin, 1856: 457.

7.   *Missionary Herald*, 1824: XX, 214–5.

8.   Ibid., 215.

9.   Cited in Bond, 1828: 317–8.

10. *Missionary Herald*, 1835: XXXI, 371.

11. Anderson, 1872: 23.

12. Ibid., 22.

13. Thomson, 1886: 123.

14. *Missionary Herald*, 1825: XXI, 346.

15. Davie, 2003: 226.

16. Debbas, 1986: 41.

17. Ibid.

18. For these and other details, see Debbas, 1986: 41–67.

19. Chevallier, 1968 :214.

20. Ibid., 208.

21. Neale, 1852: 209.

22. Ibid., 235–6.

23. Ibid., 211.

24. Ibid., 214.

25. Ibid., 217.

26. Stanhope, 1846: 216–7.

27. Chevallier, 1968: 205–22.

28. Bowring, 1840.
29. Debbas, 1986: 21.
30. Phillip, 2002.
31. Davie, 2000:14.
32. Debbas, 1986: 51–5.
33. Thomson, 1886: 49.
34. Debbas, 1986: 52.
35. Ibid., 45.
36. Ibid.
37. For these and other details, see Hanssen, 2001: 242.
38. Hanssen, 2001: 244.
39. See Khalaf and Kongstad, 1973.
40. As quoted in Hanssen, 2001: 245.
41. Hanssen, 2001:49.
42. As quoted by Hanssen, 2001: 248–9.
43. See Saliba, 1998: 30.
44. Hanssen, 2001: 251–3.
45. For further substantiation see Hourani, 1962; Owen, 1981; Salibi, 1988; Buheiri, 1987; Khalaf, 2002.
46. See Salibi, 1965; Fawaz, 1983; Sehnawi, 1981; Buheiri, 1983.
47. Hanssen, 2001: 253.
48. Girouard, 1985.
49. Davie, 2003: 211.
50. Polanyi, 1975.
51. Buheiry, 1987: 3.
52. See Buheiry, 1987: 8–9.
53. Quoted by Buheiry, 1987: 9.
54. For further details, see Davie, 2003: 209–10.
55. Davie, 2003: 223.
56. Ibid., 214.
57. See Khalaf, 1985; Salam, 1993.
58. Saliba, 1998: 12.
59. For further details see, Davie, 2003: 223–6.
60. Ghosn, 1970: 190.
61. For these and other such details, see Tabet, 1998: 84–5; Saliba, 1998: 22–8.
62. Antonius, 1965: 8.
63. For an excellent study of these issues see Hanssen, 2001.
64. Gavin, 1998: 218–9.
65. See Davie, 2003.
66. For further details, see Saliba, 2004: 37.
67. For further details, see Salam, 1993.
68. See Khalaf, 1985.
69. Owen, 2003.
70. The material collected amounted to more than twenty volumes which extended to other rural and administrative regions of Lebanon. These have been admirably contextualised and analysed by Hashim Sarkis (2004).
71. For further substantiation, see Hashim Sarkis, 1998 and 2004.
72. For further details, see Verdeil, 2003.
73. Khalaf, 1985.

74. For further details, see Nasr, 1978: 9–10.

75. For further substantiation, see Khalaf, 1985.

76. Saliba, 1998: 25.

77. Ghosn, 1970: 191.

78. Tabet, 1998: 84.

79. Ibid.

80. Saliba, 1998: 28–30.

81. Ibid.

82. Tabet, 1998: 86-7.

83. Ibid., 89.

84. See Yacoub, 2003; 975–6; Tabet, 1998.

85. Saliba, 1998: 24.

86. Ibid.

87. Tabet, 1998:91.

88. Ibid., 70.

89. For further details, see Yacoub, 2003: 381.

90. Ibid., 170.

91. André Leconte had teamed up with Auguste Perret in Paris in 1943 and carried out an archaeological mission in Syria and Lebanon at the end of the 1940s. He extended his stay in Beirut to supervise the construction of the Khaldé Airport (1948–1954). He also designed two prominent urban projects: the Lazarieh Building south of Martyrs' Square (1953), Rizk Hospital in Achrafieh (1957).

92. Arbid, 2000:7.

93. Ibid., 31.

94. For further details, see Yacoub, 2003: 787–9.

95. Yacoub, 2003: 788.

96. Ibid., 277.

Chapter Three

1. Erikson, 1976.

2. Nasr, 1993.

3. For more details, see Nasr, 1993.

4. Sarkis, 1993.

5. See Makdisi, 1990.

6. Yahya, 1993.

7. Nan, 1997.

8. Collins, 1974: 417.

9. Ibid., 416.

10. Scarry, 1985: 35.

11. Rorty, 1989. [page?]

12. Turner, 1987: 149.

13. Calinescu, 1987: 238.

14. Ibid., 228.

15. Adorno, 1973.

16. Strauth and Turner, 1988: 517.

17. Sennett, as cited in Milnar, 1996: 80.

18. DiMuccio and Rosenau, 1992: 62.

19. Barber, 1996.

20. Ibid., 8.

21. Albrow, 1977: 53.
22. For further details see Khalaf 1998:140–64.

Chapter Four

1. See Salam, 1998: 129–30.
2. Ibid., 131–3.
3. Meyer, 1999.
4. Saliba, 2004: 28.
5. For these and related details, see Saliba, 2004: 35–8.
6. Ibid., 37.
7. For further details, see Aboukhalil, 2002: 2.
8. For these and other details, see Badr 2001.
9. Badre, 2001: 18.
10. Asseily, 1998.
11. For these and other details, see Gavin and Maluf, 1996: 66.

Chapter Five

1. For further elaboration of the above and related issues, see Habermas, 1984; Calhoun, 1992; Wallace and Wolf, 1999; Turner, 2003; Scott, 1998.
2. Thompson, 2000.
3. Ibid., 179.
4. For further details, see Douaihi, 2000: 120–6.
5. Ibid.
6. I am adopting the term in its original usage as employed by Homi Bhabha (1994) and other associated typologies – see, for example Vilder (1976) and Sarkis and Rowe (1998: 275–84).
7. Mathur, 1999.
8. Illich, 1982: 18.
9. Mathur, 1999: 215.
10. al-Wali, 1993:85.
11. Poujoulat, 1986: 229.
12. Hanssen, 2001: 261.
13. Cited in Sarkis, 1998: 84.
14. Quoted by Hanssen, 2000: 268.
15. Quoted by Saliba, 2003: 35.
16. *Hadiqat al-Akhbar*, 1861.
17. *Lisan al-Hal*, 1903.
18. Zeidan, 2000: 111.
19. Yazbeq, 1958: 132.
20. For an account of the event, see *al-Ahwal*, October 1, 1908.
21. See Tueni and Sassine, 2000.
22. Habib, 2005: 8.

Chapter Six

1. Thompson, 2000: 181.
2. For these and other details, see Thompson, 2000: 180–2.
3. Aouad, 2000: 145.

4. In addition to the original four, other members of the *Usbat* might include the following: Raif Khoury, Salah Labaki, Boutros al-Bustani, Yousef Ghoussoub; Maroun Abboud, Amin Rihani and Mikhail Naimy. I say 'might', because the explicit identity of who actually constituted the proverbial 'ten' is riddled with uncertainty.

5. For further documentation, see the excellent and laborious PhD thesis in Arabic literature by Abu-Jawdeh, 1997.

6. Chabakeh, 2000: 75.

7. I am employing here Kurt Wolff's metaphor of 'surrender and catch' to highlight the creative energies made possible by such strategies (see Wolff, 1991).

8. Yahya, 2000: 110–1.

9. UNESCO statistical yearbook, 1985; Khalaf, 1992.

10. For these and other related details, see Yacoub, 2003.

11. Thompson, 2000: 200.

12. *Zahrat Suriyya* (1909), Crystal (1913), Cosmographe (1919) Chef d'Oeuvre (1919), Chautecler (1920) Familia (1920), City Palace (1920), Royal (1924), Empire (1926), Opera (1931), Roxy (1932), Rex (1933), Majestique (1934), Metropole, Dunia (1946), Schehrazade (1952), Gaumont Palace, Hollywood, Capitol (1947), Byblos, Grand Theatre, Rivoli (1946), Radio City.

13. Yacoub, 2003: 243.

14. Arabi, 1996: 38.

15. Thompson, 2000: 198.

16. *Bulletin du Circle*, 1928: 76.

17. Thompson, 2000: 203.

18. Ibid.

19. See Thompson 2000: 203, for further details.

20. Ibid., 204.

21. *Bayrut,* 1936.

22. *L'Ecran*, 1940.

23. Tarcici, 1941: 145–52.

24. Prothro and Diab, 1975.

25. Thompson, 2000: 205.

26. *al-Dabbur*, 1943:8.

27. See Daghestani, 1931: 126–131; Shaaban, 1988: 43; Woodsmall, 1936: 50–2.

28. UNESCO, 1965.

29. Barud, 1971: 5.

30. Tueni and Sassine, 2000: 114.

31. Ibid.; Hanssen, 2005: 19.

32. Jousselin, 1933:27.

33. Of the older generation, the following stood out: Hilani Aouad, Khadija Le'ou, Fatoumeh el-Halabie, Hilaneh Naccouzi, Fatmeh Hassan, etc.

34. For further such appellations, see Fouchet, 2000: 116; Tueni and Sassine, 2000.

35. See Jaber, 2000: 116–9.

36. See Weitzer, 2000: 3.

37. Khalaf, 1965.

38. Speetjens, 2004.

39. Initially, this global industry was predominantly an Asian phenomenon. Since the fall of the Berlin wall, Russians and Eastern Europeans, mostly from the Ukraine and Moldavia, have taken over.

40. For further details, see Speetjens, 2004: 46–50.

41. Rugh, 1979: 94.

42. Tarazi, 1914: 4–22.

43. For further autobiographical details, see Tueni, 1995.
44. The following were the journalists: Said Akl, Ahmad Tabbarah, Aref al-Chehabi, Betro Pouli, Jurji al-Haddad, Abdel Ghani Uraysi, Muhammad Mahmasani, Nayef Tellou, Ali Armanazi, Abdel Karim al Khalil. The identity of the remaining six could not be ascertained.
45. Tueni, 1971.
46. See Dajani, 1971: 173.
47. Tueni, 1995.
48. Rugh, 1979: 186.
49. Ibid., 185.
50. Ibid., 92–4.
51. Ibid., 186.
52. For further details, see Dajani, 2005.
53. For further details, see Tueni, 1971.
54. For other specifications, see Nabhan, 2002.
55. Issawi, 1966: 284.

Chapter Seven

1. See Gates, 1998: 117–80.
2. Owen, 1988:37.
3. Nussbaum, 1997; Edward Wolf, 2003.
4. Keane, 2001; Friedman, 1998; Young,1990.
5. Young, 1990: 250–2.
6. Friedman, 1998:33–5.
7. Fischer, 1982: 206.
8. Wirth, 1938: 155.
9. Khalaf, 2002.
10. Said, 1991: 18.
11. Ibid.
12. Sennett, 1990: 149.

Bibliography

Aboukhalil, Antoine. 2002. 'Beirut Central District and Office Space Perfection.' *Lebanon Real Estate* (Credit Libanais).

Abu-Jawdeh, Siham. 1997. 'The Literary Movement in Lebanon Between 1935–1945. as Reflected in Al-Makshouf Journal (American University of Beirut, PhD dissertation: Department of Arabic & Near Eastern Languages).

Adorno, Theodore. 1973. *Philosophy of Modern Music* (N.Y.: Seabury Press).

Albrow, M. 1977. 'Travelling Beyond Local Cultures.' In J. Eade, ed. *Living in the Global City* (N. Y. & London: Routledge).

Anderson, Rufus. 1872. *History of the Missions of the ABCFM to the Oriental Churches,* 2 Vols (Boston: ABCFM).

Appadurai, A. 1996. *Modernity at Large: Cultural Dimensions of Modernity* (Minneapolis: University of Minnesota Press).

Arabi, Afif. 1996. 'The History of Lebanese Cinema 1929–1979: An Analytical Study of the Evolution and Development of Lebanese Cinema.' (PhD dissertation, Ohio State Univesity).

Arbid, George. 2000. 'Preface' in Pierre El Khoury: *Architecture, 1959–1999* (Anis Commercial Printing Press).

Asseily, Alexandra. 1998. *The Garden of Forgiveness* (Beirut: Solidere).

Badre, Leila. 2001. 'Post-war Beirut City Centre' A Large Open-Air Museum.' *Cahiers d'Etudes.*

Barber, B. 1996. *Jihad vs McWorld* (N.Y.: Ballantine Books).

Barud, Antoine. 1971. *Shari' al-Mutanabbi, Hikayat al-Bagha' fi Lubnan* (Beirut: Haqa'iq Wa Arqam).

Bhabha, H. 1994. *The Location of Culture* (London/N.Y.: Routledge).

Bond, Alvin. 1828. *Memoir of Rev. Pliny Fisk* (Boston: Crocker and Brewster).

Buheiry, M. 1983. 'Beirut: Baroque.' (American University of Beirut).

———— 1987. 'Beirut's Role in the Political Economy of the French Mandate: 1919–39.' (Oxford: Centre for Lebanese Studies).

Bulletin du Cercle de la Jeunesse Catholique (Beyrouth, 1928–29).

Calhoun, Graig. 1992. *Habermas and the Public Sphere* (Boston: MIT Press).

Calinescu, M. 1987. *Five Faces of Modernity* (Durham, NC: Duke University Press).

De Certeau, M. 1984. *The Practice of Everyday Life* (Los Angeles, Berkely: University of California Press).

Chevallier, D. 1968. 'Western Development and Eastern Crisis in the Mid-Nineteenth-Century: Syria Confronted with the European Economy.' In Polk and Chambers, *Beginnings of Modernisation in the Middle East*.

Chiha, Michel. 1966. *Lebanon at Home and Abroad* (Beirut: Cenacle Libanais).

Collins, Jim 1995. *Architecture of Excess* (N.Y.: Routledge).

Collins, R. 1974. 'The Three Faces of Cruelty: Towards a Comparative Study of Violence' in *Theory and Society*.

Connerton, Paul. 1989. *How Societies Remember* (Cambridge University Press).

Daghestani, Kazem. 1931. *La Famille Musulmane Contemporaine en Syrie* (Paris: Librarie Ernest Le Roux).

Daher, Massoud. 1974. *Tarikh Lubnan al-Ijtima'i: 1914–1926*. (Beirut: Dar al-Farabi).

—— 1989. 'Some Remarks on the Growth of Beirut' in *Urbanism and Islam,* Vol. III (Tokyo: Middle East Culture Center in Japan).

Dajani, N. 1971. 'The Press in Lebanon.' *Gazette* 17, No. 3.

Dantons, Arthurs. 1986. 'The Vietnam Veteran Memorial' in *The Nation*. August 31: 152.

Davie, May. 1996. *Beyrouth et ses Faubourgs* (1840–1940). (Beirut: CERMOC).

—— 2003. 'Beirut and the Étoile Area.' In Nasr, J. & M. Volait (eds.) *Urbanism: Imported or Exported* (London: Wiley and Sons Ltd).

Debbas, Fouad. 1986. *Beirut, our Memory* (Beirut: Naufal Group).

DiMuccio, R.B.A & J. Rosenau. 1996. 'Turbulence and Sovereignty in World Politics.' In Z. Milnar (ed.) *Globalization and Territorial Identities* (London: Avebury).

Douaihi, Chawki. 2000. 'El-Bourj: Political Geography, Exchange of Interests and Spheres of Influence.' In Tueni & Sassine (eds.) *el-Bourj: Place de la Liberté et Porte du Levant* (Beirut: Dar An-Nahar).

L'Ecran. 1940. 'Bientôt, devant la Cour d'Appel Correctionnelle.'

Ellin, Nan. 1997. *The Architecture of Fear* (N.Y.: Princeton Architectural Press).

Erikson, K. 1976. *Everything in its Path* (N.Y.: Simon & Schuster).

Fawaz, L.T. 1983. *Merchants and Migrants in Nineteenth-Century Beirut* (Cambridge, MA: Harvard University Press).

Fischer, Claude. 1982. *To Dwell Among Friends: Personal Networks in Town and City.* (Chicago: Chicago University Press).

Forty, A. 2001. 'Introduction.' In A. Forty & S. Küchler (eds.) *The Art of Forgetting* (Oxford: Berg).

Forty, A. & Susanne Küchler (eds.) 1999. *The Art of Forgetting* (Oxford/N.Y.: Berg).

Fouchet, Max-Pol. 2000. 'Le Quartier Réservé.' In Tueni, G. and F. Sassine (eds.) *el-Bourj: Place de La Liberté et Porte Du Levant* (Beirut: Dar An-Nahar): 116.

Freud, S. 1969. *Civilization and its Discontents* (London: Hogarth Press).

Friedrich, R. 1974. *Architecture in Lebanon* (AUB Publications).

Gates, Carolyn L. 1998. *The merchant Republic of Lebanon: Rise of an Open Economy (London: I. B. Tauris)*.

Gavin, Angus. 1998. 'Heart of Beirut: Making the Master Plan for the Renewal of the Central District.' In P. Rowe & H. Sarkis (eds.) *Projecting Beirut* (Munich: Prestal-Verlag).

Gellner, E. 1988. *Culture, Identity and Politics* (Cambridge: Cambridge University Press).

Gendzier, Irene. 1990. 'The U.S. Perception of the Lebanese Civil War According to Declassified Documents: A Preliminary Account.' In Riva S. Simon, (ed.) *The Middle East and North Africa* (N.Y.: Columbia University Press).

Ghosn, R.S. 1970. 'Beirut Architecture' in Beirut College for Women (ed.) *Beirut- Crossroads of Cultures* (Beirut: Librairie du Liban).

Girouard, M. 1985. *Cities and Societies* (New Haven/London: Yale University Press).

Gulick, John. 1967. *Tripoli: A Modern City* (Cambridge: Harvard University Press).

Habermas, Jürgen. 1984. *The Theory of Communicative Action* (Boston: Beacon).

Habib, Osama. 2005. 'Solidere's Shares Jump in Kuwait Debut.' *Daily Star* (March 9).

Halbwachs, M. 1991. *On Collective Memory*, by Lewis Coser ed. (University of Chicago Press).

Hannerz, U. 1996. *Transnational Connections* (London/N.Y. Routledge).

Hanssen, J. and D. Genberg. 2002. 'Beirut in Memoriam – a Kaleidoscopic Space out of Focus.' In *Crisis and Memory: Dimensions of their Relationship in Islam and Adjacent Cultures.* A. Pflitsch and A. Neuwirth (eds.) (Berlin, Beirut: Orient Institute).

Hourani, A. 1962. *Arabic Thought in a Liberal Age* (London: Oxford University Press).

——— 1988. 'Visions of Lebanon.' In Halim Barakat (ed.) *Toward a Viable Lebanon* (London: Croom Helm).

Illich, Iran. 1982. *The Tools of Conviviality* (N.Y.: Harper & Row).

Issawi, Charles. 1966. 'Economic developement and Liberalism in Lebanon.' In Leonard Binder, ed. *Politics in Lebanon* (New York: Wiley).

Jaber, Bahjat. 2000. *Isturat Marika Isbiridom, Hikayat al-Jins wa el-Tonbah.* In Tueni, G. & Sassine, F. (eds.) *el-Bourj: Place de la Liberté et Porte du Levant* (Beirut: Editions Dar an-Nahar).

Jameson, Frederic. 1991. *Postmodernism or the Cultural Logic of Late Capitalism.* (Duke University Press).

Jarman, Neil. 2001. 'Commemorating 1916, Celebrating Difference: Parading and Painting in Befast' in A. Forty & S. Küchler *The Art of Forgetting* (Oxford: Berg).

Jessup, Henry. H. 1910. *Fifty-Three Years in Syria.* Vol. 1. (N.Y.: Fleming Revel).

Jedlowski, P. 1990. 'Simmel on Memory.' In M. Kaern, B.S. Philips and R.S. Cohen (eds.) *George Simmel and Contemporary Sociology* (Dordrecht: Kluwer).

Jousselin, J. 1933. *Enquêtes sur la Jeunesse Délinquante et la Prostitution au Liban* (Beirut: Librairie Catholique).

Keane, John. 2001. 'Global Civil Society.' In Helmut, Glasins and Kaldor, eds. *Global Civil Society* 2001. (Oxford: Oxford University Press).

Khalaf, S & P. Kongstad. 1973. *Hamra of Beirut* (Leiden: E.J. Brill).

Khalaf, Samir. 1985. 'Social Structure and Urban Planning in Lebanon' in Ann Elizabeth Mayer (ed.) *Property, Social Structure and Law in the Modern Middle East* (Albany: SUNY).

——— 1997. 'Protestant Images of Islam: Disparaging Stereotypes Reconfirmed' in *Islam and Christian-Muslim Relations.* Vol 8, No. 2.

——— 'Leavening the Levant: New England Puritans as a Cultural Transplant' in *Journal of Mediterranean Studies.* Vol. 7. No. 2.

——— 2002. *Civil and Uncivil Violence.* (N.Y.: Columbia University Press).

——2003. 'On Roots and Routes: The Reassertion of Primordial Loyalties.' In T. Hanf and N. Salam (eds.) *Lebanon in Limbo* (Baden-Baden: Nomos Verlagsesellschaft).

Khuri, F. 1975. *From Village to Suburb* (Chicago: University of Chicago Press).

King, A.D. 2003. 'Writing Transnational Planning Histories' in Nasr, J. & M. Volait (eds.) *Urbanism: Imported or Exported* (Chichester; West Sussex: John Willy and Sons Ltd)

Küchler, Susanne. 2001. 'The Place of Memory' in A. Forty & S. Küchler (eds.) *The Art of Forgetting* (Oxford/N.Y.: Berg).

Lowenthal, D. 1997. *The Heritage Crusade and the Spoils of History* (London: Viking).

—— 2001. 'Preface.' *The Art of Forgetting*, edited by A. Forty & S. Küchler (Oxford: Berg).

Lynch, Kevin. 1976. *Managing the Sense of a Region* (Cambridge, Mass.: MIT Press).

MacCannell, D. 1989. *The Tourist: A New Theory of Leisure* (N.Y.: Schocken).

Makdisi, Jean Said. 1990. *Beirut Fragments* (N.Y.: Persea Books).

Mathur, A. 1999. 'Neither Wilderness nor Home: The Indian Maidan' in James Corner (ed.) *Recovering Landscape* (Princeton Architecture Press).

Meyer, Hans. 1999. *City and Port.* (Utrecht: International Books).

Milnar, Z. 1996. *Globalisation and Territorial Identities* (London: Avebury).

Nabhan, Elie. 2002. 'An-Nahhar Returns to its Roots.' *Daily Star* (22 March).

Nan, Ellin. 1997. *Architecture of Fear* (N.Y.: Princeton Architectural Press).

Nasr, J. & M. Volait (eds.) 2003. *Urbanism Imported or Exported* (Chickester, Sussex: Wiley and Sons Ltd.).

Nasr, Salim. 1993. 'New Social Realities and Post-war Lebanon' in S. Khalaf & P. Khoury (eds.) *Recovering Beirut* (Leiden: E.J. Brill).

Neale, I.A. 1852. *Eight Years in Syria, Palestine and Asia Minor.* Vol. I, 2nd edition (London: Colburn and Co.).

al-Nusuli, Muhi al-Din. 1936. 'al-Zawaj min al- ajnabiyyat.' (Marriage to foreign Women) *Bayrut.*

Olin, Stephen. 1856. *The Works of Stephen Olin.* 2 vols (New York: Harpers).

Owen, R. 1981. *The Middle East in the World Economy; 1800–1914* (London: Methuen).

—— 1988. 'The Economic History of Lebanon, 1943–1974' in H. Barakat (ed.) *Toward a Viable Lebanon* (London: Croom & Helm).

Philipp, T. 2002. *Acre: The Rise and Fall of a Palestinian City – World Economy and Local Politics* (New York: Columbia University Press).

Poujoulat, B. 1986. *La Verité sur la Syrie et L'Expédition Française* (Beirut: Dar al Khater).

Polanyi, Karl. 1975. *The Great Transformation* (N. Y.: Octagon Books).

Prothro, E. T. & L.N. Diab. 1974. *Changing Family Patterns in the Arab World* (Beirut: American University of Beirut).

Ragheb, S. I. 1969. 'Patterns of Urban Growth in the Middle East' in Gerald Breese (ed.) *The City in Newly Developing Countries* (Englewood Cliffs, N. J.: Prentice Hall).

Robertson, R. 1992. *Globalization: Social Theory & Global Culture* (London/Delhi: Sage).

Rorty, Richard 1989. *Contingency, Irony and Solidarity* (Cambridge: Cambridge University Press).

Rugh, William. 1979. *The Arab Press: News Media and Political Process in the Arab World* (N. Y.: Syracuse University Press).

Said, Edward. 1991. 'Identity, Authority and Freedom: The Potentate and the Traveller,'

Transition. No. 54.

Salam, Assem. 1993. 'Lebanon's Experience with Urban Planning' in S. Khalaf & P. Khoury (eds.) *Recovering Beirut* (Leiden: E. J. Brill).

—— 1998. 'The Role of Government in Shaping the Built Environment' in P. Rowe and H. Sarkis (eds.) *Projecting Beirut* (Munich: Prestel).

Saliba, R. 1997. *Beirut Baroque* (Beirut: Order of Engineers & Architects).

——1998. *Beirut: 1920–1940. Domestic Architecture Between Tradition & Modernity* (Beirut: The Order of Engineers and Architects).

——2004. *Beirut City Center Recovery: The Foch-Allenby and Etoile Conservation Area* (Gottingen: Steidl).

Salibi, K. 1965. *The Modern History of Lebanon* (London: Weidenfeld & Nicolson).

—— 1988. *A House of Many Mansions* (London: I.B. Tauris).

Sarkis, Hashim. 1993. 'Territorial Claims: Post-war Attitudes Towards the Built Environment.' In S. Khalaf and P. Khoury (eds.) *Recovering Beirut* (Leiden: E.J Brill).

Sarkis, H. & R.G. Rowe. 1998. 'The Age of Physical Reconstruction.' In Peter Rowe & Hashim Sarkis (eds.) *Projecting Beirut* (Munich: Prestel).

Scarry, Elaine. 1985. *The Body in Pain: The Making and Unmaking of the World* (N. Y.: Oxford University Press).

Scott, James. 1998. *Seeing Like a State* (Yale University Press).

Sehnaoui, N. 1981. 'L'Occidentalisation de la vie quotidienne a Beyrouth, 1860–1914.' (M. A. Thesis: University of Paris).

Sennett, Richard. 1990. *The Conscience of the Eye* (N.Y.: Alfred Knopf).

Shaaban, Buthaina. 1988. *Both Right and Left Handed: Arab Women Talk About Their Lives* (Bloomington: Indiana University Press).

Short, J. R. 2001. *Global Dimensions: Space Place and the Contemporary World* (London: Reaktion Books).

Speetjens, Peter. 2004. 'Tourism's Dark Side.' *Executive* No. 63 (August).

Sovani, N.V. 1969. 'The Analysis of Over-Urbanization.' In Gerald Breese, (ed.) *The City in Newly Developing Countries* (Englewood Cliffs, N. J.: Prentice-Hall).

Stanhope, Lady Hester. 1846. *Memoirs of the Lady Hester Stanhope*. Vol.1. 2nd edition (London: Henry Colburn).

Strauth, G. & B.S. Turner (eds) 1988. 'Nostalgia, Postmodernism and the Critique of Mass Culture.' *Theory, Culture and Society*. Vol. 5.

Tabet, J. 1998. 'From Colonial Style to Regional Revivalism: Modern Architecture in Lebanon and the Problem of Cultural Identity.' In Rowe, P. & Sarkis, H. (eds.) *Projecting Beirut* (Munich-London-N. Y.: Prestel-Verlag).

Tarcici, Adnan. 1941. *L'Education Actuelle de la Jeune fille Musulmane au Liban* (Vitry-sur-Seine: Librairie Mariale).

Thompson, Elizabeth. 2000. *Colonial Citizen* (N. Y.: Columbia University Press).

Thomson, W. M. 1886. *The Land of the Book: Lebanon, Damascus and Beyond Jordan* (London: T. Nelson & Sons).

Tueni, Ghassan. 1971. *Freedom of the Press in a Developing Society* (Beirut: Dar an-Nahar).

—— 1995. *Sirr Al Mehnah Wa Asrar Oukhra* (Professional Secrets and Others) Dar an-Nahar).

—— (with F. Sassine). 2000. *Al Bourj* (Beirut: Dar an-Nahar).

————— 2000. 'A Visite D'Empereur Une Place D'Empire.' In G. Tueni & F. Sassine (eds.) *el-Bourj: Place de la Liberte et Porte du Levant* (Edition Dar An-Nahar).

————— 2000. 'Le Serail du Pouvoir et Les Jardins de la Revolte.' In G. Tueni & F. Sassine (eds.) *el-Bourj: Place de la Liberté et Porte du Levant* (Edition dar an-Nahar).

Turner, Bryan. 1987. 'A Note on Nostalgia.' *Theory, Culture and Society*. Vol. 4 (1).

Turner, Jonathan. 2003. *The Structure of Sociological Theory* (Belmont, CA: Wadsworth).

Verdeil, Eric. 2003. 'Politics, Ideology and Professional Interests: Foreign vs Local Planners in Lebanon under President Chehab' in Joe Nasr & M. Volait (eds). *Urbanism: Imported or Exported* (Chichester, England: Wiley-Academy).

Vidler, A. 1976. 'The Third Typology.' *Oppositions* 7 (Winter: 1–4).

Al-Wali, Taha. 1993. *Bayrut fi al-Tarikh wa al-Hadrah wa al-Umran* (Beirut: Dar al-'ilm lil-Malayin).

Wallace, R.A. & Alison Wolf (eds.) 1999. *Contemporary Sociological Theory* (Upper Saddle River, N.J.: Prentice Hall).

Weitzer, Ronald (2000) *Sex for Sale: Prostitution, Pornography and the Sex Industry* (N.Y., London: Routledge).

Wirth, Louis. 1938. 'Urbanism as a Way of Life.' Reprinted in Richard Sennett, *Classic Essays on the Culture of Cities* (New York: Prentice Hall, 1969).

Wolff, Kurt. 1991. 'Surrender and Catch and Sociology' in Etzkowitz, H. & Glassman, R.M. (eds.) *The Renascence of Sociological Theory* (Itasca, Ill.: F.E. Peacoch Publishers).

Wolin, S.S. 1989. *The Presence of the Past* (Johns Hopkins, 1989).

————— 'Injustice and Collective Memory' in Wolin, *The Presence of the Past* (Baltimore, Johns Hopkins University Press).

Woodsmall, Ruth. 1936. *Moslem Women Enter a New World* (N.Y. : Rond Table Press).

Yahya, Maha. 1993. 'Reconstituting Space: The Aberration of the Urban in Beirut' in S. Khalaf and Philip Khoury (eds.) *Recovering Beirut*. (Leiden: E. J. Brill).

Yates, Frances. 1966. *The Art of Memory* (Harmondsworth: Penguin, 1966).

Young, Iris Marion. 1990. *Justice and the Politics of Difference* (Princeton, N.J.: Princeton University Press).

Young, James. E. 1993. *The Texture of Memory* (New Haven & London: Yale University Press).

Yacoub, Gebran. 2003. *Architectures au Liban* (Beirut: Dar Qabis).

Yazbeq, Ibrahim. 1958. *Al-Awraq al-Lubnaniyya* Vol. 2 (Beirut).

Zaydan. J. 2000. 'Mudhakbirat.' As quoted by Tueni. G. & F. Sassine (eds.) *el-Bourj: Place de la Liberté et Porte du Levant* (Editions Dar sn-Nahar, 2000) Beyrouth.

Index

Picture Credits

Regrettably, owing to unforeseen technical considerations, it was impossible to identify the specific source for each of the images. They are here listed alphabetically with apologies for not acknowledging due credit to each plate in the text. To those interested in securing such information, kindly get in touch with cbr@aub.edu.lb.

Daher, Gaby, *Le Beyrouth des années 30*, Anis Commercial Printing Press, 1994.
Debbas, Fouad, *Beirut, Our Memory*, Naufal , 1986.
Gavin, Angus and Maluf, Ramez, *Beirut Reborn*, Archive Editions, 1996.
Khalaf, Samir, *Beirut Reclaimed*, Dar an-Nahar, 1993.
El-Khoury, Pierre, *Architecture 1959–1999*, Anis Commercial Printing press, 2000.
Al-Lahham, Khaled, *Beirut in the Popular Memory* (Arabic Edition), Sharikat al-Zawaya, 1996.
Nasr, Joe and Volait, Mercedes, *Urbanism: Imported or Exported*, John Wiley and Sons, 2003.
Rowe, Peter, and Sarkis, Hashim, *Projecting Beirut*, Prestel, 1998.
Salam, Nawwaf, and Sassine, Fares, *Lebanon: The Century in Images*, Dar an-Nahar, 2003.
Saliba, Robert, *Beirut 1920–1940, Domestic Architecture Between Tradition and Modernity*, Association of Engineers and Architects, 1998.
Saliba, Robert, *Beirut City Center Recovery*, Solidere, Steidl, 2004.
Sassine, Fares and Tueni Ghassan, *el-Bourj*, Dar an-Nahar, 2000.
Shoukair, Naim, *Beirut 1980*, Dar an-Nahar, 1980.
Skaff, Phillipe, *Joumhouriyat al-Baton* (Arabic), Dar an-Nahar, 2001.
Trawi, Ayman, *Beirut's Memory*, Anis Commercial Printing Press, n. d.
Yacoub, Gebran, *Dictionary of Twentieth-Century Architecture in Lebanon*, Alphamedia, 2003.

Casabella, International Architectural Review, no, 627, October 1995.
An-Nahar Archives.
Solidere annuals and quarterlies.